D1479454

MUSCLE CAR
CAR
CHRONICLE

BY THE AUTO EDITORS OF CONSUMER GUIDE®
WITH JAMES M. FLAMMANG

PUBLICATIONS
INTERNATIONAL, LTD.

Copyright © 1993 Publications International, Ltd. All rights reserved. This book may not be reproduced in whole or in part by mimeograph or any other printed or electronic means, or for presentation on radio, television, videotape, or film without written permission from:

Louis Weber, C.E.O.
Publications International, Ltd.
7373 North Cicero Avenue
Lincolnwood, IL 60646

Permission is never granted for commercial purposes.

Manufactured in the USA.

8 7 6 5 4 3 2 1

ISBN 0-7853-0174-7

Library of Congress Catalog Card Number 93-84370

Very special thanks to:

Chris Martin, NHRA (National Hot Rod Association)

Thanks to:

Leslie Lovett, NHRA; Bud Davis and Gerald G. Kroninger, Sunoco; Dan R. Erickson, Ford Photographic Library Services; Helen J. Earley and James R. Walkinshaw, Oldsmobile History Center; Barbara Fronczak and Brandt Rosenbush, Chrysler Historical Collection; Larry Gustin, Buick Motor Public Relations; Holley, Inc.; Rich Molan and Hector Magana, Iskenderian Racing Cams; Judy Stahl, Stahl Headers, Inc.; Kari St. Antoine and Mark Broderick, Chevrolet Public Relations; Tony Thacker, SEMA.

Technical Consultants

AMC: **Barbara Hillick**

Buick: **David W. Roman, Buick Motor Division; Terry Boyce**

Chevrolet: **Terry Boyce**

Chrysler/Dodge/Plymouth: **Jim Benjaminson**

Ford/Mercury: **Alex Gabbard**

Oldsmobile: **Helen J. Earley and James R. Walkinshaw, Oldsmobile History Center**

Pontiac: **Mike Grippo**

Studebaker: **Fred K. Fox**

PHOTO CREDITS

The editors would like to thank the following people for supplying the photography that made this book possible. They are listed below, along with the page number(s) of their photos:

National Dragster files: 22-23, 45, 47, 48, 55, 59, 60, 61, 62, 64-65, 70, 71, 77, 78-79, 85, 89, 90, 92, 93, 94, 96, 97, 99, 100-101, 107, 109, 113, 114, 116, 118, 119, 122, 123, 124, 126-127, 134, 135, 142-143, 145, 146, 147, 149, 151, 152, 155, 156, 163, 167, 173, 177, 186, 187, 188, 192, 196, 199, 200, 208, 214, 218, 244, 250, 258, 261, 262, 264, 267, 272, 279, 281, 289, 291, 301, 303, 316, 317.

Abey Studio: 128-129. **Orazio Aiello:** 135, 136, 231. **Auto Imagery, Inc.:** 315. **Greg Barrow:** 70, 83. **Scott Baxter:** 32-33, 198. **Ken Beebe/Kugler Studio:** 59, 91, 94-95, 110-111, 154, 155. **Joe Bohovic:** 123, 249, 251, 292-293. **Terry Boyce:** 48. **Scott Brandt:** 42. **Chan Bush:** 114. **David Chobat:** 241, 248. **Mitch Frumkin:** 107, 318. **Thomas Glatch:** 16, 86, 87, 161, 183, 211, 276. **Sam Griffith:** 24, 62-63, 72, 73, 80, 81, 150, 151, 176, 186, 202, 212, 213, 219, 224, 228, 229, 240, 245, 253. **Jerry Heasley:** 47, 61, 106, 118, 121, 137, 164, 165, 202, 203, 204, 206, 212, 213, 218, 230, 232. **Fergus Hernandes:** 12. **Alan Hewko/De Christopher's Studio:** 196. **Bill Hill:** 15. **Phil Hill:** 93. **S. Scott Hutchinson:** 37. **Bud Juneau:** 7, 9, 10, 11, 15, 17, 152, 153, 180, 185, 191, 203, 216, 217, 243, 245, 249, 277, 294. **Tim Kerwin:** 19. **Milton Gene Kieft:** 21, 98, 158, 179, 194, 195, 219, 310. **Dan Lyons:** 13, 19, 35, 94, 100, 101, 102, 256, 257, 311. **Vince Manocchi:** 10, 12, 16, 20, 21, 26, 56, 74, 148, 158, 231, 248, 274. **Jeff Medves:** 215. **Doug Mitchel:** 8, 11, 14, 15, 16, 17, 18, 20, 21, 22-23, 27, 29, 38, 44-45, 46, 52, 54-55, 66, 75, 76, 78, 79, 80, 81, 82, 84, 103, 104-105, 121, 124, 125, 129, 130, 140, 144, 145, 146, 152, 153, 161, 165, 169, 171, 174, 178, 181, 199, 200, 201, 203, 205, 210, 212, 215, 221, 222, 227, 228, 229, 238, 241, 244, 251, 253, 260, 261, 263, 271, 273, 278, 288, 293, 299, 300, 302, 308-309. **Mike Mueller:** 11, 15, 25, 49, 50, 51, 53, 63, 130-131, 132, 133, 156, 159, 162, 164, 165, 166, 170, 171, 190, 198, 204, 205, 207, 212, 213, 216, 225, 230, 242, 255, 259, 264, 280, 283, 295, 296. **Jay Peck:** 105. **Frank Peiler:** 113. **Photos by Morton:** 149. **Tom Salter:** 243, 244. **William J. Schintz:** 269, 282. **Rick Simmons:** 108. **Mike Slade:** 194. **Jim Smart:** 38, 43, 70, 96, 109, 114, 134, 136, 193, 197, 242, 267, 275. **Richard Spiegelman:** 99, 102, 114, 139, 196. **Studio Image:** 237. **Gerald Sutphin:** 58, 68, 69. **David Temple:** 18, 112, 282. **Bob Tenney:** 68-69. **Rithea Tep:** 295. **Jim Thompson:** 240. **Bob Trevarrow:** 96. **Andre Van De Putte:** 213. **Rob Van Schaick:** 204, 209. **Nicky Wright:** 12, 14, 16, 19, 20, 30, 31, 90, 115, 116, 141, 159, 160-161, 168, 189, 190, 192, 193, 195, 204, 205, 207, 208-209, 211, 214, 217, 226, 233, 234-235, 236, 237, 238, 239, 247, 248, 251, 264, 266, 268, 270-271, 272, 286, 287, 306, 307, 311.

Owners

Special thanks to the owners of the cars featured in this book for their enthusiastic cooperation. They are listed below, with the page number(s) on which their cars appear.

Page 7: **Cliff de Borba; Tony Capua.** 8: **Phil Kuhn; Briggs Cunningham; Philip Arneson; Bill Wagaman.** 9: **R.T. Brelsford; Doug Burnell.** 10: **John and Minnie Keys; Homer Jay Sanders, Sr.; Richard Clements; Bob Hoffman.** 11: **Stanley and Phyllis Dumes; William D. Albright; Tim Wenzlowski.** 12: **Virgil and Dorthy Meyer; Gail and John Dalmolin; Rex and Golly Gilbert; Fredrick J. Roth; Jim Van Gondon.** 13: **Chuck Sarges; Richard Kalinowski.** 14: **Otto T. Rosenbusch; Tom Franks; Richard Bourbie.** 15: **J. Cain, F. Gaugh, T. Sheafer; Roger and Connie Graeber; Ken Block; Richard Bourbie; Bill Hill.** 16: **Don Simpkin; David M. Leslie; Bob Peiler; John Krempasky; Ken Regner.** 17: **Paul Oxley; Ken Perry; Bill Bodnarchuk; Paul Armstrong; George Berg.** 18: **Z.T. Parker; Dennis McNamara; Donald Bergman; Roger Fonk; G. Bappe.** 19: **Dr. William H. Lenharth; Stephen Capone; Tom Appeal, Studebaker National Museum.** 20: **George Berg; Charles Hilbert; Dean Ullman; Barry and Barb Bales.** 21: **Bob Moore; Mervin M. Afflerback; Richard Carpenter; Don and Barbara Finn.** 22-23: **Gary Thobe.** 24: **Kenneth J. Patt.** 26: **Larri Stumpf.** 27: **Glenn Moist.** 28: **Dick Tarnutzer, Dells Auto Museum, Lake Mills, Wisc.** 29: **Dave and Norma Wasilewski.** 30, 31: **Barry and Barb Bales.** 32-33: **Jack Bratzianna.** 35: **William Korbel.** 37: **Paul Garlick.** 38: **Roger and Gerri Randolph.** 41: **George W. Rappeyea.** 42: **Robert and Karen Christanell.** 44: **Rusty Symmes.** 44-45: **Dan Mamsen.** 46: **Darryl McNabb.** 49: **Patt and J.R. Buxman.** 50, 51: **Phil Fair.** 52: **Terry D. Davis.** 53: **K. and L. Coleman.** 54-55: **Alden Graber.** 56: **Bob Mosher.** 58: **Bob Burroughs.** 59: **Frank Spittle.** 62-63: **Michael and Patricia Kelso.** 63: **Henry Hart.** 66: **Rusty Symmes.** 68-69: **Amos Minter.** 68, 69: **Bob Burroughs.** 70: **Bill Blair.** 72, 73: **Bill Jackson.** 74: **Barry Norman.** 76: **Guy Mabee.** 78, 79: **Phil Hayenga.** 80, 81: **Allen Gartzman.** 82: **Joe Zajac.** 83: **Bill Blair.** 84: **Rich Antonacci.** 86, 87: **Sam Pierce.** 90: **Jim Donaldson.** 91: **Frank Spittle.** 94: **Dick Kainer.** 94-95: **Frank Spittle.** 98: **Dennis A. Urban.** 99: **Glenn Cole.** 100, 101: **Don McLennan.** 102: **Ray and Lil Elias; Glen Cole.** 103: **Lynn Johnson.** 104-105: **Joe Kelly.** 105: **Fraser Dante Ltd.** 107: **Jerry Yonker.** 108: **Steve Shuman.** 110-111: **Frank Spittle.** 112: **Larry Barnett.** 113: **Frank Peiler.** 115, 116: **Mike Guffey.** 123: **Walter Schenk.** 124, 125: **William W. Kramer.** 128: **Alan N. Basile.** 129: **Alan N. Basile; Marvin Minarich.** 130-131: **Autoputer Inc.** 132, 133: **Dennis M. Phipps.** 135: **Ron C. Bealage.** 136: **Roger Brackett.** 139: **Glenn Cole.** 140: **Richard Hanley.** 141: **Jerry and Carol Buczkowski.**

146: **James and Mary Engle.** 148: **Harry and Virginia Demenge.** 149: **David B. Verdral.** 150, 151: **Richard Witek.** 152: **Chris Terry: Denny Allen.** 153: **Chris Terry; Denny Allen; Jeff Hare; Joe Witczak.** 154, 155: **Larry and Karen Miller.** 156: **Paul McGuire.** 157: **Ronald S. Mroz.** 158: **Bill Bush; Rich and Joan Young.** 159: **Mr. and Mrs. Richard D. Miller; Tom and Nancy Stump.** 160-161: **Bill Barnes.** 161: **Grady Hentz; Nathan Struder.** 162: **Tony and Suzanne George.** 164: **George N. Bowen.** 165: **George N. Bowen; Rich Neubauer; Tom and Katherine Stanley.** 166: **David L. Robb.** 167: **Jim LaBertew, RPM Motors.** 168: **Ross Arterbery.** 169: **John Vincent; Jeff and Trish Holmes.** 170: **Joe L. Saunders.** 171: **Joe L. Saunders; Jeff and Trish Holmes.** 174: **Jeffrey L. Hill.** 176: **James Lojewski.** 178: **Gerri Randolph.** 179: **Donald R. Crile.** 180: **Ramshead Auto Collection.** 181: **Norman Andrews.** 183: **Jim Labertew; Jeffery Baker.** 185: **Ramshead Auto Collection.** 186: **Dennis Guest.** 188: **Chris Pylar.** 189: **Chris Pylar; Kurt A. Havely.** 190: **Samuel Pampenella Jr.; Thomas S. Rapala.** 191: **Jack Karleskins.** 192: **Doug and Judy Badgley.** 193: **Doug and Judy Badgley; Dan Bohannon.** 194: **Mark Kuykendall; The Beechy Family.** 195: **Classic Car Center; The Beechy Family.** 196: **David Bartholomew.** 198: **Steve Maysonet.** 199: **Jon F. Havens; Bill Pearson; Torber Lozins; Felix Mozockie.** 200: **Gary Carlson.** 201: **Rodney Brumbaugh; Paul Gallo.** 202: **Dennis Reboletti; Dan Curry; Marion and Walter Gutowski.** 203: **Charley Lillard; Nick D'Amico; Sandy D'Amico; Dan Curry; Steven Knutsen.** 204: **Jerry Buczkowski; James E. Collins; Greg Grams, Volo Auto Museum.** 205: **Jay T. Nolan; James E. Collins; Jerry Buczkowski.** 207: **Joe L. Saunders; Robert Fraser; Steve Hinshaw.** 208-209: **Larry Bell.** 209: **Glenn Quealy; Greg Grams, Volo Auto Museum.** 210: **Andre Peterson.** 211: **Al Fraser; Thom Moerman.** 212: **Tom Shulitter; Edwin Putz; Robert Kurtz.** 213: **Glenn Moist.** 214: **Gary Pahee, Chris Duwalt.** 215: **John Cook, William Peterson.** 216: **Jack Karleskind; Carl J. Beck.** 217: **Robert and Ann Klein; Scott Campbell.** 218: **Bradd Shull; Tony Lengacher.** 219: **Robert Beechy; Rick Consiglio.** 222: **Bruce Rhoades; Greg White.** 224: **Craig P. Mentzer.** 225: **Craig P. Mentzer; Eugene Slocum; Dale Kumanchik.** 226: **Darryl A. Salisbury.** 227: **Richard P. Lambert.** 228: **Richard L. Burki; Jim and John Russell; Dan Parilli; Kent and Marsha Butterfield.** 229: **Ban Parilli.** 230: **Barry Waddell.** 231: **Dr. Mike Cruz; Michael J. Stoklosa.** 233: **Frank Kleptz.** 234-235: **Stephen Witmer.** 236: **Classic Car Centre.** 237: **Larry Bell; Joe Yanush.** 238: **Larry Bell; Greg and Rhonda Haynes; Jeff Knoll.** 239: **Greg and Rhonda Haynes; Walter P. Wise.** 240: **Bill Draper; Steve Engeman.** 241: **Jim Reilly; Bud Moore.** 242:

Steve Ames. 243: **Classic Auto Shoplace; Jack Karleskind.** 244: **Classic Auto Showplace; Dean Cardella; Fred and Kris Kuebler.** 245: **Dave Cobble II; Eric and Yoshio Nakayama.** 246: **Philip Lagerquist.** 247: **Rick Cain.** 248: **Jim Regnier; Richard Petty.** 249: **Wayne Hartye; Glen Stidger; David Arent; Richard Carpenter.** 251: **Joseph Ererle; Ronda Cunningham; Classic Car Centre.** 253: **Eric and Yoshio Nakayama; Russ Smith.** 255: **Michael S. Gray.** 256, 257: **Paul D. Pierce.** 259: **Allen Schere.** 260, 261: **David Ramally.** 263: **Odus West.** 264: **David Arent.** 265: **Yoshio and Eric Nakayama; Michael Piche.** 266-267: **Don and Karen Kerridge.** 268: **Thomas and Carol Podemski.** 269: **Dennis D. Rosenberry.** 270: **Dan Tessner.** 270-271: **Trever Badgley.** 272: **Randy O'Daniel; Trever Dadgley.** 273: **Odus West.** 274: **Jay Dykes.** 275: **Danny and Steve Runyon.** 276: **Steven Jenear.** 277: **Ray Hermand; Eric and Yoshio Nakayama.** 278: **Mary Ann and Robert Moore.** 280: **Michael S. Gray.** 282: **Jim Turner; Lou Rehrig.** 283: **Rick Cybul.** 286: **Ron Edgerly.** 287: **Terry Swisher.** 288: **Jim McCann.** 291: **William Kroncke.** 292-293: **Ralph Milner.** 293: **Kevin Kloubec.** 294: **Gregg Gyurina.** 295: **Bill Schroeder; Ron Beal.** 296: **Fernando F. Alvare.** 299: **Jim Buhle; Randy Mucha.** 200: **Dennis W. Riely.** 302: **Charles M. Kerr.** 306: **James H. Carson.** 307: **James H. Carson; Doug Schlisser.** 308-309: **Larry Rowen.** 309: **Mark and Joni Walters.** 310: **David L. Hardgrove.** 311: **Michael Rooney; Thomas and Carol Podemski.**

CONTENTS

Foreword

Foreword

To those who loved them—those who could recognize a supercar with just a glance at a fender emblem—it was as if the streets in the 1960s and early '70s were alive with muscle. Cars with roaring exhausts seemed to squeal away from nearly every stoplight.

In reality, the number of bonafide muscle cars was disarmingly low when counted against the millions of automobiles Detroit was churning out.

For example, Pontiac's 1966 GTO holds the record for the highest one-year production of any genuine supercar, with 96,946. Yet it accounted for barely 10 percent of Pontiac's sales for '66. In fact, Pontiac built 318,270 other Tempest and LeMans models alone that year. Even the most famous muscle-car engines were hardly more than footnotes to annual production tabulations. Chevrolet's storied 409-cid V-8 was installed in fewer than one percent of the cars that could be ordered with it.

But if the lore of muscle cars is out of proportion to their actual numbers, that merely underscores their impact. Indeed, these machines created an entire culture, with its own language and customs, heroes and pretenders. It is to those who loved these cars—and to those just discovering their magic—that *Muscle Car Chronicle* is dedicated.

By its narrowest definition, a muscle car was a mid-size two-door coupe or sedan with a large-displacement V-8. These types of cars had enough room underhood for huge V-8s and the generous exhaust systems the engines needed to fulfill their potential. Mid-size cars were also relatively lightweight, but distributed enough weight rearward to keep the back tires from spinning helplessly under hard acceleration.

Muscle Car Chronicle recognizes, however, that any worthwhile treatment of the subject must go beyond so confining a definition. What really counted was a car's use of high power to break away from the ordinary run of daily transportation. So here you'll find not only GTOs and GTXs, but Camaros and Chryslers, Shelby Cobras and Chevy IIs. Our story begins with the birth of mass-produced high-compression V-8s in the 1949 Oldsmobile and Cadillac, and traces muscle's fascinating journey right up to today's fuel-injected Mustangs and Z-28s.

Our mission is to celebrate all of these wonderful machines.
And our aim is to present them honestly. Unfortunately, sketchy record keeping by the manufacturers, midyear changes, and countless other variables make any reconstruction of the muscle age a slippery task.

Muscle Car Chronicle relied on data from the automakers, the National Hot Rod Association, and marque historians. We note the sources of the performance figures we quote. And we point out variances in those figures, which were not uncommon, given contemporary magazines' penchant for one-upmanship and the manufacturers' fondness for lacing the press test fleet with hopped-up ringers.

But while the details are important, the deeper satisfaction is in the color and personality of these cars. And for conveying this, the picture-laden chronicle format is uniquely suited. So study or browse, read chronologically or jump in at your favorite year. Just be ready for the ride of a lifetime!

— The Auto Editors of CONSUMER GUIDE®

1949-59

Postwar era begins with hot rodders racing 1930s roadsters with hopped-up V-8s • Organized drag racing emerges in late 1940s... National Hot Rod Association formed in 1951 • NASCAR created at Daytona Beach in 1947 • For '49, Oldsmobile stuffs 135-bhp overhead-valve V-8 into lightweight body, creating first postwar muscle machine • Step-down Hudson Hornet tears up stock-car tracks in early '50s • Chrysler launches 180-bhp "hemi" V-8 for '51 • Lincoln gets ohv V-8 for '52, wins *Carrera Panamericana* race • Ford and Mercury get ohv V-8 for '54, replacing famed flathead • First NHRA National Championship held in 1955 • '55 Chevrolet with 265-cid V-8 sets standard for burgeoning horsepower race • Chrysler introduces 300 coupe for '55, with 300-bhp hemi ... hits one horsepower per cubic inch a year later • Fuel injection goes into Chevy for '57: 283 horses from 283 cid • Daytona International Speedway opens in 1958 • 100,000 fans attend '59 NHRA Championship at Detroit ... quickest stock car's ET is just under 15 seconds; dragster hits 9.12

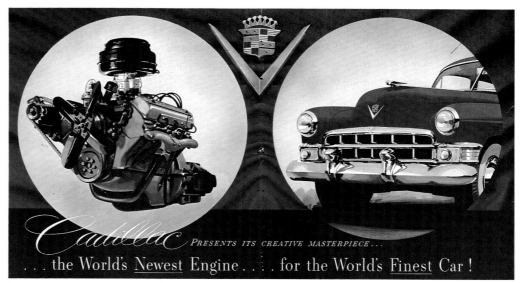

Cadillac PRESENTS ITS CREATIVE MASTERPIECE...
... the World's <u>Newest</u> Engine .... for the World's <u>Finest</u> Car!

▲ The breakthrough overhead-valve V-8s in the '49 Cadillac and Oldsmobile were light, durable, and powerful. When Olds put its "Rocket" version into the lightweight 76-series body, it created the Rocket 88, forerunner of the factory "muscle car."

▲ Tom McCahill of *Mechanix Illustrated* marveled that the sizable '49 Cadillac "out-performs just about every car." With stick shift, a Caddy could hit 60 in 12.1 seconds. The 331-cid V-8 made 160 bhp at 3800 rpm on 7.5:1 compression. This was the first year for the Coupe de Ville pillarless hardtop coupe.

▲ With two-barrel carb and 7.25:1 compression, Oldsmobile's revolutionary "Rocket" V-8 developed 135 bhp at 3600 rpm. That was fine in this 3890-pound 98, on 125-inch wheelbase—but far livelier in a 119.5-inch 88, at 265 pounds less. Four-speed Hydra-Matic was standard. Holiday hardtop coupes were new, too.

▲ A new one-piece windshield went on Cadillacs for 1950, and the 160-bhp 331-cid V-8 gave the heavy cruisers a surprising swiftness.

▲ Luxury was paramount at Cadillac, but a Series 62 model, such as this Coupe de Ville, still could do 0-60 in 13 seconds and top 100 mph.

◄ When sportsman Briggs S. Cunningham drove his highly modified Cadillac-powered special at the LeMans 24-hour endurance race in 1950, the French had an apt nickname for it: *Le Monstre*. A Cunningham-backed Caddy that looked far closer to stock took drivers Sam and Miles Collier to 10th place overall at an average 81.5 mph, with this bizarre creation finishing right behind.

▼ Specs for the 303.7-cid Olds Rocket engine, "power sensation of the nation," were unchanged from 1949, at 135 bhp and 263 lbs/ft using 7.25:1 compression and a Rochester two-barrel carb. An "export kit" included a special cam, high-compression heads, heavy-duty wheels, and other goodies.

▲ Oldsmobile touted the '50 Rocket 88's smooth ride as much as its "high-compression power" and optional "Whirlaway Hydra-Matic Drive."

▲ An Oldsmobile 88 Deluxe club sedan weighed 3486 pounds, and its fastback body looked super with options. Cadet sunvisor added $27.

▲ One of the fastest cars of its day, the Olds 88 ruled the NASCAR circuit. Two-door sedans lacked a hardtop's pizzazz, but 50,561 were built.

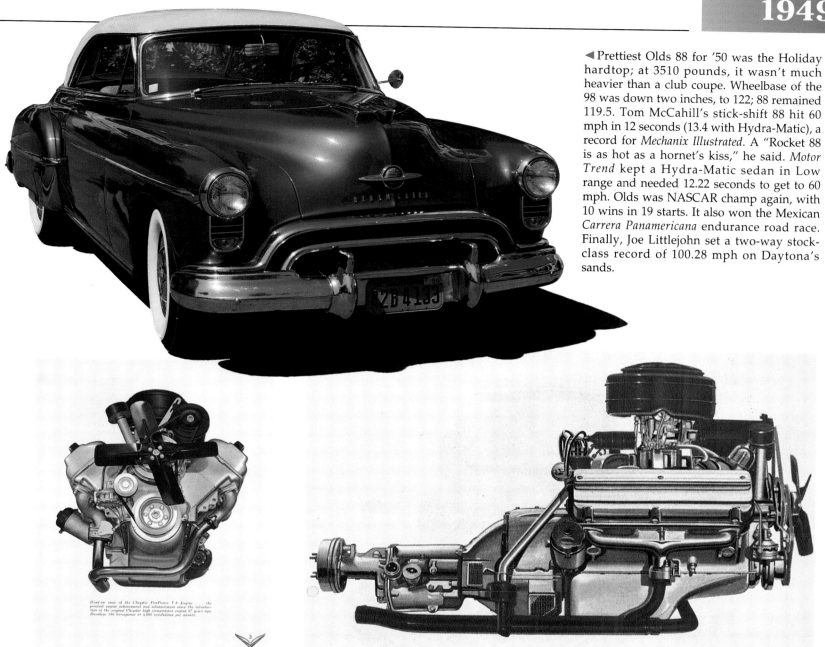

◄Prettiest Olds 88 for '50 was the Holiday hardtop; at 3510 pounds, it wasn't much heavier than a club coupe. Wheelbase of the 98 was down two inches, to 122; 88 remained 119.5. Tom McCahill's stick-shift 88 hit 60 mph in 12 seconds (13.4 with Hydra-Matic), a record for *Mechanix Illustrated*. A "Rocket 88 is as hot as a hornet's kiss," he said. *Motor Trend* kept a Hydra-Matic sedan in Low range and needed 12.22 seconds to get to 60 mph. Olds was NASCAR champ again, with 10 wins in 19 starts. It also won the Mexican *Carrera Panamericana* endurance road race. Finally, Joe Littlejohn set a two-way stock-class record of 100.28 mph on Daytona's sands.

▲For '51, Chrysler put its new FirePower V-8 into the New Yorker and the smaller Saratoga.

▲Chrysler's new V-8 not only had overhead valves, but hemispherical combustion chambers. The 331-cid "hemi" had 180 bhp at 4000 rpm via 7.5:1 compression. It helped raise Chrysler's luck in NASCAR.

▲For 1952, four Saratoga models carried the "hemi" and Fluid Torque Drive. A Saratoga could do 0-60 mph in 10 seconds.

▲A hot Hornet joined the "step-down" Hudson line for 1951 and ruled the stock-car tracks through '54 with its 308-cid L-head six.

▲ With its floor below the frame rails, Hudson had a low center of gravity for outstanding handling. The inline-six made 145 bhp at 3800 rpm on 7.2:1 compression with a two-barrel carb; Twin H-Power (dual carbs) made 170. In 35 starts, Hudson took 31 stock-car wins, 12 by Marshall Teague. Hornet for '52 included club coupe, hardtop, convertible, and this 3600-pound sedan, all on a 124-inch wheelbase.

▲ The '52 Lincoln Capri got a new 160-bhp 317.5-cid ohv V-8. Though topping two tons, hot-rod Lincolns grabbed the first five spots in the *Carrera Panamericana*. A ball-joint suspension helped handling.

▲ For '52, Oldsmobile's Super 88 got Quadri-Jet four-barrel carburetion and 160 bhp (versus 145 bhp in the regular 88). An "export kit" added a wild cam, tougher crank, and more.

▲ Cadillac's Eldorado convertible could be swift—once it got moving. The $7750 ragtop bowed for '53 with the usual 210-bhp 331-cid V-8. Touches included wire wheels, "Panoramic" wraparound windshield, cut-down doors, and metal tonneau. Just 532 were built.

▲ Chrysler shrunk its "hemi" to 241-cid and gave its restyled '53 Dodge Coronet the first ohv V-8 in the moderately priced field. Transmission choices included three-speed, overdrive, Gyro-Matic, and new Gyro-Torque automatic. A Dodge set 196 AAA stock-car speed records.

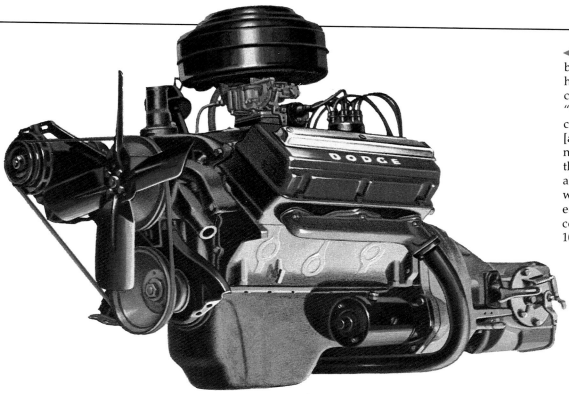

◄ Dodge's Red Ram V-8 for '53 made 140 bhp at 4400 rpm using 7.0:1 compression, hydraulic lifters, and a Stromberg two-barrel carb. It ran on regular gas, and ads touted the "triple power advantages of hemispherical combustion chambers...short-stroke design [and] high-lift lateral valves." Moreover, the new Gyro-Torque Drive had a "'Scat' gear that's plain greased lightning." The "hemi" also had smooth manifolding, large and widely separated valves, and centrally located spark plugs. On the down side, it was costly to build. Danny Eames took one to 102.62 mph on a California dry lake.

▲ A Dodge Coronet convertible went for $2494 in 1953. Wheelbase was 114 inches on two-door Dodges, 119 on four-doors. Dodge promised a "magnificent reserve of acceleration" with the Red Ram V-8.

▲ At 3530 pounds on a 124-inch wheelbase, a '53 Hornet club coupe was no featherweight, but the 7-X engine helped it to 21 NASCAR wins. Stick-shifts worked through a fluid-cushioned clutch.

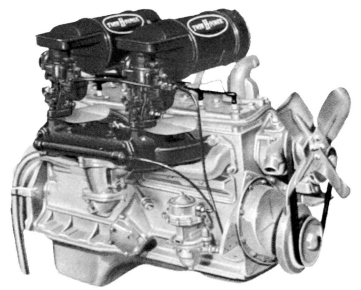

▲ A Hornet engine with Twin H-Power was easy to spot. Hudson made "severe usage" parts available to racers. The 7-X six featured a .020-inch overbore, special cam, and headers—for about 210 bhp.

▲ Olds still was losing to Hudson on stock-car tracks in 1953; the 165-bhp V-8 in the Super 88 (and bigger 98) wasn't enough. A new J-2 option added 8.5:1 heads, solid lifters, and full-race cam.

11

▲ New heads, four-barrel, and dual exhausts gave the '54 New Yorker's "hemi" 235 bhp. "Anything less is Yesterday's Car!" said ads. Chryslers averaged 118.18 mph in a 24-hour endurance run.

▲ Replacing the hallowed flathead for '54 was Ford's new 130-bhp ohv 239-cid, the hottest V-8 in the low-priced field. A 256-cid Police V-8 had 160 bhp. Ball joints replaced kingpins. Ford-O-Matic cost $184.

▲ A '54 Hudson Hornet Hollywood hardtop sold for $2988. Its 308-cid engine was the biggest L-head six at the time. It had 160 bhp with 7.5:1 compression and two-barrel carb. Twin H-Power added 10 bhp.

▲ Hornet ragtop sold for $3288. Hudson took 17 NASCAR wins in its last year of factory race support. On May 1, 1954, it merged with Nash to form American Motors. This was the step-down design's last year.

▲ The Hot One! Chevrolet triggered the horsepower race in 1955 with a magnificent new 265-cid V-8. It had 162 bhp with a two-barrel and 180 with the four-barrel, dual-exhaust "Power Pack." A V-8 Bel Air Sport Coupe cost $2166 and weighed 3165 pounds—less than a Ford or Plymouth hardtop. *Road & Track's* Power Pack Two-Ten with overdrive did 0-60 in 9.7 seconds and 17.4 at 77 mph in the quarter-mile.

▲ A '55 Bel Air convertible went for $2305. At midyear, Chevy advertised a special-order Power Kit to boost output to 195 bhp.

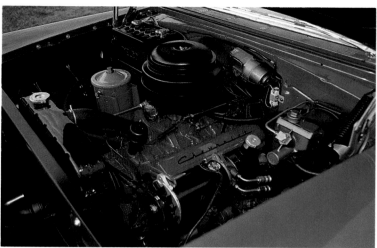

▲ Chevy's '55 V-8 weighed less than a six. Its thinwall castings, stud-mount rocker arms, and hollow pushrods could handle 5500 rpm.

▲ Luxury and performance combined in the 300-bhp, leather-lined Chrysler C-300 of '55. Just 1725 were built, priced at $4110.

▲ "America's Most Powerful Stock Car," crowed the ads. C-300s won 37 stock-car races and finished 1-2 at over 130 mph in Daytona's flying mile.

◄ Despite its two-ton heft, the C-300 plundered the nation's stock-car tracks. This is Tim Flock ripping through a turn at the original Daytona Beach track. Buck Baker was among the other legends to win with a C-300. A street-ready version could accelerate to 60 mph in 9 seconds and top out at 130 mph. A 300 set a class standing-start quarter-mile record at 76.84 mph. The godfather of the magazine road test, Tom McCahill, was a fan. He said the C-300 was "as solid as Grant's Tomb and 130 times as fast." He called it "a hardboiled, magnificent piece of semi-competition transportation."

▲ For the C-300, the 331-cid "hemi" made 300 bhp at 5200 rpm, versus 250 bhp in the New Yorker. It used solid lifters, 8.5:1 compression, a full-race cam, and twin four-barrel carbs.

▲ Built on New Yorker's 126-inch wheelbase, the C-300 had PowerFlite and a 150-mph speedometer. Wire wheels cost extra, but air conditioning, outside mirrors, and backup lights weren't factory-available.

▲ Ford dropped the 239-cid ohv V-8 after one season, turning to a 272-cid enlargement with 162 bhp at 4400 rpm, or 182 with Power Pack.

▲ The new Fairlane topped the line of restyled '55 Fords and took some styling cues from the just-introduced Thunderbird. The Sunliner convertible went for $2324 with a V-8 and weighed 3382 pounds. Overdrive added $110; Ford-O-Matic, $178.

▲ Pontiac was restyled for '55. This is the $2691 Star Chief convertible. Midyear brought a four-barrel Power Pack and 200 bhp.

▲ With stick shift, Pontiac's new "Strato Streak" 287.2-cid V-8 for 1955 had 173 bhp at 4400 rpm on a 7.4:1 compression. Hydra-Matic upped the ante to 180 bhp at 4600 rpm via an 8.0:1 squeeze.

It *looks* high priced—but it's the new Chevrolet "Two-Ten" 4-Door Sedan.

For sooner and safer arrivals!

It's so nimble and quick on the road . . .

Of course, you don't have to have an urgent errand and a motorcycle escort to make use of Chevrolet's quick and nimble ways. Wherever you go, the going's sweeter and safer in a Chevy.

Power's part of the reason. Chevrolet's horsepower ranges up to 205. And these numbers add up to *action*—second-saving acceleration for safer passing . . . rapid-fire reflexes that help you avoid trouble before it happens!

True, lots of cars are high powered today, but the difference is in the way Chevrolet *handles* its power. It's rock-steady on the road . . . clings to curves like part of the pavement. That's *stability*—and it helps make Chevrolet one of the few great road cars!

Highway-test one, soon. Your Chevrolet dealer will be happy to arrange it. . . . Chevrolet Division of General Motors, Detroit 2, Mich.

THE HOT ONE'S EVEN HOTTER

Traffic-test it—it's a beautiful thing to handle!

▲ Cheaper and less bold than a Bel Air, a '56 Two-Ten was a threat with the right V-8 as Chevy brought performance to the people.

▲ A '56 Bel Air Sport Coupe went for $2275 with the 162-bhp, 265-cid V-8. Powerglides had 170. New options brought 205 bhp with a four-barrel, or 225 with dual quads and 9.25:1 compression.

▲ Complementing the 300B for '56 was DeSoto's Adventurer. It had a 320-bhp, 341-cid dual-quad V-8. Only 996 were built.

▲ Enlarging the "hemi" to 354 cid and adding a high-lift camshaft gave Chrysler's 300B 340 bhp—or 355 bhp with optional 10.0:1 compression.

▲ In addition to one horsepower per cubic inch, 300B buyers could now get air conditioning and a 6.17:1 (!) axle. Pushbutton three-speed TorqueFlite was standard, but manual was offered.

◄ Buick had switched from straight-eight to V-8 power in 1953. For '56, the 322-cid V-8 in the Super, Roadmaster, and Century yielded 255 bhp.

▶ Dodge got noticed in '56 not only for its new fins and tri-tone color schemes, but for a D-500 option that added 8.5:1 compression and Carter dual quads to the 315-cid V-8. It made 295 bhp and was offered on any model, including this Royal Lancer. Super Red Ram 315 continued with 230 bhp.

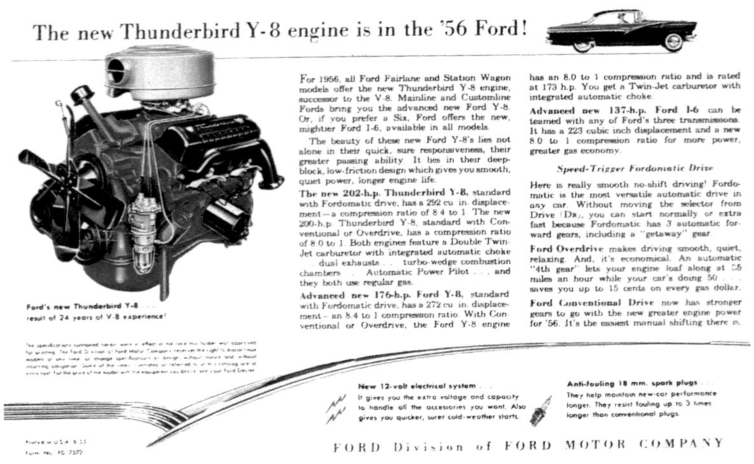

The new Thunderbird Y-8 engine is in the '56 Ford!

(Ford advertisement text, partially legible)

FORD Division of FORD MOTOR COMPANY

▲ Ford's new '56 Y-8 V-8 had 200 bhp, 202 with Fordomatic.

▲ At midyear, even the Customline two-door could get the 292-cid V-8.

▲ Mercury's '56 Montclair with Merc-O-Matic had a 225-bhp version of the "Safety-Surge" 312-cid V-8. A 260-bhp edition came later.

▲ *Auto Age* saw 0-60 mph in 12.2 seconds with a 225-bhp Montclair. Mercury won five NASCAR Grand National races in 1956.

▲ Packard's '56 Caribbean had motoring's largest V-8, at 374 cid.

▲ With 10.0:1 compression and dual quads, the 374 made 310 bhp.

▲ Leading the '56 Pontiac lineup was the Star Chief convertible. It had a 227-bhp version of the 316.6-cid V-8. Nearly all had Hydra-Matic.

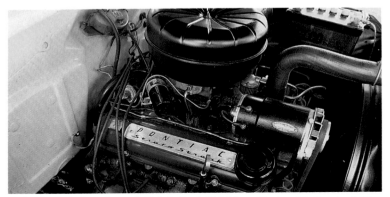

▲ Stick-shift four-barrel 316.6s had 216 bhp, Hydra-Matics had 227. Special version got dual quads, 10.0:1 compression, and 285 bhp.

▲ Fury joined the '56 Plymouth line and got exclusive use of a 240-bhp, 303-cid, four-barrel V-8. Zero-60 mph took 9 seconds, the quarter, 16.5.

▲ With its 275-bhp, 352-cid, four-barrel Packard V-8, Studebaker's '56 Golden Hawk was good for 0-60 mph in 8.7 seconds. Other Hawks had Stude V-8s.

▲ Chevy's '57 was a future classic, but notable, too, was the newly enlarged 283-cid V-8, which had up to 270 bhp with dual quads.

▲ Hottest of the 283s was the fuel-injected version. With 10.5:1 compression and high-lift cam, it made a super-efficient 283 bhp.

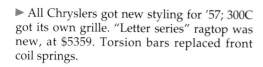

▲ Chevy's 283-bhp "fuelie" had to use a three-speed manual. A 250-bhp version could have automatic.

▶ All Chryslers got new styling for '57; 300C got its own grille. "Letter series" ragtop was new, at $5359. Torsion bars replaced front coil springs.

▲ Enlarged to 392 cid, the 300C's dual-quad hemi made 375 bhp on 9.25:1 compression, 390 on 10.0:1. Zero-60 mph took 8.4 seconds with TorqueFlite.

◀ DeSoto's stylish Adventurer hardtop (and new ragtop) got 345 bhp from a 345-cid V-8.

▲ A '57 Ford Fairlane 500 Victoria hardtop with the 272-cid V-8 cost $2439; 292- or 312-cid "go" was optional. Ford outsold Chevy in '57.

▲ Ford's '57 312-cid four-barrel "Thunderbird" V-8s had 245, 270, and 285 bhp; a Paxton supercharger gave 300 bhp, with 330 on tap for NASCAR racers.

▲ Olds enlarged its 324-cid V-8 to 371 cubes for '57, biggest among GM cars. It had 277 bhp with a four-barrel in this Super 88.

▲ Olds' three-deuce J-2 option made 300 bhp. Zero-60 mph took 9 seconds. Lee Petty hit 144.9 mph on Daytona salt with one, but NASCAR banned the J-2.

▲ For 1957, the V-8 in the stunningly restyled Plymouth Fury grew to 318 cid and 290 bhp. *Motor Trend*'s stick-shift Fury hit 60 mph in 8.7 seconds.

▲ Available in any '57 Plymouth, the new 318 had dual quads, high-lift cam, dual exhausts, and 9.25:1 compression. New TorqueFlite cost $220.

▶ The limited-edition Bonneville convertible joined Pontiac during the '57 season. It cost $5782 and only 630 were built, all with a fuel-injected V-8. The 370-cid mill delivered 310 bhp at 4800 rpm, 400 lbs/ft of torque at 3400, but had to haul 4285 pounds of Bonneville. A lighter Pontiac Chieftain with the 347-cid V-8 and Tri-Power could beat the Bonnie's 18-second quarter-mile time by 1.2 seconds. Pontiac issued three Tri-Power engines for '57, but two were for NASCAR.

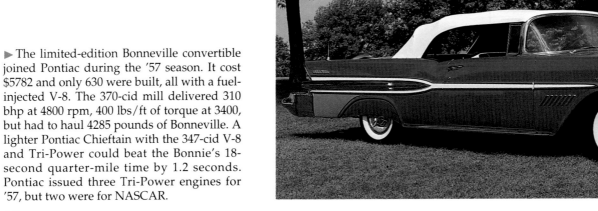

▲ Rebel's V-8 had 255 horsepower at 4700 rpm, 9.5:1 compression, solid lifters, and a four-barrel. Only 1500 were built, priced at a hefty—for Rambler— $2786.

◄ Early muscle from Rambler! Squeezing the big Nash Ambassador's new 327-cid V-8 into a light Rambler body produced the '57 Rambler Rebel. Zero-60 times were close to 7 seconds—second only to a fuelie Corvette, according to *Motor Trend*.

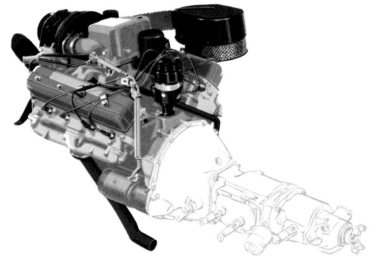

▲ Studebaker gave its '57 Golden Hawk bigger tail feathers, and trimmed some weight by substituting its own V-8 for the Packard power of '57. Handling improved, and 0-60 still took about 9 seconds, the quarter, 17.3 seconds.

▲ In the Golden Hawk, Stude's 289-cid V-8 used a "Jet-Stream" supercharger to get 275 bhp at 4800 rpm and 333 lbs/ft of torque at 3200 rpm. An overdrive manual or Flight-O-Matic slushbox were offered.

▲ Overshadowed in later years by '57 models, the heavier '58 Chevy pleased buyers with its 2.5-inch longer wheelbase, smoother ride, and bigger size. Impala (shown) bowed as the new top-line hardtop and convertible.

▲ Big news under Chevy hoods for '58 was the 348-cid V-8 with up to 315 bhp from three deuces and 11.0:1 compression. A '57 283 fuelie was faster, but *Motor Trend*'s 348 still did 0-60 in 9.1 seconds and the quarter in 16.5.

▲ A jump to 10.0:1 compression gave the Chrysler 300D's hemi 380 bhp, up by 5, for '58. A few came with Bendix fuel injection.

▲ Ford engine options in '58 grew to include a 332-cid V-8 with 240 or 265 bhp, and a new FE-series 352-cid big-block with 300 bhp.

▲ Super 88 had chromey, barge-like styling—and the optional continental kit didn't help—but Olds advanced to fourth in sales for '58, partly on the strength of more potent 371-cid V-8s.

▲ The Rocket 371 made 305 bhp in the Super 88 and 312 in the 98, which rode a four-inch longer wheelbase.

▼ Bonneville became a separate Pontiac series for '58. The fancy convertible and hardtop used the Chieftain's 122-inch wheelbase (two less than Star Chief's). A Tri-Power ragtop paced the Indy 500.

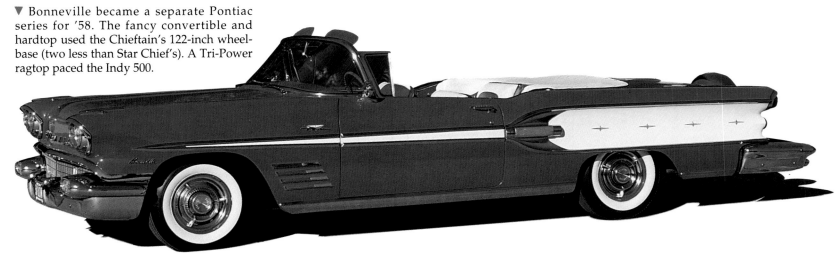

▲ In Bonneville, Pontiac's 370-cid V-8 ranged from 255 bhp with a four-barrel to 300 with Tri-Power. About 200 Bonnevilles had Rochester fuel injection, available for $500 and good for 310 bhp.

▲ Pontiac's $93.60 Tri-Power option used three two-barrel Rochesters, 10.5:1 compression, and a high-lift cam to get 300 bhp at 4600 rpm. Two NASCAR-certified V-8s arrived during the year, with 315/330 bhp.

▲ "Batwing" fins and a "nostril" grille drew the eye to the '59 Chevy Impala, but buyers also savored an even dozen engine options.

▲ Chevy's 348-cid V-8 now had 250 to 335 bhp, depending on carburetion and compression (up to 11.25:1). Four 283s were sold, at 170-290 bhp.

▲ Engineer Robert M. Rodger with the dual-quad 413-cid wedge that replaced the hemi in Chrysler's '59 300E. Horsepower was still 380.

▲ Late-1950s automotive styling themes reached a crescendo with the 1959 Custom Royal Lancer. D-500 power gave the Dodge some bite.

▲ Dodge buyers got a 326-cid V-8, a 361 (295/305 bhp), or this 320-bhp D-500 383 (345 bhp with dual quads).

▼Pontiac enlarged its V-8 to 389 cid. Bonneville had from 260 bhp to this 345-bhp Tri-Power. The new Catalina had 215.

▲ Chrysler built just 140 of its $5749 300E ragtops for '59. The new wedge V-8 was 100 lbs. lighter than the 392-cid hemi, and had 450 lbs./ft. of torque, up 15, so acceleration was even quicker.

▲ Pontiac unveiled two trademarks for '59: a split grille and a "Wide-Track" chassis. Bonneville again topped the line, at $3257 for the Sport Coupe.

1960

Compact Chevrolet Corvair and Ford Falcon debut • Ram Induction launched on Chrysler 300F, yielding 375 or 400 bhp • Dodge and Plymouth get Ram Induction for their big V-8s • Lee A. Iacocca, appointed Ford Division's general manager, helps rekindle interest in performance • Smooth Ford Starliner appears, eager for NASCAR superspeedways • Ford announces triple two-barrel setup as dealer-installed option • Hurst-Campbell markets Dual-Pattern floor-shift conversion • Drag-oriented Pontiac with Tri-Power belts out 348 bhp • Pontiac develops racing chassis, offers Borg-Warner four-speed • Jim Wangers drags Pontiac to Super/Stock and stock eliminator wins at NHRA Nationals

1960 CHEVROLET HIGH-PERFORMANCE ENGINES							
TYPE	CID	BORE× STROKE	BHP @ RPM	TORQUE @ RPM	FUEL SYSTEM	COMP. RATIO	AVAIL.
ohv V-8	283	3.88 × 3.00	230 @ 4800	300 @ 3000	1 × 4bbl.	9.5:1	full size
ohv V-8	348	4.13 × 3.25	250 @ 4400	355 @ 2800	1 × 4bbl.	9.5:1	full size
ohv V-8	348	4.13 × 3.25	305 @ 5600	350 @ 3600	1 × 4bbl.	11.0:1	full size
ohv V-8	348	4.13 × 3.35	320 @ 5600	358 @ 3600	1 × 4bbl.	11.25:1	full size
ohv V-8	348	4.13 × 3.35	280 @ 4800	355 @ 3200	3 × 2bbl.	9.5:1	full size
ohv V-8	348	4.13 × 3.35	335 @ 3600	362 @ 3600	3 × 2bbl.	11.25:1	full size

▼ The ultimate in big Chevy style and speed for '60 was an Impala Sport Coupe with the Special Super Turbo-Thrust 348. It made 335 bhp with Tri-Carb induction, solid lifters, and 11.25:1 compression. A four-speed manual gearbox also was available.

▲ Chevrolet toned down Impala's "batwing" tail for 1960. All full-size convertibles were Impalas.

▲ This was El Camino's last year as a full-size model. Chevy called it a "two-door sedan pickup."

▼ The Bel Air Sport Coupe debuted for '60 with Impala styling and available V-8 power starting at $2596, versus $2704 for the Impala Sport Coupe.

▲ Chevy's 348-cid V-8 had its moments. Here, Terry Prince in the Prince & Nicholson '60 Bel Air (left) launches on his way to the B/S title at the 1962 NHRA Winternationals. The two-door sedan turned 13.50s at 103 mph.

▶ Early Chrysler muscle was best expressed by a series of big, stylish two-door hardtops starting with the 1955 C-300 and its 300-bhp Hemi. By 1960, the "letter series" cars had progressed to the 300F. It continued the tradition of opulence and muscle, though front-end styling was now more similar to that of other Chryslers. Chrysler adopted unibody construction for '60, which weighed less than the former body-on-frame designs. At a princely $5411, the spirited 300 hardtop was "highly impractical—and definitely desirable," said *Car Life*. Pushbutton TorqueFlite automatic was standard, but a French-built Pont-a-Mousson four-speed manual transmission (as in Facel Vega) was optional for just this season, ending up in only seven 300Fs.

▼ Ram Induction was the big news under Chrysler 300F hoods. With long tubes, the 413-cid V-8 delivered 375 bhp. Optional short-ram tubes added 25 horses. A 375-bhp 300F could hit 60 mph in 7.1 seconds and do the quarter-mile in 16 flat. *Car Life* claimed a 0-60 time of 6.8 seconds—in a drizzle!

▲ Slipping into the four-place 300F was a snap, with automatic-swiveling front seats pointing the way. A full-length console was standard, along with a tachometer and an electro-luminescent instrument panel.

▲ Torsion-bar front suspension helped give the hot Chrysler its road-hugging ride. *Car Life* noted that body roll was "barely noticed," due partly to "extraordinary bucket seats." 300Fs took the top six spots in Daytona's flying mile, led by a record 144.927 mph with Gregg Ziegler behind the wheel.

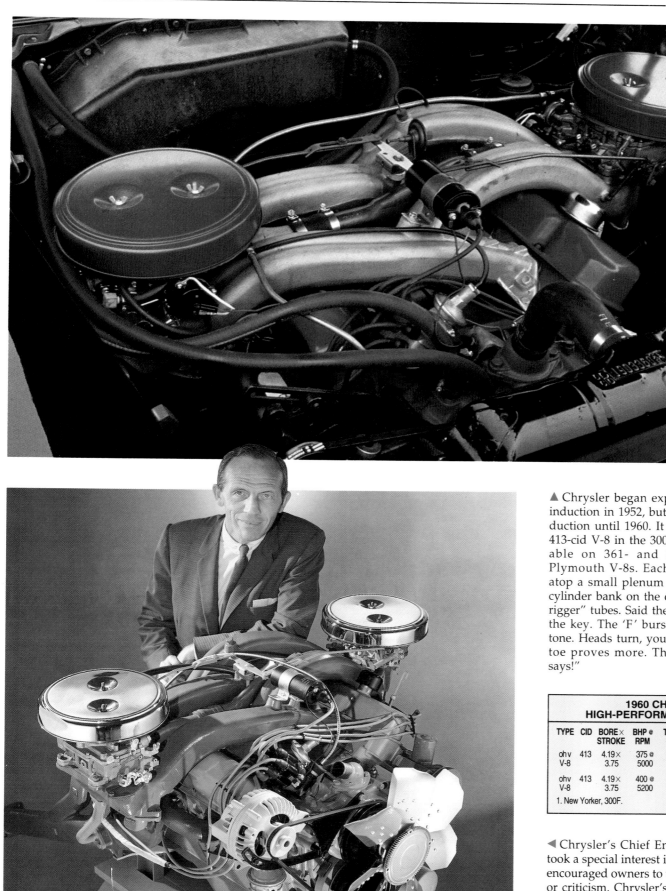

▲ Chrysler began experimenting with ram induction in 1952, but didn't put it into production until 1960. It came standard on the 413-cid V-8 in the 300F, and was also available on 361- and 383-cid Dodge and Plymouth V-8s. Each four-barrel carb sat atop a small plenum chamber, and fed the cylinder bank on the opposite side via "outrigger" tubes. Said the 300F brochure: "Turn the key. The 'F' bursts into a throaty baritone. Heads turn, you tingle. A touch of the toe proves more. This car means what it says!"

1960 CHRYSLER HIGH-PERFORMANCE ENGINES

TYPE	CID	BORE × STROKE	BHP @ RPM	TORQUE @ RPM	FUEL SYSTEM	COMP. RATIO	AVAIL.
ohv V-8	413	4.19 × 3.75	375 @ 5000	495 @ 2800	2×4bbl.	10.0:1	1
ohv V-8	413	4.19 × 3.75	400 @ 5200	465 @ 3600	2×4bbl.	10.0:1	300F
1. New Yorker, 300F.							

◄ Chrysler's Chief Engineer, R.M. Rodger, took a special interest in the "letter" cars, and encouraged owners to write with suggestions or criticism. Chrysler's ram induction recognized that pressure waves within the intake system could produce a "supercharging" effect. To yield peak power at mid-range speeds—when it's needed for highway acceleration—a 30-inch tube was optimum. One drawback: The ram effect occurs only in a rather narrow rpm range, so it had less impact as the engine revved.

▲ Sedate appearances can deceive, as in the case of this fawn/white Dodge Polara Suburban wagon with seating for nine. Under the hood dwells a 383-cid D-500 engine with ram induction, hooked to the usual TorqueFlite automatic. Luxury extras include swivel seat, rear air, and power locks. This restored wagon spent time in a junkyard.

▶ Fitted with cast aluminum ram induction, Dodge's 383 earned the D-500 badge and 330 bhp. With short-ram induction whipping up 340 bhp, a Dart Phoenix could storm to 60 mph in 8.5 seconds and turn 16.3 in the quarter. The larger Matador carried a 295-bhp 361 V-8, while full-size Polaras came only with 383s, either 325 or 330 bhp.

▲ Dart sedans, hardtops, and coupes had a 118-inch wheelbase, four inches shorter than the larger and heavier Matador and Polara. This Dart Phoenix hardtop coupe weighed 3605 pounds and listed for $2727 with V-8.

1960 DODGE HIGH-PERFORMANCE ENGINES

TYPE	CID	BORE × STROKE	BHP @ RPM	TORQUE @ RPM	FUEL SYSTEM	COMP. RATIO	AVAIL.
ohv V-8	361	4.13 × 3.38	295 @ 4600	390 @ 2400	1×4bbl.	10.0:1	Matador
ohv V-8	361	4.13 × 3.38	310 @ 4800	435 @ 2800	2×4bbl.	10.0:1	Pioneer, Phoenix
ohv V-8	383	4.25 × 3.75	330 @ 4800	465 @ 2800	2×4bbl.	10.0:1	1
ohv V-8	383	4.25 × 3.75	325 @ 4600	435 @ 2800	1×4bbl.	10.0:1	Pioneer, Polara
ohv V-8	383	4.25 × 3.75	330 @ 5200*	425 @ 3600	1×4bbl.	10.0:1	Pioneer, Phoenix

* 340 bhp with long-ram induction. 1. Pioneer, Phoenix, Matador, Polara.

◀ The Seneca was at the bottom of the Dart line, below the Pioneer and Phoenix. At 3530 pounds, the two-door Seneca sedan was the lightest Dodge available with a V-8 engine, though it was limited to the 230-bhp 318-cid unit. To get the 383, you had to move up to the Phoenix.

► Fords were restyled for '60. Wheelbase grew one inch, to 119, and overall length was up by nearly six. The Galaxie Starliner coupe had a slippery roofline tailored for NASCAR superspeedways.

▲ The 360-bhp "Interceptor 360" 352-cid V-8 was Ford's first performance engine since 1957. It had a Holly four-barrel on an aluminum intake manifold. Triple two-barrels became a midyear dealer option.

▲ Ford judged its Cruise-O-Matic automatic gearbox too weak for the Interceptor 360, so the engine initially was sold only with a Borg-Warner T-85 manual with three speeds or with overdrive (shown).

▼ A 360-bhp Ford Starliner averaged 142 mph at Daytona for 40 laps. Karol Miller drove one to a record 157.902 mph on the Bonneville flats. Ford's 15 wins topped the Grand National stock-car tour in 1960.

1960 FORD HIGH-PERFORMANCE ENGINES

TYPE	CID	BORE × STROKE	BHP @ RPM	TORQUE @ RPM	FUEL SYSTEM	COMP. RATIO	AVAIL.
ohv V-8	352	4.00 × 3.50	300 @ 4600	381 @ 2800	1×4bbl.	9.6:1	full size
ohv V-8	352	4.30 × 3.70	360 @ 6000	380 @ 3400	1×4bbl.	10.6:1	full size

▲ Olds' "Regular Rocket" 371-cid V-8 (left) had up to 260 bhp; "Premium Rocket" 394 had 315.

▲ A Ninety-Eight convertible paced the Indy 500. It rode a 126.5-inch wheelbase and weighed 4349 pounds. Lighter and smaller were the Dynamic 88 and the Super 88. They had a 123-inch wheelbase. Oldsmobile's top performer was the Super 88 fitted with the optional 315-bhp, four-barrel 394-cid V-8.

1960 OLDSMOBILE HIGH-PERFORMANCE ENGINES

TYPE	CID	BORE × STROKE	BHP @ RPM	TORQUE @ RPM	FUEL SYSTEM	COMP. RATIO	AVAIL.
ohv V-8	371	4.00 × 3.69	240 @ 4400	375 @ 2800	1×4bbl.	8.75:1	Dynamic 88
ohv V-8	371	4.13 × 3.69	325 @ 4600	435 @ 2800	1×4bbl.	9.75:1	Super 88
ohv V-8	394	4.13 × 3.69	315 @ 4600	435 @ 2800	1×4bbl.	9.75:1	Super 88,89

▶ Plymouth's most potent engine to date was the 383-cid V-8 with ram induction, here tagged "SonoRamic." Similar to the system installed on Chrysler 300F engines, its dual quads and long intake tubes produced up to 330 bhp. Plymouth was beginning to shake its staid, family-car image.

► Its longhorn, cross-ram manifolds packing a pair of big four-barrels, "SonoRamic" induction served as the opening salvo of Plymouth's performance makeover in the 1960s. With a single four-barrel, the 383 still made a respectable 310 bhp. The compact Valiant also debuted this year. A "Hyper-Pak" option for its 170-cid "slant six" borrowed the ram-induction principle and increased horsepower from 101 to 148 with a 10.0:1 compression.

▼ Plymouth went to unibody construction for 1960, but the styling was garish as tailfins had their last hurrah. This is the mid-line Belvedere hardtop.

1960 PLYMOUTH HIGH-PERFORMANCE ENGINES

TYPE	CID	BORE × STROKE	BHP @ RPM	TORQUE @ RPM	FUEL SYSTEM	COMP. RATIO	AVAIL.
ohv I-8	170	3.40 × 3.13	148 @ 5200	153 @ 4200	1×4bbl.	10.5:1	Valiant
ohv V-8	361	4.12 × 3.38	305 @ 4800	369 @ 3000	1×4bbl.	10.0:1	full size
ohv V-8	361	4.12 × 3.38	310 @ 4800	435 @ 2800	2×4bbl.	10.0:1	full size
ohv V-8	383	4.24 × 3.38	330 @ 4800	460 @ 2800	2×4bbl.	10.0:1	full size
ohv V-8	383	4.24 × .3.38	325 @ 4600	435 @ 2800	1×4bbl.	10.0:1	full size
ohv V-8	383	4.24 × 3.38	330 @ 5200	435 @ 3600	2×4bbl.	10.0:1	full size

▲ The Sport Fury was gone, but carrying on as Plymouth's cousin to the Dodge Dart was the 118-inch-wheelbase Fury, here in convertible form. At $2967, it was Plymouth's most expensive non-station wagon model. A 310-bhp Fury could manage 7.5 seconds to 60 mph, and 15.6 for the quarter-mile.

1960 PONTIAC HIGH-PERFORMANCE ENGINES

TYPE	CID	BORE× STROKE	BHP @ RPM	TORQUE @ RPM	FUEL SYSTEM	COMP. RATIO	AVAIL.
ohv V-8	389	4.06× 3.75	281 @ 4400	407 @ 2800	1×4bbl.	8.6:1	Bonneville
ohv V-8	389	4.06× 3.75	283 @ 4400	413 @ 2800	1×2bbl.	10.25:1	1
ohv V-8	389	4.06× 3.75	303 @ 4600	425 @ 2800	1×4bbl.	10.25:1	2
ohv V-8	389	4.06× 3.75	318 @ 4600	430 @ 3200	3×2bbl.	10.75:1	3

1. Catalina, Ventura, Star Chief. 2. Bonneville, Bonneville Safari.
3. Catalina, Ventura, Star Chief, Bonneville.

fresh point of view

...from Pontiac 1960

THE ONLY CAR WITH WIDE-TRACK WHEELS

▶ Pontiac sales overtook Oldsmobile and Buick in 1959 and would continue to climb well into the decade. The '60s were basically facelifted '59s, though the Ventura trim level joined the line for this year only. Inside, the floor tunnel was lowered thanks to a redesigned Hydra-Matic transmission, and a removable "Sportable" transistor radio was optional.

▼ Pontiac temporarily dumped its split grille for a full-width design that helped to emphasize the wide-track theme. Wheelbase was 122 inches on Catalina and Ventura, 124 on Star Chief and Bonneville (shown). All used a 389-cid "Tempest" V-8. It came with a four-barrel on the Bonneville and made 281 horsepower with manual shift, 303 bhp with Hydra-Matic. Special four-barrel versions also came in 333-bhp tune, while Tri-Power setups yielded 318 or 348 bhp, with some sources listing up to 363 bhp.

▲ Only the $3530 Custom Safari wagon cost more than the $3476 Bonneville ragtop. Pontiac's other convertible was the $3078 Catalina. On Bonneville, leather upholstery with "Morrokide" accents was standard and fabric tops were available in six colors. The Bonneville drop top weighed 4030 pounds.

Why ladies like the security of Wide-Track driving

A wider track is a wider stance. A wider stance is stability, safety, balance, less lean and sway, easier maneuvering, better control, more confidence and security at the wheel. Pontiac has a wider stance than any other car. A very pleasant demonstration of Wide-Track driving is yours for the asking. See or call one of our fine dealers this week.

With the widest track of any car, Pontiac's width is on the road—where it gives you better stability. Wide-Track widens the stance, not the car.

PONTIAC THE ONLY CAR WITH WIDE-TRACK WHEELS

◀While Pontiac ads sang the praises of security and even fuel economy, it was a different tune at racetracks. For example, Smokey Yunick's '60 Catalina led the Daytona 500 at an average of nearly 160 mph until he spun out nine laps from the finish.

▲ At 3835 pounds, a Catalina two-door hardtop was the lightest Poncho. On Labor Day at Detroit Dragway, Jim Wangers won NHRA top-stock eliminator in one. And a 333-bhp 389 street version was timed at 7.8 seconds 0-60, and 16 seconds flat in the quarter-mile.

1961

Chevrolet turns to the 409—an engine soon to be immortalized in song as well as stats ● Super Sport trim option debuts on all Chevrolet Impala models ● Chrysler 300G offered in both convertible and hardtop form ● Dodge and Plymouth start with 383-cid V-8s, later add 413 wedge ● Dodge Lancer Hyper-Pak option wrings 196 bhp out of 225-cid six ● Bore/stroke boost transforms Ford's 352-cid V-8 into a 390 ● 401-bhp triple two-barrel Ford V-8 added during model year—deemed legal for drag racing ● Ford offers its first four-speed ● 375-bhp Ford Starliner exceeds 153 mph at Daytona ● Sporty Falcon Futura appears with bucket seats but puny power ● Oldsmobile adds "personal" Starfire convertible ● Downsized bodies boost performance from Pontiac's hot 389s ● Pontiac wins record 30 of 52 NASCAR Grand National stock-car starts ● Compact Pontiac Tempest debuts

▲ Chevrolet full-size models got a big dose of sportiness in mid-1961 with the Super Sport option. Available on any Impala for $53.80, it included a host of styling and mechanical alterations. Inside was a Corvette-type grab-bar in front of the passenger, some special trim, and a 7000-rpm tachometer.

▶ The Super Sport package was ordered on just 453 '61 Impalas, most of them coupes, with a handful of convertibles getting the option. This striking example carries the full load of SS equipment, including sintered metallic brake linings. Also part of the package: special body trim, simulated knock-off spinner wheel covers, power steering/brakes, heavy-duty springs/shocks, and 8.00×14 whitewalls.

▲ Hottest 348-cid V-8 had 350-bhp with Tri-Power and solid lifters; the four-barrel gave 340 bhp. Both demanded manual shift, but the 305-bhp version could have Powerglide automatic. At mid-year, the 348 was bored and stroked to become the fabled "409," which had 360 bhp with a single four-barrel.

▼ Big Chevys kept their 119-inch wheelbase for '61, but got shorter, narrower bodies. Top Impala was the Sport Coupe. This one has the SS option, T-10 four-speed, and 3.70:1 Positraction axle.

▲ Chevrolet dealers handled installation of this year's Super Sport option kits. They were available only on Impalas with the 348 or 409, though the 348 could in fact be ordered on any full-size Chevy. That meant those triple carbs beneath the hood could imbue even a garden-variety Biscayne with enough firepower to surprise anyone who mistakenly thought you had to have SS icing to get 350-horse muscle.

▲ Impala Sport Coupe started at $2704 with V-8, and weighed 3534 pounds. Like all big Chevys, it had new vent openings over the grille, but triple tailights identify Impalas from lesser models.

▲ Bel Air Sport Coupe shared Impala's graceful greenhouse, but was the mid-range model, with Biscayne the low-priced entry. Chevy's base V-8 was a 283, but fuel injection was no longer offered.

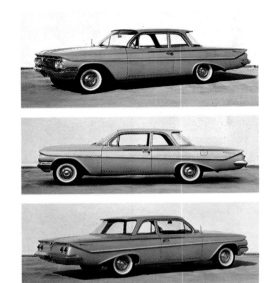

▲ Bel Air two-door sedans came only with the more conservative roofline and wraparound rear window. These sedans started at $2491 and were available with all engines except the Impala SS-only 409.

◄ Introduction of the SS kit coincided with the unveiling of the 409, and the tandem made for one of the coolest combinations on wheels. Only 142 409s were installed for '61, but they set the stage for the coming Super Sport mystique. Manufacturing problems kept initial production small, so most early 409s went to racers and road-testers. Belting out 360 bhp at 5800 rpm and a whopping 409 pounds/feet of torque, the hot V-8 could send an Impala to 60 mph in 7.8 seconds and through the quarter-mile in 15.8. Features included a dual-snorkel air cleaner, forged aluminum pistons, wild cam, solid lifters, Carter AFB carb, and 11.25:1 compression.

IT FEELS GOOD, LOOKS BETTER and GOES GREAT!

Take any one of Chevy's five '61 Impalas, add either the new 409-cubic-inch V8 or the 348-cubic-inch job and a four-speed floor-mounted stick, wrap the whole thing in special trim that sets it apart from any other car on the street, and man, you have an Impala Super Sport! Every detail of this new Chevrolet package is custom made for young men on the move. This is the kind of car the insiders mean when they say Chevy, the kind that can only be appreciated by a man who understands, wants, and won't settle for less than REAL driving excitement.

Here are the ingredients of the Impala Super Sport kit* • Special Super Sport trim, inside and out • Instrument Panel Pad • Special wheel covers • Power brakes and power steering • Choice of five power teams: 305 hp. with 4-speed Synchro-Mesh or heavy-duty Powerglide. 340 hp. with 4-speed only. 350 hp. with 4-speed only. 360 hp. with 4-speed only • Heavy-duty springs and shocks • Sintered metallic brake linings • 7,000-RPM Tach • 8.00 x 14 narrow band whitewalls • Chevrolet Division of General Motors, Detroit 2. Michigan.

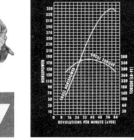

CHEVROLET

1961 CHEVROLET HIGH-PERFORMANCE ENGINES							
TYPE	CID	BORE×STROKE	BHP @ RPM	TORQUE @ RPM	FUEL SYSTEM	COMP. RATIO	AVAIL.
ohv V-8	283	3.88× 3.00	230 @ 4800	300 @ 3000	1×4bbl.	9.5:1	full size
ohv V-8	348	4.13× 3.25	250 @ 4400	355 @ 2800	1×4bbl.	9.5:1	full size
ohv V-8	348	4.13× 3.25	305 @ 5600	355 @ 3400	1×4bbl.	9.5:1	full size
ohv V-8	348	4.13× 3.35	340 @ 5800	326 @ 3600	1×4bbl.	11.25:1	full size
ohv V-8	348	4.13× 3.35	280 @ 4800	355 @ 3200	3×2bbl.	9.5:1	full size
ohv V-8	348	4.13× 3.35	350 @ 6000	364 @ 3600	3×2bbl.	11.25:1	full size
ohv V-8	409	4.31× 3.50	360 @ 5800	409 @ 3600	1×4bbl.	11.0:1	full size

▶ Canted quad headlamps led the way for this year's Chryslers, including the 300G. Again powered by the 375-bhp 413-cid V-8, the big sports-luxury coupe ran to 60 mph in 8.2 seconds and needed only 16.2 to finish the quarter-mile. An optional 400 bhp was again offered. Production of the 300 increased to 1617, 337 of them convertibles. Both body styles rode the New Yorker's 126-inch wheelbase.

▼ A chrome spear through a "300" badge again helped identify Chrysler's performance flagship, though the fake spare tire cover was excised from the trunk lid and 15-inch wheels returned for the first time since 1956. The 300G coupe cost $5441 with a curb weight of 4260 pounds. The rarer convertible went for $5841 and weighed 4315 pounds. The four-place cabin sports beige leather upholstery, a full-length console, power windows, and swivel power front seats.

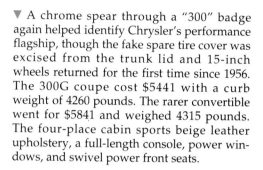

1961 CHRYSLER HIGH-PERFORMANCE ENGINES							
TYPE	CID	BORE× STROKE	BHP @ RPM	TORQUE @ RPM	FUEL SYSTEM	COMP. RATIO	AVAIL.
ohv V-8	413	4.19× 3.75	375 @ 5000	495 @ 2800	2×4bbl.	10.0:1	300G
ohv V-8	413	4.19× 3.75	400 @ 5200	465 @ 3600	2×4bbl.	10.0:1	300G

▲ The hallowed "300" insignia stood for panache and power. A slightly modified 300G piloted by Gregg Ziegler rocketed through Daytona's flying mile at 143.027 mph. A stock version driven by Bud Faubel hit 90.7 mph in the standing mile.

▶ Dual quads and the signature long-ram induction tubing teamed 375 horses with a stout 495 pounds/feet of torque at just 2800 rpm. A three-speed manual with floor shift replaced the rare four-speed unit, though most buyers specified TorqueFlite automatic.

THIS IS THE NEW 300G BY CHRYSLER

A car that heats up your blood. The 300-G . . . the 1961 version of Chrysler's championship breed of motorcars. A car that can take its well-proportioned heft and go record-breaking at Daytona Beach.* The rare American that's turned out one at a time; a few thousand times a year. You'll find this tiger powered by the latest in Chrysler's brilliantly engineered ram-injection V-8s. With a full 375 horsepower that you manage with incredible ease. Power brakes and steering help. But the real clue to the "G's" handling genius is its superbly balanced suspension. Conveniences are complete. Comfort is served in typical 300 style: four leather-lined, foam-padded bucket seats. This is a total machine. The one that can tour confidently with the best automobiles the world has to offer. The 300-G . . . a rare kind of car for a rare kind of man.

▲ Chrysler touted its 300G as a well-rounded car, able to "tour confidently with the best automobiles the world has to offer." Though, apparently, as "a rare kind of car for a rare kind of man," women drivers need not apply.

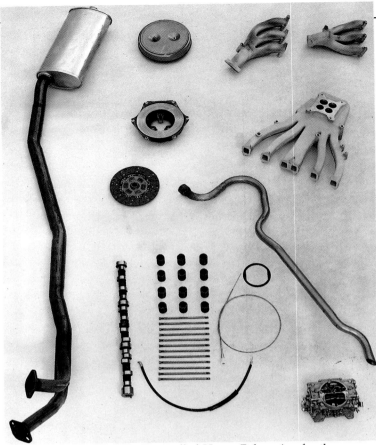

▲ Dodge offered this dealer-installed Hyper-Pak option for the venerable 225-cid "slant six" engine. An aggressive cam, four-barrel carb, long-ram manifold, and tuned headers helped boost horsepower from 145 to 196—nearly one bhp per cubic inch.

▲ Reverse-swept fins and a freshened nose gave the full-size Dodges a new look. Dart (above) road a 118-inch wheelbase and was the make's low-priced entry. Returning was the 325-bhp 383-cid D-500 V-8 option, available with dual-quad ram induction for 330 bhp, or 340 bhp with short-ram tubes. That gave the Dart roughly 10 pounds per horsepower, about the same as a 360-bhp/409 Impala.

▶ *Hot Rod* magazine ran a fully stock two-door Dart with Ram-equipped 383 and TorqueFlite through the quarter-mile in 15.25 seconds, hitting 89.59 mph. Later in the year, Dodges could be ordered with a 413-cid V-8 (right). Breathing through a single four-barrel carb, this Super D-500 engine yielded 350 horsepower. Optional Ram induction boosted it to 375 bhp.

▲ A stock D-500 383 powers this original Vermillion Red Dodge Polara convertible, with bright red deluxe interior. Three-speed TorqueFlite sends its 325 horses to a "Sure-Grip" 3.23:1 limited-slip axle. In addition to the D-500 package, options included power windows, brakes, steering and seats; "Auto Pilot"; "Safe-T-Matic" door locks; "Hi Way Hi-Fi" (a 16 2/3-rpm under-dash record player); "Aero wheel" squared-off steering wheel; bumper guards; spinner wheel covers; "Astrophonic" radio; "Mirromatic" rear-view mirror; and extended rocker-molding trim.

▲ Polara rode a 122-inch-wheelbase and was Dodge's flagship (the Matador model was dropped). Polaras nonetheless looked similar to Darts, and both could be fitted with the D-500 V-8s.

1961 DODGE HIGH-PERFORMANCE ENGINES

TYPE	CID	BORE × STROKE	BHP @ RPM	TORQUE @ RPM	FUEL SYSTEM	COMP. RATIO	AVAIL.
ohv V-8	383	4.25 × 3.75	325 @ 4600	425 @ 2800	1×4bbl.	10.0:1	Dart, Polara
ohv V-8	383	4.25 × 3.75	330 @ 4600	460 @ 2800	2×4bbl.	10.0:1	Dart, Polara
ohv V-8	383	4.25 × 3.75	340 @ 5000	440 @ 2800	2×4bbl.	10.0:1	Dart
ohv V-8	383	4.25 × 3.75	340 @ 5000	440 @ 2800	2×4bbl.	10.0:1	Dart
ohv V-8	383	4.25 × 3.75	330 @ 5200	425 @ 3600	1×4bbl.	10.0:1	Dart
ohv V-8	413	4.18 × 3.75	350 @ 4600	470 @ 2800	1×4bbl.	10.0:1	Dart
ohv V-8	413	4.18 × 3.75	375 @ 5000	465 @ 2800	2×4bbl.	10.0:1	Dart
ohv V-8	413	4.18 × 3.75	375 @ 5200	450 @ 2800	1×4bbl.	10.0:1	Dart

▲ With a single four-barrel carburetor instead of Ram Induction and with 10.0:1 compression, Dodge's basic 383-cid D-500 cranked out 325 bhp and 425 pounds/feet of torque. It was one of the era's most durable engines, but it didn't help Dodge sales, which slumped more than 25 percent. Dodge styling wasn't popular, competition increased, and sales were sluggish industry-wide. Still, 1961 marked the first time Dodge could take advantage of the 413 V-8, which previously had been installed only in big, heavy Chryslers. The 413 would quickly evolve into a series of Ramcharger powerhouses.

▲ Shorter by nearly four inches overall, and two inches narrower, big Fords sported a handsome facelift with round taillights and modest canted fins. Wheelbase was unchanged at 119 inches. This is the semi-fastback Starliner roof. A bore/stroke boost turned the FE-series 352-cid V-8 into a 390, ranking with Pontiac's 389. Two versions went on sale, at 300 and 375 bhp, plus the 330-bhp Police Special. All Ford V-8s adopted the "Thunderbird" designation.

◄ Ford's big gun as the year opened was the "Thunderbird 390 Super," packing a 375-bhp wallop at 6000 rpm and 427 pounds/feet of torque at 3400. Power brakes and steering and air conditioning were unavailable with this engine. Described by *Hot Rod* as a "real charger," the 375-bhp V-8 had 10.6:1 compression, cast iron headers, and a Holley four-barrel. If that didn't satisfy, midyear brought triple Holley two-barrels and higher compression, good for 401 horses at 6000 rpm and 430 pounds/feet of twist. At NHRA Winternationals, Les Ritchey ran a tri-carb Ford to a 13.33-second ET at 105.50 mph.

▲ Full-size traditional-roof two-doors came in Custom 300, Fairlane, Fairlane 500, and Galaxie trim. Galaxie (shown) weighed 3537 pounds and cost $2538; the 390 four-barrel added $197.

▲ Two-tone upholstery added flash to a Sunliner ragtop; the available 390 V-8 could add dash, especially with Ford's first four-speed manual gearbox, a Borg-Warner T-10, added late in '61.

▲ Sunliner convertibles started at $2849, and found 44,614 customers. Less popular was the $2599 Starliner hardtop; with just 29,669 built, it would be dropped after this model year.

▲ Legendary stock-car racer Fred Lorenzen piloted Holman-Moody Fords to three Grand National wins in '61, driving both the ragtop and the Starliner. Ford took seven NASCAR victories that season.

1961 OLDSMOBILE HIGH-PERFORMANCE ENGINES							
TYPE	CID	BORE × STROKE	BHP @ RPM	TORQUE @ RPM	FUEL SYSTEM	COMP. RATIO	AVAIL.
ohv V-8	394	4.13 × 3.69	250 @ 4400	405 @ 2400	1 × 2bbl.	8.75:1	Super 88
ohv V-8	394	4.13 × 3.69	325 @ 4600	435 @ 2800	1 × 4bbl.	10.0:1	1
ohv V-8	394	4.13 × 3.69	330 @ 4600	440 @ 2800	1 × 4bbl.	10.25:1	Starfire
1. 88, Super 88, 98.							

▲ This Dynamic 88 Holiday hardtop coupe shows the crisp lines that freshened Oldsmobile's full-size roster. It started at $2956, weighed 3981 pounds, and was Olds' best-selling hardtop. The Super 88 line spawned a Starfire convertible at midyear. It was priced at $4647 and weighed 4330 pounds.

1961 FORD HIGH-PERFORMANCE ENGINES							
TYPE	CID	BORE × STROKE	BHP @ RPM	TORQUE @ RPM	FUEL SYSTEM	COMP. RATIO	AVAIL.
ohv V-8	352	4.00 × 3.50	220 @ 4400	336 @ 2400	1 × 2bbl.	8.9:1	full size
ohv V-8	390	4.05 × 3.78	300 @ 4600	427 @ 2800	1 × 4bbl.	9.6:1	full size
ohv V-8	390	4.05 × 3.78	375 @ 6000	427 @ 3200	1 × 4bbl.	10.6:1	full size
ohv V-8	390	4.05 × 3.78	401 @ 6000	430 @ 3500	3 × 2bbl.	10.6:1	full size

▲ All big Oldsmobiles used 394-cid V-8s. Standard on the Dynamic 88 was a 250-bhp unit. Standard on the Super 88 and on the Ninety-Eight, and optional on the Dynamic 88, was a 325-bhp version. The Starfire boasted a special 330-bhp variant and about 7600 of the sporty convertibles were built. For '62, the Starfire model would become a separate series with both a ragtop and a hardtop. They were Oldsmobile's most expensive cars.

▶ "Fins vanish, fangs remain," was *Motor Life*'s take on Plymouth's reskinned Fury. A 330-bhp 383-cid Fury two-door hardtop turned a respectable 0-60-mph time of 7.4 seconds, with 15.1 in the quarter-mile. Even with the tamer 305-bhp "Golden Commando" 361-cid mill, a Fury could hit 60 in 9.3 seconds.

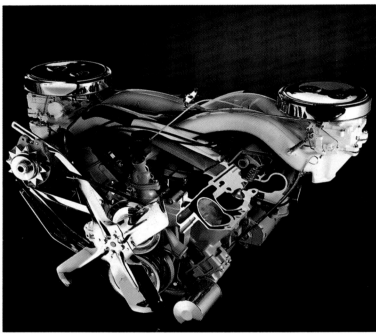

▲ The 383 had 325 bhp with a single four-barrel, 330 with long-tube ram induction, and 340 with a short-ram. But Ford now had 390 cid and Chevrolet added a 409, so Plymouth answered with the 350-bhp 413 at midyear.

1961 PLYMOUTH HIGH-PERFORMANCE ENGINES

TYPE	CID	BORE× STROKE	BHP @ RPM	TORQUE @ RPM	FUEL SYSTEM	COMP. RATIO	AVAIL.
ohv V-8	361	4.12× 3.38	305 @ 4800	395 @ 3000	1×4bbl.	9.0:1	full size
ohv V-8	383	4.24× 3.38	330 @ 4800	460 @ 2800	2×4bbl.	10.0:1	full size
ohv V-8	383	4.24× 3.38	340 @ 5000	440 @ 2800	1×4bbl.	10.0:1	full size
ohv V-8	383	4.24× 3.38	330 @ 5200	425 @ 3600	2×4bbl.	10.0:1	full size
ohv V-8	413	4.18× 3.75	350 @ 4600	470 @ 2800	1×4bbl.	10.0:1	Fury
ohv V-8	413	4.18× 3.75	375 @ 5000	465 @ 2800	2×4bbl.	10.0:1	Fury
ohv V-8	413	4.18× 3.75	375 @ 5200	450 @ 2800	1×4bbl.	10.0:1	Fury

This Tri-Power Pontiac packs one horse for every 10½ pounds

Figure it out for yourself: a Catalina Sports Coupe at 3680 lbs., powered by the 348 H.P. Trophy V-8 = 1 H.P. per 10.57 lbs. Even most sports cars wish they could match it!

We trimmed off every bit of excess weight. There's less weight over-all and more of it is sprung between the wheels for a lot better balance.

Make no mistake: This is a big car—nearly 4000 pounds worth of solid road machinery, give or take a few depending on model and equipment. But the pay-off is how Pontiac moves its weight.

The 348 H.P. Trophy V-8 puts out one horse for every 10½ pounds. And other Pontiac V-8's (11 in all to choose from) have power-to-weight advantages that come close to matching it.

Stack Wide-Track up against all the others and you'll see no other car packs or pulls its weight so well. Test for yourself at your Pontiac dealer's.

PONTIAC MOTOR DIVISION OF GENERAL MOTORS CORPORATION

MOTOR TREND/APRIL 1961 **87**

▲ Pontiac returned to the split grille for '61, but it was on a revamped line of full-size models. Wheelbases shrunk, and restyled bodies lost four inches of length, two-and-a half inches of width, and one inch of height, yet taller roofs and lower floors actually made interiors larger. Ads like this helped enthusiasts zero in on one welcome effect of such downsizing: Performance. It touted the 389-cid, 348-bhp Tri-Power Trophy V-8 in a 3680-pound Catalina Sports Coupe and calculated that it was good for one horsepower per 10.5 pounds. "Even most sports cars wish they could match it!" bragged Pontiac.

1961 PONTIAC HIGH-PERFORMANCE ENGINES							
TYPE	CID	BORE × STROKE	BHP @ RPM	TORQUE @ RPM	FUEL SYSTEM	COMP. RATIO	AVAIL.
ohv V-8	389	4.06 × 3.75	235 @ 3600	402 @ 2000	1×4bbl.	8.6:1	1
ohv V-8	389	4.06 × 3.75	267 @ 4200	405 @ 2400	1×2bbl.	10.25:1	2
ohv V-8	389	4.06 × 3.75	283 @ 4400	413 @ 2800	1×2bbl.	10.25:1	3
ohv V-8	389	4.06 × 3.75	303 @ 4600	425 @ 2800	1×4bbl.	10.25:1	4
ohv V-8	389	4.06 × 3.75	287 @ 4400	416 @ 2400	1×4bbl.	10.25:1	2
ohv V-8	389	4.06 × 3.75	318 @ 4600	430 @ 3200	3×2bbl.	10.75:1	full size
ohv V-8	389	4.06 × 3.75	333 @ 4800	425 @ 2800	1×4bbl.	10.75:1	full size
ohv V-8	389	4.06 × 3.75	348 @ 4800	430 @ 3200	3×2bbl.	10.75:1	full size
ohv V-8	421	4.09 × 4.00	405 @ 5600	425 @ 4400	2×4bbl.	11.0:1	5

1. Bonneville. 2. Catalina, Ventura. 3. Star Chief.
4. Bonneville, Bonneville Safari. 5. Catalina cpe.

▲ Ponchos were racetrack regulars in '62. Above, two '61s storm out of the hole at the NHRA Winternationals, where Lloyd Cox took Super Super/Stock Automatic with a 13-second ET at 107.78 mph. And on the NASCAR circuit, Pontiacs won a record 30 of 52 Grand National races, including Marvin Panch's Daytona 500 crown.

▶ Pontiac performance at the start of '61 meant the Tri-Power 389-cid V-8, which made up to 348 bhp from the factory, or 363 with a dealer-installed Super-Duty package. Pictured in a factory-prepared drag car is a Tri-Power 389 pegged at 368 bhp.

▼ Pontiac prepared a handful of lightweight drag Catalinas with aluminum front sheet-metal and drilled-out "Swiss-cheese" frames. This example also has the rare eight-lug aluminum wheels. Late in '61, Pontiac unleashed the Super Duty 421-cid V-8, rated at 405 bhp with dual quads.

▲ Teaming with ever-stronger engines was the weight-losing cutback in size. Bodies were trimmer on wheelbases that shrank from 123 inches to 119 on Catalina and Ventura (shown) and from 124 to 123 on Star Chief and Bonneville. This is a Sport Coupe.

▲ A Borg-Warner four-speed manual was now a production Pontiac item, having previously been a special-order factory option. Three-speed Hydra-Matic and beefed-up Super Hydra-Matic were the available automatics. Performance didn't have to be accompanied by austerity, as the interior of this well-equipped, air-conditioned Ventura demonstrates.

▶ A stock Ventura hardtop with a Tri-Power 348-bhp 389 like this one could run 0-60 mph in 8.2 seconds and turn a 15.5-second quarter-miie. Muscle like this and youthful new styling were making it increasingly difficult for street racers to ignore Pontiac. At sanctioned drag events, meanwhile, the aluminum-component Catalinas were good for ETs in the low 12s and trap speeds in excess of 116 mph.

▲ Bucket seats were part of Pontiac's new youthful image—an image fueling a sales upturn. Ventura models blended Bonneville luxury with Catalina svelteness.

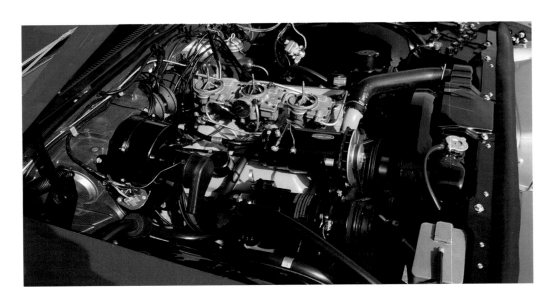

1962

Performance gets the nod in this watershed year, as Big Three automakers pass the 400-cid mark ● Beach Boys belt out their ode to Chevy's "real fine" 409, now able to crank out 409 bhp—the mystical 1 hp per cubic inch ● New 327-cid V-8 replaces the venerable Chevrolet 348 mill ● Chrysler markets low-bucks 300 as well as another "letter-series" ● Downsized Dodges are treated to hopped-up Ram-Charger 413 engine—ready to terrorize dragstrips ● Plymouth gets its own version of 413, known as Super/Stock ● 406-cid V-8 lurks under Ford hoods—up to 405 horses on tap ● Ford drops slippery Starliner; sells only square-cut models ● Glamorous Ford 500XL hardtop and ragtop get midyear debut, a sales generator pioneered by Lee Iacocca ● Mid-size Ford Fairlane bows, but muscular editions will come later ● Oldsmobile introduces turbocharged F-85 Jetfire with fluid injection; performance fails to excite ● Pontiacs earn 22 NASCAR victories out of 53 starts; Fireball Roberts wins Daytona 500 in one ● Pontiac Grand Prix debuts

ac·cel′er·a′tor

One who or that which accelerates; specif.: **a** On automobiles, a foot-operated throttle. **b** (*pron.* ak-sel′er-a′ter; *L.* ak-sel′er-a′tor) *Anat.* Any muscle or nerve that hastens a motion. **c** *Chem.* A substance that hastens a reaction. **d** *Physics.* Any device used to impart high speeds to charged particles. (Webster's New Collegiate Dictionary) *CHEVROLET* All the above is true, as far as it goes. What it doesn't say is that an Impala Super Sport has even more going for it than performance. It's a swinging car in every way. Bucket seats, special interior, distinctive exterior trim, all part of the Super Sport kit, optional at extra cost on Impala Sport Coupes and Convertibles, and it proclaims to the world that this machine doesn't take a back seat to anybody. To understand, you'll just have to try an Impala Super Sport, that is, step on that accelerator. You'll be impressed, or our name isn't Chevrolet Division of General Motors, Detroit 2, Michigan.

CHEVROLET IMPALA

MOTOR TREND/APRIL 1962 **19**

▲ Simple and understated, this ad went right to the heart of the matter. And greater availability of Chevy's 409-cid V-8 lent credence to the claim. In '61, only 142 cars got the 409. In '62, it went onto 15,019 Chevys.

1962 CHEVROLET HIGH-PERFORMANCE ENGINES							
TYPE	CID	BORE × STROKE	BHP @ RPM	TORQUE @ RPM	FUEL SYSTEM	COMP. RATIO	AVAIL.
ohv V-8	327	4.00 × 3.25	250 @ 4400	350 @ 2800	1 × 4bbl.	10.5:1	full size
ohv V-8	327	4.00 × 3.25	300 @ 5000	360 @ 3200	1 × 4bbl.	10.5:1	full size
ohv V-8	409	4.31 × 3.50	380 @ 5800	420 @ 3200	1 × 4bbl.	11.0:1	full size
ohv V-8	409	4.31 × 3.50	409 @ 6000	420 @ 4000	2 × 4bbl.	11.0:1	full size

▲ Sing along: "She always turns in the fastest time. My four speed, dual quads, positraction 409. Giddy up, giddy up, giddy up 409...."

▲ Lighter in weight and $100 cheaper than an Impala, Chevrolet's Bel Air sport coupe was the "sleeper" choice among 409 buyers, many of whom ordered the optional 7000-rpm tach, which showed a 6200-rpm redline. The base single-quad 409 had 380 bhp. With twin Carter AFB four-barrels and a wild cam, the 409 developed a rated 409 horsepower at 6000 rpm, and 420 lbs/ft of torque at 4000, on 11:1 compression.

▲ At the 1962 NHRA Winternationals, "Dyno Don" Nicholson won the Stock Eliminator title for the second straight year behind the wheel of a super-tuned 409.

▲ Hayden Proffitt drove this four-speed Bel Air 409 to Stock Eliminator honors at the '62 U.S. Nationals. His winning ET was 12.83 seconds at 113.92 mph.

▲ Asking for a 409 added $428 to the price of any full-size Chevrolet; $60 more bought this dual-quad edition. A four-speed cost $188 extra.

▲ *Motor Trend* ran a Chevy hardtop with the 409-bhp 409 to 60 mph in 6.3 seconds and recorded a 14.9-second quarter-mile at 98 mph.

▼ The Impala's formal hardtop roof mimicked a top-up convertible, but serious racers preferred the Bel Air's slantback profile. Black-wall tires and taxi-cab-grade hubcaps only enhanced the no-frills, no-nonsense image. The 409 was the first engine of the muscle age to acquire an identity all its own.

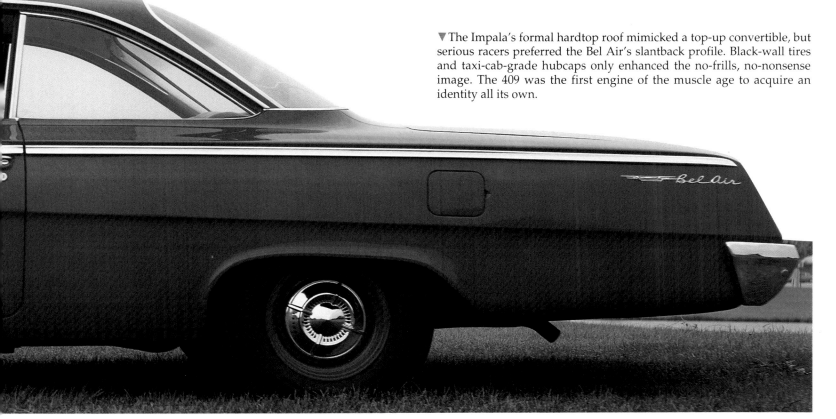

▲ The only Impala two-doors for '62 were the convertible and this Sport Hardtop. Crossed flags above a 409 label identified the Impala as a machine to be reckoned with. And Super Sport versions were recognized by "spinner" wheelcovers, "SS" emblems, and anodized aluminum bodyside moldings.

▲ On the Impala, bucket seats were a $102 option and were often ordered along with the Super Sport package. The SS package itself was a $54 option for Sport Coupes or convertibles and again included a center console and passenger grip bar. A tachometer was another factory option and mounted to the steering column.

▲ Pick a 409 back in '62 and you had to take manual shift. Four-speed units were quickly becoming the racers' choice, although a three-speed gearbox was now available, too. After limited exposure in cars intended for sanctioned drag racing and for press-review, the Turbo-Fire 409 V-8 became a regular-production option for '62. Compared to the seldom-seen '61 edition, it had a stronger block and tougher cast alloy heads, plus revised pistons.

◄ *Car and Driver* ran a 380-bhp 409 to 60 mph in 7.3 seconds and finished the quarter-mile in 14.9 at 94 mph. Late in the model year, Chevy built a limited run of lightweight 409 specials with aluminum front-end parts that shaved 130 pounds from the nose. Aluminum body panels could also be bought over the counter at Chevrolet dealerships.

▲ Attention-seekers couldn't ask for much more in '62 than an Impala SS 409 convertible. With a V-8, the ragtop started at $3026 and tipped the scales at 3560 pounds. Turbo-Fire 409s got the raves, but the Super Sport package actually was available with any Impala engine—even a puny six. Many buyers ordered the new 327-cid V-8, which replaced the 348. The 327 came in 250- or 300-bhp tune. It was more flexible than the 409 at low speeds, had excellent mid-range punch, and was more refined on the highway. And of course, it cost less and used less gas.

▶ "Dyno Don" Nicholson took this 409 Impala Sport Coupe to the B/FX class title at the '62 U.S. NHRA Nationals. Nicholson ran a 12.93-second quarter-mile at 113.63 mph. Bel Airs snared Super/Stock and stock eliminator honors at the Nationals, and a Bel Air was the S/S champ at the Winternationals. Meanwhile, in the stock-car-racing wars, the 409 powered Chevrolets to 14 NASCAR victories, most of them short-track events.

▲ The Chevy II compact bowed for '62, with four- and six-cylinder power. It wasn't long before hot rodders stuffed in 327s. Dick Rutherford ran this one with a fuel-injected 327 Corvette engine in A/FX (factory experimental) competition at the '62 Winternationals. Another 360-bhp conversion, by Bill Thomas, recorded a 0-60 mph time of 5.2 seconds.

▲ Chrysler's 300H coupe and ragtop again came with the 413 cid V-8, now at 380 bhp in standard tune. But "letter series" fans hissed when Chrysler applied the 300 label—without the H—to a series that included a four-door hardtop and standard 383 cid V-8. The 300 cost $1700 less than the "H," and both could get the 413, so only 558 300Hs were ordered.

▶ When "factory" street/strip goodies didn't pass muster, aftermarket firms were eager to fill the gap. Ed Iskenderian of Inglewood, California, earned a name for his roller cam kits. Young racers pored through each new "Isky" catalog, which featured tuning tips from the pros. And decals like this showed up on the back window of many a muscle car.

			1962 CHRYSLER				
			HIGH-PERFORMANCE ENGINES				
TYPE	CID	BORE×STROKE	BHP @ RPM	TORQUE @ RPM	FUEL SYSTEM	COMP. RATIO	AVAIL.
ohv V-8	413	4.19×3.75	380 @ 5200	450 @ 3600	2×4bbl.	10.0:1	full size
ohv V-8	413	4.19×3.75	405 @ 5400	373 @ 3600	2×4bbl.	10.0:1	300H

▲ Full-size Chryslers were becoming rare at the track, but Gary Nichols drove this one in the top-stack automatic class at the '62 Winternationals. A street 300H, with its 380 bhp, could hit 60 in 7.7 seconds and do the quarter in 16. The dual-quad 413 V-8 also was available in 405-bhp form.

▼ A chop in wheelbase from 118 inches to 116 and downsized sheetmetal shrunk the standard-size Dodge Polara (shown) and Dart to mid-size dimensions. Mainstream customers found this as controversial as the rather odd new styling. But racers liked the weight loss—and the revitalized 413-cid V-8.

▲ A watershed engine for Mopar—the Max Wedge 413. The 413-cid V-8 dated from 1959, but only this one was bred to go racing. It was rated at 410 bhp.

▲ Apart from tall floor shift and bucket seats, little inside this Polara's cabin suggests the thrills that await a tromp on the gas pedal.

▲ Chrysler chief designer Virgil Exner's styling was as flamboyant from the rear as the front. But this was the only view some got of a Max Wedge Polara.

▲ Dart was the cheapest "big" Dodge, and was 200 pounds lighter than a Chevy Bel Air. A stock stripper Dart two-door sedan like this one with the 410-bhp 413 pulled only 8.4 pounds per horsepower, making possible a blistering 5.8-second 0-60 mph time and an spine-mashing 14.4-second quarter-mile ET.

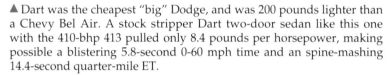

▲ Dodge tagged its hot 413 the Ram-Charger. It cost $374.40 more than a Dart with the 230-bhp 318-cid V-8. With dual 650cfm Carter four-barrels, solid lifters, aluminum pistons, and an 11.0:1 compression, the 413 cranked out 410 bhp. Special pistons gave 415 or 420 bhp (depending on the source).

▲ All 413s had wedge-shaped combustion chambers, but the Ram-Charger 413 was designed for "maximum" performance, hence, the unofficial "Max Wedge" title. Chrysler intended it for "sanctioned acceleration trials," not for the street; but more than a few Darts conducted "trials" away from the strip.

◄ Ram-Charger 413s set four NHRA class records in '62, including Dick Landy's 12.7-second ET with a three-speed manual, and Bill Golden's 12.5 with automatic. Ads claimed a Ram Dart "has about the best power-weight ratio ever offered on a production car."

▲ Bodyside "fins," "turbine" taillamps—love 'em or hate 'em. But there was no debate that this was, as its maker claimed, "The lean new breed of Dodge!" Wheelbase was a half-inch shorter than Ford's new intermediate Fairlane. "More live action because there's less dead weight," said Dodge.

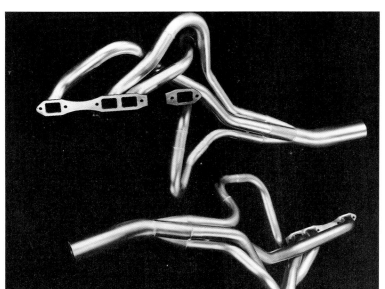

▲ Ram-Chargers earned their name partly from the "ram's-horn" sweep of their three-inch headers, necessary to fit into a 413 Dodge's engine bay. *Motor Trend* called the upswept exhaust the "most efficient and beautiful ever put on an American car."

▲ A three-speed manual floor-shift was standard, but this Dart has the optional TorqueFlite automatic. It was controlled by dashboard buttons, as on other Dodges, but was fortified for high-upshift abuse. A 3.91:1 axle was standard, but ratios from 2.93:1 to 4.89:1 could be ordered.

				1962 DODGE HIGH-PERFORMANCE ENGINES			
TYPE	CID	BORE×STROKE	BHP @ RPM	TORQUE @ RPM	FUEL SYSTEM	COMP. RATIO	AVAIL.
ohv V-8	361	4.12× 3.38	305 @ 4800	395 @ 3000	1×4bbl.	9.0:1	full size
ohv V-8	361	4.12× 3.38	310 @ 5200	390 @ 3400	2×4bbl.	10.0:1	full size
ohv V-8	383	4.25× 3.75	330 @ 4600	425 @ 2800	1×4bbl.	10.0:1	full size
ohv V-8	383	4.25× 3.75	335 @ 5000	420 @ 3600	2×4bbl.	10.0:1	full size
ohv V-8	413	4.18× 3.75	365 @ 4600	460 @ 2800	1×4bbl.	11.0:1	full size
ohv V-8	413	4.18× 3.75	380 @ 5200	455 @ 3600	2×4bbl.	11.0:1	full size
ohv V-8	413	4.18× 3.75	410 @ 5200	460 @ 4400	2×4bbl.	11.0:1	full size

▲ Ford answered Chevy's 409 and Chrysler's Max Wedge 413 with its first 400-plus-cid V-8. Delivered part-way through the '62 model year, it was basically a Ford 390-cid V-8 bored out to 406 cid. It had a .080-inch larger bore (now 4.13), but retained the 390's 3.78-inch stroke. Called the Thunderbird 406 High-Performance V-8, but available only in the new facelifted Galaxie, it signaled a fresh performance push for the blue-oval brigade.

1962 FORD HIGH-PERFORMANCE ENGINES

TYPE	CID	BORE × STROKE	BHP @ RPM	TORQUE @ RPM	FUEL SYSTEM	COMP. RATIO	AVAIL.
ohv V-8	390	4.05 × 3.78	300 @ 4600	427 @ 2800	1 × 4bbl.	9.6:1	full size
ohv V-8	406	4.13 × 3.78	385 @ 5800	440 @ 3800	1 × 4bbl.	11.4:1	full size
ohv V-8	406	4.13 × 3.78	405 @ 5800	448 @ 3500	3 × 2bbl.	11.4:1	full size

▲ Gold-colored "406" bird emblems on front fenders marked the hottest Fords; 390s used silver. The complete 406 package cost $379.70, and required not only the four-speed manual gearbox but either 6.70 or 7.10 × 15 tires (replacing the standard 14-inch rubber). Also included were heavy-duty shock absorbers and springs, fade-resistant drum brakes, a larger fuel line, heavier clutch, stabilizer bar, and high-capacity radiator.

▶ Breathing through a single Holley four-barrel carburetor (shown), the 406 was rated at 385 bhp at 5800 rpm. As the Super High-Performance Tri-Power, it wore three Holley two-barrels and was rated at 405 horses and 448 pounds/feet of torque. Both versions had an 11.4:1 compression ratio, and cast-in headers that led to low-restriction dual exhausts. *Motor Trend* did 0-60 in 7.1 seconds with a 406 Galaxie sedan, lending weight to Ford's '62 sales theme: the "Lively Ones."

▲ Ford Division General Manager Lee Iacocca pioneered the spring-time product introduction, and in mid-'62 he unveiled the Galaxie 500XL Victoria hardtop coupe and 500XL Sunliner convertible. The "500" stood for the grueling 500-mile trek around a NASCAR oval. "XL" could have meant "extra lively." This Sunliner, with its optional stainless steel fender skirts, was among 13,108 XL convertibles built.

▲ Ford's 406 has "something like Ferrari performance at a fifth of the price," said *Motor Trend*. This is the tri-carb 405-bhp edition.

▲ In addition to bucket seats and a console, Ford's 500XL could be ordered with a Borg-Warner four-speed manual and optional 8000-rpm tach.

▼ Galaxies wore round taillamps above semi-circular bumper cutouts. "Powered by one of the optional Thunderbird 406 High-Performance V-8s," said the sales brochure, a "Sunliner moves with a nimbleness and flight-like quality rivaled by only one other...the Thunderbird itself!"

SLEEPER !

To the old carnival guessing game of "Which shell is the pea under?" you can add another—"Which Galaxie is hiding the new six-barrel?"

You can get a very precise answer, it's true, when one of these sleepers suddenly goes "zzz-z-z-ZOW!" and vanishes. But that leaves you sitting foolishly in the middle of a lot of empty landscape.

Better to know beforehand. But how? You'd think 405 horsepower, header exhausts, six-barrel carbs, 406 cubic inches and 11.4 compression couldn't be hidden. But Ford's V-8 magicians have brewed up a real street machine—no wild 2000 r.p.m. idle, no dragster noises, no battle to fire it up. Girls drive these things down to the supermarket and never suspect they are a half-throttle away from escape velocity.

Of course, you do get a clue watching one straighten out a corner. They handle! Because this engine (and the 4-barrel version) come only as a package with Heavy Duty shocks, springs, driveshaft, U-joints, brakes —plus 15-inch wheels and nylon tires. That's what makes the tab of $379.70* so fantastic—and why there are so many Galaxie sleepers around to embarrass you. But why be dominated? Get your own 406 and you won't need to guess which Galaxie has the six-barrel.

A PRODUCT OF (Ford) *FORD MOTOR COMPANY*

*Manufacturer's suggested list price for extra equipment

FORD V-8

MOTOR TREND/APRIL 1962 **11**

◀ Ford's copywriters played it both ways. The "six-barrel" 406-equipped Galaxie was actually a tame beast that bared its fangs only on demand. After all, Ford wanted to sell cars to "girls" and grandmas, too, not just dragstrip dudes. Sleepers they may have been, but 406 Galaxies still were too heavy to outgun the lighter 413 Dodges and Plymouths and the new Pontiacs. Ford did shave 164 pounds by offering aluminum bumpers and fiberglass body panels, but in quantities too small to rank as "production." So the NHRA put those cars into experimental classes, where the going was very tough.

▼ The oval air cleaner marks this 406 as the tri-carb sizzler. *Hot Rod* ran a 385-bhp version to 60 mph in 7.1 seconds, turning the quarter-mile in 15.3 at 93 mph. *Motor Trend* responded with a 6.5-second 0-60 time in a 405-bhp 406, but its quarter-mile was a 15.6 at 92. Early 406s were fragile, but heavier main webs and four-bolt caps remedied that as Ford's high-performance department, guided by NASCAR experience, began to get it in gear.

▼ All Galaxies wore a single wide bodyside molding, but lesser models lacked the XL's extra trim and bucket seats. Only the initiated knew at a glance that this plain-vanilla hardtop carried a 406—and in knockout-punch 405-bhp tune, to boot. Axle ratios as low as 4.11:1 could replace the standard 3.50:1 cog.

▲ Dick Heyler is pictured in his Cruise-O-Matic 406 Galaxie running in SS/SA at the '62 Winternationals. His sponsor, Ford dealer Ben Alexander, had costarred with Jack Webb in the '50s TV version of *Dragnet*.

▲ At 430 bhp in NASCAR tune, the 406 was still shy of the 465-bhp, 421-cid Pontiacs, and Ford stock-car wins, so important for publicity, were rare. NASCAR thwarted an effort to fit convertible Galaxies with aerodynamic "fastback" rooflines. So Ford enlarged the 406 to 483 cid and tested it for 500 miles on the Bonneville Salt Flats. It averaged 164 mph and saw 182 mph. But NASCAR never allowed the 483.

▲ Galaxies had nicely appointed interiors, and this one has the optional Ford air conditioning, as well as the extra-cost column-mounted tachometer kit. Since it's a 406, Ford's Borg-Warner T-10 four-speed (now a factory installation) was mandatory. Cruise-O-Matic three-speed automatic was okay with other engines.

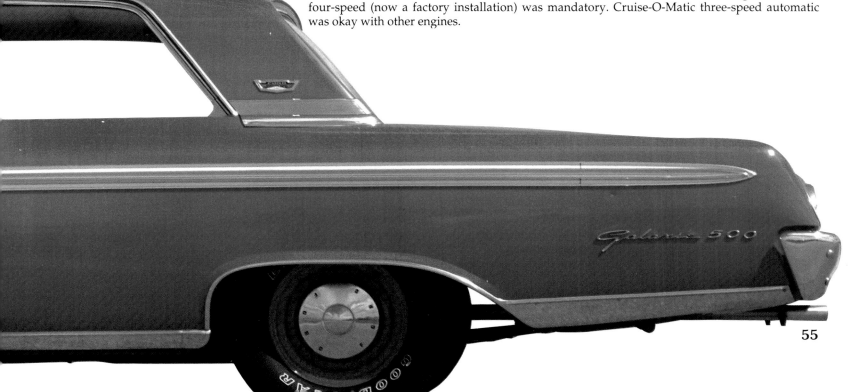

meet a new Plymouth Sport Fury!

◀ Plymouth revived a name from 1959 for its new top-line '62s. Unlike lesser models, which came with a Slant Six, Sport Fury carried a standard 305-bhp 361 "Golden Commando" V-8, with options including a pair of 383s and the mighty 413. Interiors featured smart, two-tone vinyl buckets and center console. The coupe started at $2851, the convertible at $3082.

▼ Full-size Plymouths were seven inches shorter this year, and up to 400 pounds lighter. Combine that with Mopar's newly fortified 400-bhp-plus 413-cid V-8, and Plymouth was now in the muscle big leagues. Plymouth called its version of this engine the Super Stock 413, and though relatively few were built, many of those that were went into bare-bones two-door sedans like this Belvedere. No stripes. No badges. Just thunder waiting to happen. It's a classic example of the unassuming look preferred by serious street racers. A 335-bhp 383-cid V-8 also was offered.

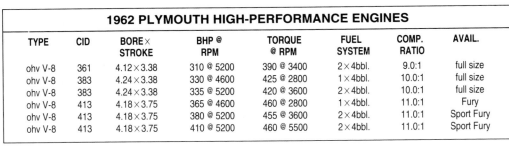

1962 PLYMOUTH HIGH-PERFORMANCE ENGINES

TYPE	CID	BORE × STROKE	BHP @ RPM	TORQUE @ RPM	FUEL SYSTEM	COMP. RATIO	AVAIL.
ohv V-8	361	4.12 × 3.38	310 @ 5200	390 @ 3400	2 × 4bbl.	9.0:1	full size
ohv V-8	383	4.24 × 3.38	330 @ 4600	425 @ 2800	1 × 4bbl.	10.0:1	full size
ohv V-8	383	4.24 × 3.38	335 @ 5200	420 @ 3600	2 × 4bbl.	10.0:1	full size
ohv V-8	413	4.18 × 3.75	365 @ 4600	460 @ 2800	1 × 4bbl.	11.0:1	Fury
ohv V-8	413	4.18 × 3.75	380 @ 5200	455 @ 3600	2 × 4bbl.	11.0:1	Sport Fury
ohv V-8	413	4.18 × 3.75	410 @ 5200	460 @ 5500	2 × 4bbl.	11.0:1	Sport Fury

▼ Like Dodge, Plymouth downsized for '62, cutting the wheelbase of the Savoy, Belvedere, and Fury by two inches, to 116, and shedding pounds in the process. The Sport Fury coupe and convertible were midyear additions.

◄ Drag racing can be a family sport, as this 1962 portrait of a happy—and winning—Ohio clan proves. Only a few years earlier, Plymouth victories in such volume would have been unheard of. But Mopar was coming on strong, and 413 Plymouths were shattering NHRA Super Stock/Automatic records. Interestingly, Plymouth opened the '62 model year with the 305-bhp 361 V-8 as its top engine. Then, to remain competitive on the strip, it issued a batch of lightweight "Super/Stock" specials with the short-ram 413. Output was rated 410 bhp, but actually ran closer to 500 bhp. Super/Stock was the class in which they raced. At the time, the NHRA classified cars based on pounds per advertised horsepower. Chrysler's push-button TorqueFlite automatic was the hot choice behind the 413; the three-speed manual was actually slightly slower in the quarter, and a four-speed wasn't offered.
1962-52 (6 x 23.1):

▲ A lightweight Savoy two-door with the limited-production Super/Stock 413 V-8 made for a tough-to-beat combination on street or strip. At around 3200 pounds the Savoy weighed even less than its Dodge Dart cousin, and could be lightened further by being ordered without heater, radio, and sound deadening.

▶ Not an uncommon view to those who squared off against a Super/Stock 413 Savoy. Though they were available in the flashy Sport Fury, most of the beefed-up 410-bhp motors went into stripper two-doors aimed at the dragstrip. Owners took to calling these hot Dodge/Plymouth engines "Max Wedge," but Chrysler never used that designation.

▲ In a Savoy, both the grocery-getter and the go-getter shared the simplest of instruments and controls—though a tap on the gas would quickly make clear if there were a slant-six or a 413 beneath the hood. Racers rejoiced, but customers shunned this year's downsized models, and Plymouth sunk to No. 8 in sales.

▲ Plymouth's "RB-Block" 413 was known as the "Ram-Charger" over at Dodge. Both had a 4.19-inch bore and 3.75-inch stroke, with solid lifters and dual valve springs to halt valve float past 6000 rpm. Rods were magnafluxed, and short-ram intake manifolds carried twin 659cfm Carter AFB four-barrels. Cast-iron headers were routed upward to fit into the tight engine bay.

▲ Plymouth power and light weight paid off in a historic quarter-mile run by Tom Grove in July 1962. Grove drove his Super Stock Belvedere to an ET of 11.93 seconds at 118.57 mph. His was the first stock passenger automobile to beat 12 seconds in the quarter-mile. Here, Grove is behind the wheel of his "Melrose Missile II" at the '62 Winternationals.

▶ The extra gauges and the roll-cage members betray this '62 Fury as something special. It is in fact the Bonneville Salt Flats special in which Andy Granatelli hit 194 mph. And it's street legal! Power comes from a 413 bored to 480 cid, with twin McCulloch-Paxton superchargers feeding Carter dual quads, which were mounted on a modified Chrysler 300 intake manifold. A Hurst three-speed and 2.93:1 gears complete the drivetrain.

▼ Horsepower of the Fury's engine is uncertain, but it had to be substantial to push such an un-aerodynamic shape to more than 190 mph. Air intakes in place of headlamps, full-dish wheelcovers, and slight suspension modifications were the only other changes. At Riverside International Raceway, this car burned a 12.51 quarter-mile at 117.41 mph—not bad, considering the Bonneville gearing.

▶ At Pontiac, the push for performance had become relentless. After finishing 1-2-3 in the Daytona 500 in '61, and becoming one of the cars to beat on the drag strips and boulevards, it moved aggressively to develop and market speed equipment. The principal venue was the Catalina, which grew an inch in wheelbase, to 120, but was still three less than the bigger, heavier Star Chief and Bonneville. A minor restyle included a return to the popular split grille. Catalina was the only Pontiac eligible for the Super Duty engines: the 421-cid V-8, which again boasted 405 bhp, and the tough four-barrel 389-cid V-8, which was good for 385 bhp.

moving machine
either side of the line!

Pontiac Catalina

There's a good deal more to driving than a straight-line quarter-mile, and nobody knows that better than the performance-minded. Which is why Pontiac's Catalina shows up so often among you people.

One of the reasons for this popularity is the choice of engine/transmission teams. Standard equipment is a 215-hp Trophy V-8 hooked up to a three-speed stick, of course. But you can get a storming 405-horse engine and heavy-duty four-speed as extra-cost options. And other extra-cost options blanket the area in between, including automatics.

Wide-Track and Pontiac's own special handling precision come standard with the Catalina, naturally. So does

a fat helping of pure luxury, without which you shouldn't allow yourself to be.

The great thing is that a new Catalina goes easy on your bankroll—this is Pontiac's lowest-priced full-sized series. Talk it over with your Pontiac dealer first chance you get. Plan to spend some time with him—you could use up a whole day just looking through that list of options, and a happier time you couldn't imagine.

(Oh, and if you'd like to check your Cat against the clocks, feel free. No fair making the Catalina do the pushing while the dragster has all the fun.) Pontiac Motor Division, General Motors Corporation.

MOTOR TREND/APRIL 1962 **7**

▼ Mickey Thompson, aboard the Royal Tempest Tiger, is on his way to eliminating Bill Lawton's Tasca Ford "Orbiter I" in the A/FX class at the '62 U.S. Nationals. Pontiac had chosen Ace Wilson's Royal Pontiac dealership in Royal Oak, Michigan, as ground zero for the distribution and promotion of its burgeoning catalog of speed equipment. Royal sold special Pontiac performance parts through the mail and over the counter. It also super-tuned Ponchos for the street and campaigned modified versions made all the hotter through the close cooperation of Pontiac engineers.

▶ At 16 years of age, Don Gay was probably the youngest Pontiac drag racer and was certainly among the fastest, with an A/S class time of 12.81 seconds at 111.52 mph in his 421 Catalina. Gay went on to fame as a Funny Car driver and dragstrip owner. Elsewhere, a "Royal Bobcat" Catalina hardtop with a 370-bhp 389 recorded a 6.5-second 0-60 mph run and a 14.5-second quarter-mile. And at the Detroit Dragway, Jim Wangers's Royal Bobcat Super Duty Catalina turned a 12.38-second quarter at 116.23 mph. Over in NASCAR, Pontiac took 22 checkered flags in 53 starts, including Fireball Roberts's victory in the Daytona 500. Joe Weatherly became the first Pontiac driver to win the Grand National driving title.

▲ This is one of a handful of lightweight '62 Catalinas that used aluminum for the hood, front bumpers, and front fenders. Aluminum fender liners and trunk lid, as well as aluminum intake and exhaust manifolds, also were offered. Weight shavings of 150 pounds or more were possible. Finally, a special dual-quad 421 was available at a breathtaking $2250—for the engine alone.

▲ Deadliest of the Super Duty 421s was a race-ready—but street-legal—version with four-bolt mains, forged rods and crank, solid lifters, and NASCAR heads. Two Carter 1000cfm AFB four-barrels rode a Mickey Thompson aluminum intake manifold. It was rated at 405 bhp, but real output was around 450.

1962 PONTIAC HIGH-PERFORMANCE ENGINES

TYPE	CID	BORE× STROKE	BHP @ RPM	TORQUE @ RPM	FUEL SYSTEM	COMP. RATIO	AVAIL.
ohv V-8	389	4.06× 3.75	305 @ 4600	425 @ 2800	1×4bbl.	10.25:1	full size
ohv V-8	389	4.06× 3.75	318 @ 4600	430 @ 3200	3×2bbl.	10.75:1	full size
ohv V-8	389	4.06× 3.75	333 @ 4800	425 @ 2800	1×4bbl.	10.75:1	full size
ohv V-8	389	4.06× 3.75	348 @ 4800	430 @ 3200	3×2bbl.	10.75:1	full size
ohv V-8	389	4.06× 3.75	385 @ 5200	430 @ 3200	1×4bbl.	10.75:1	1
ohv V-8	421	4.09× 4.00	405 @ 5600	425 @ 4400	2×4bbl.	11.0:1	2

1. Catalina Super Duty. 2. Catalina cpe.

▼ Semon E. "Bunkie" Knudsen, in his final season as Pontiac general manager, earned credit for sensible marketing of the Grand Prix "personal-luxury" coupe, which bowed mid-way through the '62 model year. Grand Prix followed the path of Ford's four-seat Thunderbird. Essentially, it was a Catalina hardtop with unique styling touches, bucket seats, and a console with tach and gauge package. No two-tone colors were used. Starting at $3835, the Grand Prix was a success.

▶ Grand Prix was available only with Pontiac's Trophy 389-cid V-8, but it was offered in a host of forms, from a 230-bhp two-barrel to the 348-bhp Tri-Power. A three-speed stick was standard, but most Grand Prixs carried the new "Roto" three-speed Hydra-Matic, which cost the same $231 as a four-speed manual floor-shift. Pontiac built 30,195 Grand Prixs in '62, and the division itself now ranked third in sales, up from a dismal ninth just six years earlier.

▼ Off the line at the '62 U.S. Nationals is Les Ritchey and the Ed Martin Ford against Ace Wilson's Royal Pontiac in SS/S eliminations. "Race on Sunday, Sell on Monday" had become more than wishful thinking. It was hard fact, and dealers knew that customers were paying attention to the publicity that came with competition. The link was perhaps strongest in stock-car racing, and here Pontiac was a real force. In winning Daytona, the Smokey Yunick-prepared Super Duty 421, running a single four-barrel as NASCAR required, pounded out some 440 bhp and qualified at 158.7 mph. A stock 421 Catalina averaged a record 113.2 mph in a 500-mile endurance test at Indianapolis.

▲ Pontiac hardtop coupes, including this Catalina, got a new convertible-inspired roofline. Though their impact was great, only about 200 Super Duty 421s actually were built, and there were even fewer Super Duty 389s.

▲ Clean lines and modest weight made the '62 Catalina hardtop a tempting machine, and there was little outward sign of whether it carried one of the many 389s or a gunslinger 421. Small hubcaps helped keep it mysterious.

▲ *Motor Trend* ran a dual-quad Super Duty 421 Catalina to 60 mph in a mere 5.4 seconds, blasting through the quarter-mile in just 13.9 at 107 mph. Those were superior numbers, given the poor traction afforded by tires of the day.

▲ The hottest Catalinas needed that big tach above the column to keep track of revs, especially when shifting a Borg-Warner/Hurst close-ratio four-speed. Otherwise, the interior was strictly stock Pontiac.

1963

Ford, GM, and Chrysler advertise 425 horsepower for hottest stock mills; experts know true figures are far higher ● Displacement war escalates as Ford elbows its 406-cid V-8 to 427 cubic inches, and Mopar wedge grows from 413 to 426 cid...Chevrolet stands pat at 409 cid, except for rare 427-cid Z-11 ● Race sanctioning bodies impose 427-cid limit ● GM management orders all corporate-sponsored race activity halted ● Chevy's lightweight Z-11 drag car arrives in small numbers for Super/Stock, with 427-cid V-8 and 430 unfettered horses underhood ● Ford debuts semi-fastback Galaxie 500 and 500XL hardtops at mid-year ● Special lightweight Catalinas save some 300 pounds, strike terror at dragstrips with Super Duty 421 V-8 ● At NASCAR, Chevy's Impala 427 Mark IV qualifies fastest, but Fords end season with 23 victories, versus Plymouth's 19 (14 by Richard Petty) ● Fords sweep first five spots in Daytona 500 ● ETs of rail dragsters threaten 8-second mark, topping 180 mph...in stock classes, only a handful squeeze past 12 seconds

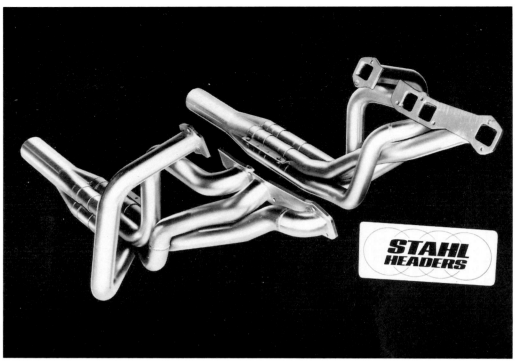

▲ Such goodies as Stahl exhaust headers helped send a stream of 409-equipped Chevrolets to the winner's circle. A record 16,902 of the 409s went to buyers, rated 340-, 400-, or pavement-stomping 425 bhp.

1963 CHEVROLET HIGH-PERFORMANCE ENGINES							
TYPE	CID	BORE×STROKE	BHP @ RPM	TORQUE @ RPM	FUEL SYSTEM	COMP. RATIO	AVAIL.
ohv V-8	327	4.00×3.25	250 @ 4400	350 @ 2800	1×4bbl.	10.5:1	full size
ohv V-8	327	4.00×3.25	300 @ 5000	360 @ 3200	1×4bbl.	10.5:1	full size
ohv V-8	409	4.31×3.50	340 @ 5000	420 @ 3200	1×4bbl.	10.0:1	full size
ohv V-8	409	4.31×3.50	400 @ 5800	425 @ 3600	1×4bbl.	11.0:1	full size
ohv V-8	409	4.31×3.50	425 @ 6000	425 @ 4200	2×4bbl.	11.0:1	full size
ohv V-8	427	4.41×3.50	430 @ 5800	430 @ 4000	2×4bbl.	13.5:1	Impala Sport Coupe

▲ Most teens merely swooned over factory-stock muscle, but some hit the strips themselves. Here, 18-year-old Butch Leal runs the Del Munson Stock Eliminator Chevy at the '63 Winternationals. Leal became one of the best-known players in NHRA Super Stock, A/FX, and Pro Stock. Over in NASCAR, Junior Johnson won two races in Chevrolets, helping give the automaker eight victories.

▼ Chevy unleashed a 427-cid version of the 409 under the Z-11 label. The limited-production dual-quad mill had 430 bhp at 6000 rpm, 425 lbs/ft of torque at 4200. Here, Ronnie Sox wheels the Friendly Chevrolet-backed "Mr. 427" in an A/FX showdown against Len Richter's Ford at the '63 U.S. Nationals. Sox would go on to become a Mopar hero after this season.

▲ Chevrolet's bubble-roof '62 Bel Air hardtop (rear) was gone, leaving only the squared-off Impala. Deceptively ordinary, this '63 Impala contains the Z-11 drag package. About 100 were built for Super/Stock, typically with an aluminum hood, front fenders and bumpers, to cut 180 pounds. The 427-cid engine matched the new NASCAR and NHRA displacement limits.

▲ Intended for competition only, Z-11s like this one were sold only to factory-approved buyers. On the street, Chevy's 340-bhp version of the 409, with hydraulic lifters and lower compression (10:1 instead of 11:1), proved more practical. *Car Life* smoked one to 60 mph in 6.6 seconds with Powerglide, while *Motor Trend* managed a 15.9-second quarter-mile.

◄ This mockup of Sunoco's "Magic 8" custom-blending dial was used to help educate sales reps at a meeting in Atlantic City. As compression ratios rose in the early 1960s, higher-octane gasoline became mandatory. In fact, some truly tight high-performance V-8s demanded aviation fuel.

▶ "When the 'Orange Monster' strikes," ads warned, "records topple!" The monster was Chrysler's new Ram Charger 426-cid wedge, basically a bored 413, but with internal hop-ups and more power. Dodge ads claimed the Ram Charger would "burn rubber as long as you let it." (Below right): Herman Mozer's Super Stock Automatic dropped teammate Jim Thornton for Top Stock Eliminator at the '63 NHRA Nationals, then jailed "Lawman" Al Eckstrand with a 12.22 at 116.73 mph.

THE DEPENDABLES FROM DODGE !

A WOLF...

IN STREET CLOTHING

Stock car racing is the ultimate measure of a car's capabilities. And the '63 Dodge has been doing very well, thank you. Fact is, it's chewing up competition on tracks all over the country. We aren't the least bit surprised. Racing takes raw power and Dodge has it. Racing takes control. Dodge has that, too. Experts call its torsion-bar suspension the best in the business. Racing demands toughness. Dodge's unitized body is welded, one piece. Tough, tight. As rattle-free as can be. What's best is this: All the things that make Dodge such a wolf on the tracks make it a model of deportment for your everyday driving. Performance? You've got it—with a wide choice of prize-winning V8 power. You've got a lot more going for you, too. Maneuverability, money-saving dependability and something extra nice—a low price. Dodge is on the move, all right. And we urge you to sample some of its high adventure soon. See your Dodge Dealer. He's got The Dependables in a size to suit you. Compact Dart. Standard-size Dodge. Big 880. Pick a size, pick a price, pick a Dodge.

HOT 1963 DODGE

DODGE DIVISION **CHRYSLER** MOTORS CORPORATION | '63 DODGE: A FULL LINE OF CARS IN THE LOW-PRICE FIELD. THREE SERIES: 24 MODELS. HARDTOPS, SEDANS, CONVERTS, WAGONS.

Jim Thornton and Herman Mozer (979) coming off the line in S/SA class.

Some days you win

Mozer and Al Eckstrand in final run for Top Stock Eliminator title.

Some days you lose

The fortunes on the straight and narrow warpath change as quickly as the gears in the go-box! Today you tear 'em up. Tomorrow is another day. Your machine has got to be mean ... you've got to be good ... and you've got to come out of the hole with more togetherness than Amos and Andy! That's the drama of the drag strip, man and machine.

That's why more than 100,000 buffs bulged the track at Indy for the NHRA's big showdown—the world championships.

And what a showdown! On Saturday, Jim Thornton in a '63 Dodge downed his Ramcharger teammate, Herman Mozer, on his way to royalty in the Super Stock Automatic Class. Next day, running for the meet's most coveted honor—Top Stock Eliminator—Mozer turned the tables and gave Thornton the thumb. But the event was far from over. Mozer still had to face the present "Mr. Eliminator," Al Eckstrand in Lawman, another specially equipped '63 Dodge. And another winner is defeated. Mozer edged him by 1/100th of a second with an e.t. of 12.22.

Some days you win. Some days you lose. That's what keeps the quarter-mile jaunt so interesting. But have you noticed? When a Dodge loses these days ... it's another Dodge.

Hot Dodge

DODGE DIVISION **CHRYSLER** MOTORS CORPORATION

▲ Sagging '62 sales taught Dodge its lesson. Styling for '63 was toned down, and the wheelbase of its standard-size cars grew by three inches, to 119. They were called 330, 440, and Polara (shown).

◄ The 426 had 415 bhp on 11.0:1 compression; or 425 bhp on 13.5:1. Stage II and Stage III versions followed during the year, with larger-bore Carter carbs. Valve lift and duration grew, tightest compression dropped to 12.5:1, and recast heads were installed.

RAMCHARGER 426

1963 DODGE HIGH-PERFORMANCE ENGINES

TYPE	CID	BORE × STROKE	BHP @ RPM	TORQUE @ RPM	FUEL SYSTEM	COMP. RATIO	AVAIL.
ohv V-8	383	4.25 × 3.75	325 @ 5200	420 @ 3600	2×4bbl.	11.0:1	full size
ohv V-8	426	4.25 × 3.75	370 @ 4600	460 @ 2800	1×4bbl.	11.0:1	full size
ohv V-8	426	4.25 × 3.75	375 @ 4600	465 @ 2800	1×4bbl.	13.5:1	full size
ohv V-8	426	4.25 × 3.75	415 @ 5600	470 @ 4400	2×4bbl.	11.0:1	full size
ohv V-8	426	4.25 × 3.75	425 @ 5600	480 @ 4400	2×4bbl.	13.5:1	full size

▲ "Strictly business" was the rule when a customer ordered a Stage II or III Ramcharger V-8 in a basic Dodge 330 two-door. This factory-built 3200-pound light-weight racer wears an aluminum front end and deletes the radio and heater.

▶ Hood scoops to feed the ram-inducted carbs are the sole clue that 425 ramcharged horses wait in ambush. Heavy-duty TorqueFlite sent all that action to a 4.56:1 axle in this installation, but others had a close-ratio three-speed floor shift.

▲ The colorful "Candymatic" Dodge drag car was a national Top Stock Eliminator. Its name combined the candy-stripe theme with the idea of an automatic transmission, in this case controlled by Hurst's new shifter.

▲ Stock-car racing, declared a Dodge ad, proved "the ultimate measure of a car's capability." Perhaps, but many savored the straight-line thrill of cars like "Candymatic" at the strip, and of their own Dodges on the street.

▶ Detroit lawyer Elton A. "Al" Eckstrand's "Ramchargers" Polara was top Stock Eliminator at the '63 NHRA Winternationals in Pomona, California. His ET was 12.44 seconds at 115.08 mph. This car used a Hurst Dual Gate shifter. This popular aftermarket piece combined the set-and-forget convenience of a regular automatic with an adjacent "gate" into which the shift lever could be moved and then slammed manually through rapid 1-2-3 upshifts.

▼ This is how the "Ramchargers" drag car looked in its original livery, before adopting the "Candymatic" name and awning-stripe paint scheme. Though professionally tuned, its engine was basically the same as that available to anyone through the factory. Brochures warned that the 426 Ramcharger warmed up slowly (having no heat applied to the manifold) and was "not a street machine." Rather, it was "designed to be run in supervised, sanctioned drag-strip competition by those qualified....Yet, it is stock in every sense of the word."

▲ Ford came on strong in NASCAR for '63, with "Tiny" Lund winning the Daytona 500 in a Galaxie. In drag racing, however, the competition weighed about 3200 pounds, some 300 less than a Galaxie. Ford fought back with a series of 50 lightweight Galaxies with fiberglass front body panels and aluminum front bumpers that slashed about 174 pounds. These 3425-pound race-only Fords ran 12.07-second ETs at 118 mph, but still weren't fast enough to win any NHRA national titles. This is Dick Brannan giving it his best in one of the '63 lightweights.

◄ Shelby's AC Cobra sports car was bred for twisty-course road racing, but in Dragonsnake form, it was ready to take on the quarter-mile. Dragonsnakes were made available for 1963 and were sold with 23 options designed specifically for drag racing. Their Ford HiPo 289-cid V-8 was available in four stages of tune: 271, 300, 325, and 380 bhp. Dragonsnake prices ranged from $6795 to $8995.

▲ Based on the British AC Ace roadster, the Shelby Cobra was the product of Ford V-8 power and the imagination of a race-car driver and builder from Texas, Carroll Shelby. They were expensive, exclusive, and fast.

▲ The Cobra sports car was in a way a classic example of the muscle car philosophy: scads of horsepower in the lightest car to be found. Earliest examples used Ford's 260-cid, then the 289, and finally the mighty 427.

Full-size Fords entered '63 with carried-over '62 powertrains. But those soon were joined by a brutal new 427 V-8, which ostensibly was the 390/406 FE-series bored by .010-inch. Actually, the new block was freshly cast and carried a forged steel crankshaft, cross-bolted main bearing caps, forged aluminum pistons, and aluminum intake manifold. Though called 427, actual displacement was 425 cubic inches. The lightweight valvetrain and high-lift, solid-lifter camshaft could withstand 7000 rpm. An oval air cleaner held an exposed filter element between aluminum upper and lower sections. The strongest 427 used a pair of 652cfm Holley four-barrels for an advertised 425 bhp at 6000 rpm and 480 pounds/feet of torque at 3700. With a single 780cfm Holley, the engine had 410 bhp at 5600 and 476 lbs/ft. Both versions ran 11.5:1 compression. Chromed valve covers were included.

▲ Ordering a 427 for $405.70 ($56 more for twin-carb) brought a tougher suspension, rear axle, and brakes; heavy-duty driveshaft and U-joints; and 15-inch wheels. A four-speed manual was mandatory.

1963 FORD HIGH-PERFORMANCE ENGINES

TYPE	CID	BORE × STROKE	BHP @ RPM	TORQUE @ RPM	FUEL SYSTEM	COMP. RATIO	AVAIL.
ohv V-8	260	3.80 × 2.87	260 @ 5800	281 @ 3300	1 × 4bbl.	10.5:1	Cobra
ohv V-8	289	4.00 × 2.87	271 @ 6000	312 @ 3400	1 × 4bbl.	10.5:1	full size, Cobra
ohv V-8	390	4.05 × 3.78	330 @ 5000	427 @ 3200	1 × 4bbl.	9.6:1	full size (police)
ohv V-8	390	4.05 × 3.78	340 @ 3200	430 @ 3200	3 × 2bbl.	10.5:1	full size
ohv V-8	406	4.13 × 3.78	385 @ 5800	440 @ 3800	1 × 4bbl.	11.4:1	full size
ohv V-8	406	4.13 × 3.78	405 @ 5800	448 @ 3500	3 × 2bbl.	11.4:1	full size
ohv V-8	427	4.23 × 3.78	425 @ 6000	480 @ 3700	2 × 4bbl.	11.5:1	full size (race)

▲ In February 1963, Ford introduced slanted rear rooflines for the "1963 ½" Galaxie 500 (shown) and 500XL series. Called the Sports Hardtop, the semi-fastback was two inches lower than the equivalent notchback and allowed a great aerodynamic advantage on NASCAR superspeedways.

▲ A precursor to the 1964 Fairlane Thunderbolt was this '63 run by Rhode Island Ford dealer Bob Tasca. With the factory's help, Tasca squeezed a 427 into the intermediate and unveiled it on Labor Day Weekend at the NHRA Nationals in Indianapolis. Running in factory experimental, it turned a 12.21 at 118.42, but still got beat by a Z-11 Chevy. Production Fairlanes were offered with a 271-bhp version of the 289 V-8. With a four-barrel and 11.0:1 compression, it was Ford's first performance engine in a mid-size.

▶ Camshaft profiles could easily spell the difference between winning and losing—at the strip or on the street. Iskenderian, one of the best-known aftermarket firms, rode to the rescue with its line of mild to moderate to wild racing cams. If the stock bumpstick just wouldn't do, an "Isky" cam could increase valve duration and lift for better breathing and more power.

Authorized Dealer

ISKENDERIAN

OFFICIALLY AMERICA'S FASTEST!

World's Fastest RACING CAMS

▲ Both the 427-cid V-8 and the Galaxie fastback-style roofline debuted in mid-'63. The hot new engine and aerodynamic roof were an inspired duo in stock-car racing and carried the blue oval to the 1963 NASCAR championship.

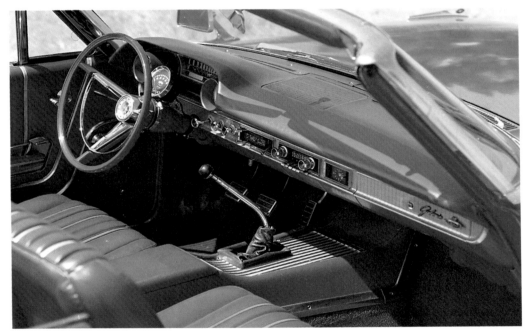

▲ All full-size Fords got fresh sheetmetal for '63, and after midyear were known as the "Super Torque" Galaxies. Engine choices started with a 260-cid V-8, soon replaced by the 289; but pedal-down Ford fans could reach all the way to the carryover 406, or the new 427. This Rangoon Red 500XL drop top represents big Ford style and muscle at its most stylish. It has the 406-cid V-8 with Tri-Power carburetion.

◄ Fast fun in the sun. This Galaxie 500XL convertible has the $188 optional Borg-Warner four-speed manual transmission, with a big 8000-rpm Rotunda tachometer above the steering column to help the driver get the most out of that stout 406. Lesser V-8s were offered with automatic, either the $212 Cruise-O-Matic three-speed or the $190 Ford-O-Matic two-speed. This ragtop has the rare $94 Ford AM/FM radio, but not the $102 power windows.

▶ While the new 427 grabbed the headlines at midseason, Ford's familiar 406-cid V-8 carried the ball early in the year. When equipped with the three-deuce setup, as is this one, it again delivered an attention-getting 405 bhp. The four-barrel 406 made 385 bhp. Incidently, the tri-carb hardware was shipped from the factory in the car's trunk, to be installed by the dealer's service department. Dealers could also install a nasty set of exhaust cutouts, for $55, though Ford urged buyers not to use them on the street. By spring 1963, Ford advertisements no longer mentioned either 406. One more performance-packed engine had faded into history, giving way to a brash newcomer.

Mercury's new sizzler the...

Marauder

A new breed of scat!

Note the sleek, racy design of Mercury's newest hardtop: the 1963½ Marauder. Aerodynamic styling cuts air resistance, takes full advantage of Mercury's brilliant new V-8's.

No matter which Mercury V-8 engine you choose, you get brilliant performance! A big 390 V-8 is standard on the Marauder hardtop model. On S-55 bucket-seaters, the standard engine is a 4-barrel Super Marauder 390 V-8. Optional engines range up to a 427 V-8.

Marauder transmission choices include multi-drive Merc-O-Matic and 3- and 4-speed fully synchronized manual shifts. Looking for a top performer? See your Mercury dealer.

FACTS ON SUPER MARAUDER 427 V-8: Displacement: 427 cu. in. • 4.23 bore x 3.78 stroke • 425 hp @ 6000 rpm • 480 lb-ft torque @ 3700 rpm • dual 4-barrel carburetors • compression ratio 11.5:1 • mechanical valve lifters • fully synchronized 4-speed stick shift transmission.

COMET • METEOR • MERCURY: PRODUCTS OF *Ford* MOTOR COMPANY • LINCOLN-MERCURY DIVISION
FOR 60 YEARS THE SYMBOL OF DEPENDABLE PRODUCTS

1963 MERCURY HIGH-PERFORMANCE ENGINES							
TYPE	CID	BORE× STROKE	BHP @ RPM	TORQUE @ RPM	FUEL SYSTEM	COMP. RATIO	AVAIL.
ohv V-8	427	4.23× 3.78	410 @ 5600	476 @ 3400	1×4bbl.	11.5:1	full size
ohv V-8	430	4.30× 3.70	320 @ 4600	465 @ 2600	1×4bbl.	10.1:1	full size

◀ Mercury's counterpart to the 1962½ Galaxie Sport Hardtop was the Marauder, a new nameplate that eschewed the reverse-slant "Breezeway" roof of other big Mercs. Engine choices began with a 250-bhp V-8, but stretched to the dual-quad, solid-lifter 427. Pioneer auto writer Tom McCahill said the big 427 Marauder "has more hair on its chest than a middle-aged yak."

1963 OLDSMOBILE HIGH-PERFORMANCE ENGINES							
TYPE	CID	BORE× STROKE	BHP @ RPM	TORQUE @ RPM	FUEL SYSTEM	COMP. RATIO	AVAIL.
ohv V-8	215	3.50× 2.80	215 @ 4600	300 @ 3200	1×1bbl.*	10.25:1	Jetfire
ohv V-8	394	4.13× 3.69	330 @ 4800	440 @ 2800	1×4bbl.	10.25:1	S-88, 98
ohv V-8	394	4.13× 3.69	345 @ 4800	440 @ 3200	1×4bbl.	10.5:1	Starfire
* Turbocharged.							

▲ There's "nothing like it on the road today," claimed Olds. The Jetfire used a four-barrel carb, but also injected a mixture of distilled water and methyl alcohol into the fuel/air charge. This kept the combustion chamber cool enough to prevent knock under the 10.25:1 compression.

◀ Oldsmobile took a different high-performance tack: turbocharging. Its F-85 Jetfire, unveiled in spring 1962 and carried over for '63 (left), turbocharged a 215-cid aluminum V-8 for 215 bhp, 60 more than the non-turbo version. Fitted with buckets and console, Olds said the $3049 hardtop aimed at "the man who thrives on high adventure." But most testers were disappointed with the Jetfire's 8-10-second 0-60s and near 19-second quarter-miles.

▲ Plymouth's full-size line lost some of its eccentric styling for '63 and gained the 426 Super Stock wedge as a new high-performance engine. It made 415 or 425 bhp, depending on tune, and would turn this and other similarly plain Belvederes into a real pavement rippers.

▲ Little inside suggested the thrills awaiting a stab at the accelerator. The floor-mounted shift lever for the three-speed 'box may have been a clue, however. Four-speed transmissions hadn't yet arrived on Chrysler products.

▲ Plymouth's Super Stock 426 breathed through twin Carter AFB four-barrels offset atop a cross-ram manifold. Exhaust was handled by the ram's-horn headers. The 415 bhp was from 11:1 compression, the 425 bhp from 13.5:1.

◄ Tom Grove, of Union City, California, was one of the West Coast's quickest Mopar drag racers. Here, Grove's "Melrose Missile III" Plymouth takes on Bill Hanyon's Fury at the '63 NHRA Winternationals. "Street" versions of this car were available through any dealer. At the Pomona dragstrip, *Hot Rod* took a 426 Super Stock Plymouth with automatic and 4.56:1 axle to a 12.69-second ET at 112 mph. The magazine explained that the 13.5:1-compression 426 "is strictly a ¼-mile sprinter and not designed for street driving. Plymouth recommends that full throttle bursts be limited to 15 seconds and then only if the gasoline used is 102 octane or better." Even the 11:1 Super Stock was "a thoroughbred designed for the track, not a workhorse for pulling a plow." Mopar 426 Wedge engines set eight NHRA records in 1963.

1963 PLYMOUTH HIGH-PERFORMANCE ENGINES

TYPE	CID	BORE× STROKE	BHP @ RPM	TORQUE @ RPM	FUEL SYSTEM	COMP. RATIO	AVAIL.
ohv V-8	383	4.24× 3.38	330 @ 4600	425 @ 2800	1×4bbl.	10.0:1	full size
ohv V-8	426	4.25× 3.75	370 @ 4600	460 @ 2800	1×4bbl.	11.0:1	full size
ohv V-8	426	4.25× 3.75	375 @ 4600	465 @ 2800	1×4bbl.	13.5:1	full size
ohv V-8	426	4.25× 3.75	415 @ 5600	470 @ 4400	2×4bbl.	11.0:1	full size
ohv V-8	426	4.25× 3.75	425 @ 5600	480 @ 4400	2×4bbl.	13.5:1	full size

▲ Any win is a good win, and Plymouth's were not confined to the dragstrips in '63. The Chrysler division came on strong in oval racing, especially on the shorter tracks. Here, A.J. Foyt steers one between turns. Plymouth took the USAC Manufacturers' Trophy, while Richard Petty was at the wheel in 14 of Plymouth's 19 NASCAR wins, a total second only to Ford's 23 victories.

▼ "Golden Commando" was the tag Plymouth gave to its 383-cid V-8, a consistent performer that in 330-bhp form could take a Sport Fury hardtop to 60 mph in 7.2 seconds and to a 15.9-second quarter-mile. Hamilton Motors of Detroit sponsored a series of drag Plymouths under the "Golden Commando" banner, including this 426 wedge Super Stock Automatic car. Drivers such as Al Eckstrand, Bill Shirey, Forest Pitcock, and John Dallafior put in seat time with these potent Plymouths.

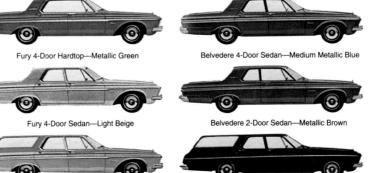

1963 PLYMOUTH LINEUP

Fury Convertible—Dark Metallic Blue

Belvedere 2-Door Hardtop—Medium Beige

Fury 2-Door Hardtop—Ruby

Fury 4-Door Hardtop—Metallic Green

Belvedere 4-Door Sedan—Medium Metallic Blue

Savoy 4-Door Sedan—Light Green

Sport Fury Convertible—Ebony

Fury 4-Door Sedan—Light Beige

Belvedere 2-Door Sedan—Metallic Brown

Savoy 2-Door Sedan—Ruby

Sport Fury 2-Door Hardtop—Coppertone

Fury 4-Door Station Wagon—Light Blue

Belvedere 4-Door Station Wagon—Ebony

Savoy 4-Door Station Wagon—Metallic Brown

▲▼ Arlen Vanke ran one of the quickest—and cleanest—Plymouths in the NHRA wars. Cars with the basics of his two-door 426-cid Savoy were offered to the public. They were among 105 lightweight Plymouths that saved 150 pounds through the use of front fenders and a scooped hood made of aluminum, and by deleting most every convenience item. At midyear came the Stage III 426, a more radical wedge with larger primary bores for its twin Carter AFBs, a higher-lift (.520-inch) camshaft, and larger-chamber heads.

▲ Despite the polished brightwork, the 426 in Vanke's Plymouth was not pretty to competitors. These mills held a host of super-tough internal components.

▼ Tom Grove's "Melrose Missile IV" was a 12.37-second Super/Stock threat, but that still wasn't enough to beat Dave Strickler's lightning-fast "Old Reliable" Chevy for NHRA's U.S. Nationals Top Stock title in '63.

▲ Though the 426-cid Super Stock engine wasn't recommended for street use, it was nevertheless available on uplevel Plymouths. Witness this striking Sport Fury ragtop with its 425 bhp and TorqueFlite automatic.

▲ Bright and sassy, this Super Stock Sport Fury is a very pretty sleeper. Note the automatic transmission's pushbutton gear selection aligned vertically to the left of the steering wheel.

▲ Few believed the conservative figures, but Super Stock 426 engines were rated at 415 bhp with 11:1 compression, or 425 with 13.5:1. "Getup and go Plymouth!" was one slogan this year. And how!

▼ With the Super Duty 421 underhood, this was Pontiac's seat of power for '63. The clean Catalina goes with a rugged four-speed manual hooked to a 4.30:1 Positraction rear axle. The factory tachometer and vacuum gauges were new options for '63 (a tilt steering wheel also was new). Bucket seats are tritone white/burgundy/wine. An AM/FM radio completes the picture.

▲ Full-size Pontiacs got new sheetmetal from the beltline down and adopted the stacked headlamps that would become their trademark for the next several years. All big Ponchos could get the 421-cid V-8. It was offered in 353-bhp form with a four-barrel, or as the 421 HO (High Output) in 370-bhp guise with a Tri-Power setup. This particular Catalina, however, has the rare 405-bhp Super Duty 421, which was intended for the dragstrip. Note the desirable eight-lug wheels.

▲ *Motor Trend* ran a four-speed dual-quad Super Duty Catalina to a 0-60 run of 5.4 seconds and a quarter-mile of 13.9 seconds at 107 mph—on street tires. Even the "ordinary" 370-bhp Tri-Power 421 could turn ETs in the mid-14s.

◄ Only 88 Super Duty engines were built for '63. Most went into Catalinas. They came in three levels of tune, each with less torque— but more horsepower and a higher rev capability—than a regular 421. Pontiac's Special Equipment catalog warned that Super Dutys were "designed only for all-out performance enthusiasts."

1963 PONTIAC HIGH-PERFORMANCE ENGINES

TYPE	CID	BORE × STROKE	BHP @ RPM	TORQUE @ RPM	FUEL SYSTEM	COMP. RATIO	AVAIL.
ohv V-8	389	4.06 × 3.75	313 @ 4600	430 @ 3200	3×2bbl.	10.25:1	full size
ohv V-8	421	4.09 × 3.75	353 @ 5000	455 @ 3400	1×4bbl.	10.75:1	full size
ohv V-8	421	4.09 × 3.75	370 @ 5200	460 @ 3800	3×2bbl.	10.75:1	full size
ohv V-8	421	4.09 × 4.00	390 @ 5800	425 @ 3600	1×4bbl.	12.0:1	1
ohv V-8	421	4.09 × 4.00	405 @ 5600	425 @ 4400	2×4bbl.	12.0:1	1
ohv V-8	421	4.09 × 4.00	410 @ 5600	435 @ 4400	2×4bbl.	13.0:1	1

1. Catalina cpe.

Here's one Pontiac Catalina that wasn't intended for Sunday drives—unless those journeys were taken in 1320-foot bites. Ultra-light bucket seats, T-handle shifter, oversized tachometer, radio-delete, auxiliary gauges, and, of course, the racing helmet, attest to its mission as a quarter-mile warrior.

▶ In place of the back seat, this fierce Catalina sports a set of support braces to help maintain solidity in case of mishap. The fire extinguisher could come in mighty handy, too. All-synchro four-speeds were the racers' choice on the strip, but conventional Catalinas might have a three-speed manual gearbox or Super Hydra-Matic.

▲ Riding a 120-inch wheelbase, the comparatively lightweight Catalina was the sensible choice to carry Super Duty power. Still, a stock hardtop tipped the scales at 3725 pounds, so every bit of weight-cutting helped when performance was at stake. Special Catalinas built for dragging saved 300 pounds through use of aluminum bumpers and bucket seats, bell housing, front-end sheetmetal, and axle centers. Frames were lightened, batteries moved to the trunk, and insulation and sound deadening omitted.

◀ Most ferocious of the Super Duty 421 V-8s was this dual-quad trooper. It ran a 13.0:1 compression, good for 410 bhp at 5600 rpm and a walloping 435 pounds/feet of torque at 4400. At 12.0:1 compression were the single-carb Super Duty, with 390 bhp at 5800 rpm, and the other dual-quad, with 405 bhp at 5600. Both of those "lesser" Super Duty V-8s delivered 425 pounds/feet of torque.

▲ As it turned out, Pontiac Motor Division wasn't quite as "passionate" about racing as this Catalina's nomenclature suggests. Early in 1963, GM ordered a halt to factory participation in racing and a de-emphasis on high performance. Pontiac did drop out of direct involvement in racing, but the 421 engine remained available, and in fact was offered in all the full-size models for the first time in '63. This drag car's "Swiss Cheese" license tag refers to its frame, portions of which were drilled through with holes at the factory to reduce weight.

▲ "Here's What The Other '63s Wished They Looked Like," promised Pontiac ads. Well, perhaps not exactly like this particular Catalina, which sacrificed some of its beauty for a two-fisted drag-strip wallop. This Catalina drag car boasts 405 horsepower, but as usual, actual output was anybody's guess. Catalina and Grand Prix rode a 120-inch wheelbase, three inches shorter than the Bonneville and Star Chief.

▲ The lightest, cheapest two-door Catalina with a High Output Tri-Power 421 HO and four-speed could turn mid-14s right out of the box. The 421 HOs were available with three- or four-speed manual or Super Hydra-Matic automatic. Pontiac recommended a 3.42:1 axle as a good acceleration/cruising compromise, though dealer-installed ratios up to 4.44:1 were available. This Marlin Aqua Sports Sedan spent four years of its early life racing in A/Stock; it has less than 6000 miles on the odometer.

◄ The tri-carb 421 HO had 370 bhp at 5300 rpm, and 460 lbs/ft of torque at 3800 with three Rochester two-barrels and 10.75:1 compression. The four-bolt block had a forged crank and hydraulic lifters. It cost $404 to $445 more than a 389-cid, depending on the combination of equipment.

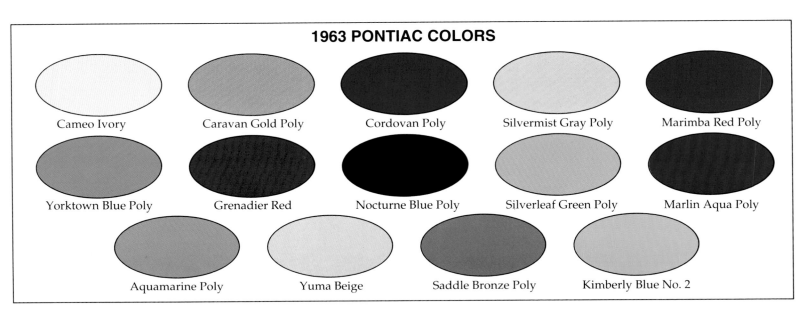

1963 PONTIAC COLORS

Cameo Ivory | Caravan Gold Poly | Cordovan Poly | Silvermist Gray Poly | Marimba Red Poly

Yorktown Blue Poly | Grenadier Red | Nocturne Blue Poly | Silverleaf Green Poly | Marlin Aqua Poly

Aquamarine Poly | Yuma Beige | Saddle Bronze Poly | Kimberly Blue No. 2

Two New Cars are Born

Avanti-inspired...
Bonneville-tested!

**R2 SUPER LARK
R2 SUPER HAWK**

▲ A hero to Pontiac partisans in 1963—and for years afterward—was "Akron Arlen" Vanke. His A/FX "Tin Indian III" is shown at the NHRA Winternationals. A fellow Pontiac driver, Bill Shrewesberry, took A/FX honors at the '63 Winternationals with a torrid 12.04-second ET at 116.27 mph. Big Ponchos were out-digging plenty of rivals, but the high-performance focus would soon be shifting to mid-size cars—a shift for which Pontiac itself could take credit. In a hint of what was to come, 11 Super Duty V-8s were installed in compact Tempests.

◄ Studebaker soon would fade from the American scene, but its R2 supercharged editions were quick at the Bonneville Salt Flats: 132 mph for the sedate Super Lark, 140 for the sleek Super Hawk. Meanwhile, an R3 Studebaker Avanti did a record 168.15 mph for the flying kilometer. Occasionally, a tame-looking R2 Lark would blow away a scoffing rival at the dragstrip, but as on the street, it was too little, too late.

We designed two new cars—and built a lot of our record-setting Avanti into them. Added the supercharged Avanti R2 engine.

...And took them to the Flats for final evaluation and endurance tests. The results surprised even us: R2 Super Lark—132 mph! R2 Super Hawk—140 mph! With 2 up. Under bad weather and surface conditions—even snow. USAC timed the bit, official.

That kind of performance told us these cars were ready to join the Studebaker line. R2 Super Lark and R2 Super Hawk are now available on special order at your Studebaker dealer's.

The package of pow and pizazz:
R-2 blown mill, 4-speed box, Avanti wheels inside 6.50-15's. Anti-sway rod forward; trac rods, rear. HD springs and shocks at both ends. Our disc binders. Belts. (Now installed on **all**

cars from Studebaker, by the way.) Sundry little signs on each car to tell the peasantry you've got an extreme automobile. When parked. Under way, they'll know without sign language. Warning: The color choice is limited. But you have your own spray gun, don't you?

Studebaker
CORPORATION

1963 STUDEBAKER HIGH-PERFORMANCE ENGINES							
TYPE	CID	BORE × STROKE	BHP @ RPM	TORQUE @ RPM	FUEL SYSTEM	COMP. RATIO	AVAIL.
ohv V-8	289	3.56 × 3.63	240 @ 4800	305 @ 3200	1×4bbl.	10.25:1	1
ohv V-8	289	3.56 × 3.63	290 @ 5200	330 @ 3600	1×4bbl.	9.0:1*	1
*Supercharged. 1. Hawk, Lark, Avanti.							

1964

425 horsepower remains top advertised industry figure; displacement race also stands pat ● Crafty Pontiac launches legendary GTO as Tempest LeMans option with 389-cid V-8 ● Mustang unveiled as 1964½ model ● Mid-size Chevelle debuts with available 283-cid V-8, but soon a trio of 327s deliver up to 365 bhp... Malibu hardtop and ragtop offered with Super Sport package ● Hemi V-8 returns to Dodge/Plymouth ranks after five-year absence; leads Chrysler to 26 NASCAR victories—but Ford wins 30 ● Tamer "Street Wedge" debuts under Dodge/Plymouth hoods ● Ford tries to legalize SOHC (overhead-cam) 427 for oval tracks; NASCAR nixes the notion ● Race-ready Thunderbolt Fairlane sends Ford back to the winner's circle at dragstrips with ETs in the 11s ● A/FX (Factory Experimental) compact Ford Falcons and Mercury Comets hit dragstrips with 427-cid engines ● Richard Petty wins his first Daytona 500 in a Hemi Plymouth ● At Tucson Dragway, a Dodge Charger sets S/FX quarter-mile record of 135.55 mph

▲ Full-size Chevrolets adopted a larger, more formal look as the mid-size Chevelle targeted the burgeoning youth market. This Meadow Green Biscayne two-door sedan carries the hottest 409 V-8, again rated at 425 horsepower and hooked to a Muncie four-speed and 3.70:1 Positraction axle. The 409 also came in 340- and 400-bhp configurations, but quarter-mile rivals were tougher than ever. The 409's days were numbered.

1964 CHEVROLET IMPALA SS CONVERTIBLE

1964 CHEVROLET IMPALA SS COUPE

▲ Chevrolet's full-size Super Sport became a distinct Impala series, not an option package. Offered as hardtop or convertible, a new AM/FM radio was offered, while a walnut-grained steering wheel added class.

▲ A total of 185,325 SS Impalas went to customers in '64, typically loaded with luxury rather than strict stand-on-the-pedal power. Only the tamest 340-bhp 409 could be ordered with air conditioning.

▲ Open the early-muscle dictionary to "sleeper" and this may be what you'll see: Budget-model Biscayne body; blackwall tires; taxi-cab hub caps. Open the throttle on this car, however, and you'll surely have to hang on as 425 pounds/feet of torque turn those skinny bias-plies into gummy smoke generators. Still, times were changing, and production of the 409 fell 48 percent, to 8864 installations for '64.

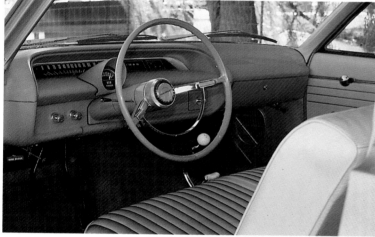

▲ A big tachometer and a dash without a radio is one way to spot a muscle-car interior. Another is the M20 four-speed gearbox. The close-ratio M21 could have a 4.11:1 or 4.56:1 axle with Positraction.

▲ Full-size Chevrolets were fading from the performance scene, but the 409 maintained the sales catalog's promise that it would be "especially saucy in highway passing situations." The sizzling 427 Z-11 option was killed.

▲ Street racers learned the signs. A burbly exhaust note and a lumpy idle would be the first clues, and the crossed-flags 409 insignia would confirm it: One of these 425-bhp heavyweights was not to be taken casually.

1964 CHEVROLET HIGH-PERFORMANCE ENGINES

TYPE	CID	BORE × STROKE	BHP @ RPM	TORQUE @ RPM	FUEL SYSTEM	COMP. RATIO	AVAIL.
ohv V-8	283	3.88 × 3.00	220 @ 4800	295 @ 3200	1 × 4bbl.	9.25:1	Chevelle
ohv V-8	327	4.00 × 3.25	250 @ 4400	350 @ 2800	1 × 4bbl.	10.5:1	full size, Chevelle
ohv V-8	327	4.00 × 3.25	300 @ 5000	360 @ 3200	1 × 4bbl.	10.5:1	full size, Chevelle
ohv V-8	327	4.00 × 3.25	365 @ 6200	350 @ 4400	1 × 4bbl.	11.0:1	Chevelle
ohv V-8	409	4.31 × 3.50	340 @ 5000	420 @ 3200	1 × 4bbl.	10.0:1	full size
ohv V-8	409	4.31 × 3.50	400 @ 5800	425 @ 3600	1 × 4bbl.	11.0:1	full size
ohv V-8	409	4.31 × 3.50	425 @ 6000	425 @ 4200	2 × 4bbl.	11.0:1	full size

▲ The engine bay of Chrysler's letter-series cars still was an eye-opener with the ram-inducted twin-quad setup that added 30 bhp to the standard 360-bhp 413-cid V-8. And an optional four-speed manual replaced a three-speed. But while 3647 300Ks were sold for '64—compared to just 400 300Js for '63—Chrysler's proud letter-series model was not the hot rod its forbearers had been.

▶ A drop in power and deletion of such standard items as leather upholstery reduced letter-series prices and increased sales to record levels. The hardtop listed for $4056. The convertible returned after a one-year absence. It started at $4522, and 625 were sold. Still, few two-ton 300Js went to dragstrips, as performance buyers turned elsewhere. This was the last of the "true" letter-series 300s.

ISKY RACING ★ CAMS ★

1964 CHRYSLER HIGH-PERFORMANCE ENGINES

TYPE	CID	BORE × STROKE	BHP @ RPM	TORQUE @ RPM	FUEL SYSTEM	COMP. RATIO	AVAIL.
ohv V-8	383	4.25 × 3.38	305 @ 4600	410 @ 2400	1 × 2bbl.	10.0:1	full size
ohv V-8	413	4.19 × 3.75	340 @ 4600	470 @ 2800	1 × 4bbl.	10.0:1	full size
ohv V-8	413	4.19 × 3.75	360 @ 4800	470 @ 3200	1 × 4bbl.	10.0:1	300K
ohv V-8	413	4.19 × 3.75	390 @ 4800	485 @ 3600	2 × 4bbl.	10.0:1	300K

▲ Backed by Hodges Dodges, the "Original Ramchargers" Candymatic Mopar invariably hung on into the late rounds at major NHRA events. That's what it's doing at the Pomona Winternationals against a Ford Thunderbolt. The Dodge 330 two-door sedan carried Chrysler's 426-cid Super Stock wedge V-8.

▲ One of the best-known Chrysler Corporation racers on the West Coast was "Dandy Dick" Landy, seen here in full flight at the '64 Winternationals.

This is a Top Stock Eliminator. What did he eliminate? And why.

Dave Strickler in his '64 Dodge Ramcharger. Top Stock Eliminator in the 1964 AHRA Phoenix Dragstrip Championships.

On a straightaway track, from a standing start, he beat another car to the finish line one quarter of a mile away. He continued to beat (and eliminate) one car after another in his class. Until only he was left.

Dragstrip racing—America's newest million-fan sport—operates under clearly defined, rigidly enforced rules. It is a supreme challenge in acceleration.

It was not surprising that a competition equipped Dodge won. It would be highly unusual if a Top Stock Eliminator was not a Dodge or Plymouth.

Dragstrip competition, stock car races, and road rallies continue to confirm the excellence of Chrysler Corporation engineering, developed through years of extensive research and testing in the laboratory and on the proving grounds.

Want to eliminate all other cars? Test drive a '64 from Chrysler Corporation.

Plymouth · Dodge · Chrysler · Imperial

 **CHRYSLER CORPORATION**

Visit Chrysler Corporation's "Autofare" at the N. Y. World's Fair

▲ Dodge not only informed readers that Dave Strickler won Top Stock Eliminator in the AHRA's Phoenix Dragstrip Championship, it told them what that meant. Some Super Stock Dodges used aluminum doors, front fenders, and hood.

▲ Roger Lindamood's "Color Me Gone" Dodge turned an 11.31 at 127.84 mph at the NHRA Nationals and beat Jim Thornton and the Ramchargers for Top Stock.

▲ An altered wheelbase gave Dave Strickler's "Dodge Boys" coupe better weight distribution, helping him take A/FX honors at the '64 NHRA Nationals.

Dick Landy
"Landy's Dodge"

Bill Flynn
"Yankee Peddler"

Mary Ann Foss
"Go-Hummer"

Bill Golden
"Little Red Wagon"

Bob Harrop
"Flying Carpet"

Roger Lindamood
"Color Me Gone"

Sam Kennedy
"Hemi-Charger"

Shirley Shahan
"Drag-On-Lady"

▲ Men dominated this gallery of early Mopar drivers, but an increasing number of women were able to match reflexes and skill with the best of them to the delight of drag-strip crowds.

▲ George Hurst developed and marketed high-performance shifters, and promoted them vigorously. Here he is in a Polara convertible—complete with Miss Golden Shifter—at the '64 Winternationals. Hurst awarded a Polara hardtop to the team of Sox and Martin, who won Super Stock in a '64 Mercury Comet.

▲ For '64, big Dodges got a smoother front end, as seen on this Polara 500 convertible, while two-door hardtops got a new reverse-taper rear roof pillar. Returning for its last season was the raucous 426-cid wedge with 425 bhp and 13.5:1 compression. An easier-to-manage 365-bhp "Street Wedge" variant with 10.3:1 compression, milder cam, and single four-barrel without ram induction was also made available.

▶ The new 426 Street Wedge had a chrome air cleaner and valve covers, but not the upswept headers. Brochures warned that sale of the dual-quad 426 wedge was "limited to recognized and qualified competition participants only." But they had a cautionary note about the new wedge, too. "Quite frankly," Dodge said, "it is recommended for the performance specialist only."

		1964 DODGE HIGH-PERFORMANCE ENGINES					
TYPE	CID	BORE × STROKE	BHP @ RPM	TORQUE @ RPM	FUEL SYSTEM	COMP. RATIO	AVAIL.
ohv V-8	383	4.25 × 3.75	330 @ 4600	425 @ 2800	1×4bbl.	10.0:1	full size
ohv V-8	426	4.25 × 3.75	365 @ 4800	470 @ 3200	1×4bbl.	10.3:1	full size
ohv V-8	426*	4.25 × 3.75	415 @ 5600	470 @ 4400	2×4bbl.	11.0:1	full size
ohv V-8	426	4.25 × 3.75	425 @ 5600	480 @ 4400	2×4bbl.	12.5:1	full size
ohv V-8	426*	4.25 × 3.75	425 @ 6000	480 @ 4600	2×4bbl.	12.5:1	full size

* Hemi.

▲ King Kong returns! Chrysler revived its mighty Hemi V-8 for '64, unveiling it at Daytona in February 1964, where it promptly swept the first three places in NASCAR's biggest race. The 426-cid monster still was a few years away from street duty, but did find a home beneath the hood of a few special drag-prepped 330/440/Polara Dodges. This 330 two-door is one of those factory-built race cars.

▲ Called the Maximum Performance Package, Dodge's drag-ready Hemi setup used lightweight Dodge van bucket seats and eliminated the rear seat, radio, heater, and carpeting.

▲ Though it resembled the hemi-head Mopars of the 1950s, this one was based on the RB wedge. Dodge claimed 425 bhp at 6000 rpm with 12.5:1 compression, and 415 bhp with an 11.0:1 squeeze. Actual outputs were closer to 570 bhp.

▲ The Maximum Performance Package moved the battery to the trunk and used aluminum for the hood, front fenders, doors, and some minor body panels.

▲ Spotter's guide: The hood scoop on Ramcharger 426 wedges had two distinct openings. The 426 Hemis could be identified by their single large opening.

▲ Hemis used the new heavy-duty-side-loading Chrysler four-speed manual or the three-speed TorqueFlite, which was in its last year with pushbuttons.

▲ The Hemi's large, half-arc combustion chambers allowed fuel to burn quicker and more completely with reduced risk of dangerous knocking. Breathing and heat dissipation at high rpm also were outstanding, though the complex valve network with dual rocker shafts helped push manufacturing cost high.

▲ After setting a slew of quarter-mile records with automatic, Dodge announced its new four-speed.

▲ NASCAR versions of the Hemi used a single Holley four-barrel atop a dual-plane high-rise intake manifold. Drag Hemis used a ram-tuned aluminum induction system with Carter dual quads. These heavily modified "Dodge Chargers," however, had superchargers.

▲ The S/FX Chargers had 850-900 bhp. At 135.33 mph in the quarter, no stock-body car was faster.

▲ Trophies by the truckload: Hemis powered Jim Thornton (above) among others to NHRA titles, while in NASCAR, Richard Petty road one to his first Daytona 500 flag.

FORD GALAXIE 500 2-DOOR HARDTOP

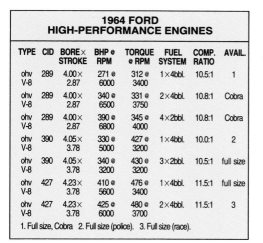

**1964 FORD
HIGH-PERFORMANCE ENGINES**

TYPE	CID	BORE × STROKE	BHP @ RPM	TORQUE @ RPM	FUEL SYSTEM	COMP. RATIO	AVAIL.
ohv V-8	289	4.00 × 2.87	271 @ 6000	312 @ 3400	1×4bbl.	10.5:1	1
ohv V-8	289	4.00 × 2.87	340 @ 6500	331 @ 3750	2×4bbl.	10.8:1	Cobra
ohv V-8	289	4.00 × 2.87	390 @ 6800	345 @ 4000	4×2bbl.	10.8:1	Cobra
ohv V-8	390	4.05 × 3.78	330 @ 5000	427 @ 3200	1×4bbl.	10.0:1	2
ohv V-8	390	4.05 × 3.78	340 @ 3200	430 @ 3200	3×2bbl.	10.5:1	full size
ohv V-8	427	4.23 × 3.78	410 @ 5600	476 @ 3400	1×4bbl.	11.5:1	full size
ohv V-8	427	4.23 × 3.78	425 @ 6000	480 @ 3700	2×4bbl.	11.5:1	3

1. Full size, Cobra   2. Full size (police).   3. Full size (race).

"3½-speed" box—and no charge

Every standard-shift Ford has Synchro on Low gear. Same for V-8 version of Fairlane and Falcon. That takes the old three-speeder out of Dullsville; making the bottom cog a *driving* gear instead of just a start-up gear is like adding half a ratio to the box and even the most basic Ford you can buy gets a good chunk of that sports car feeling.

How do you explain this to mama, who thinks Synchro is a new detergent?

Well, you can take her out in a '64 Ford and say: "Look, here I am almost stopped and the light goes green—so I pop it into Low and away we go; no 'crr-r-runch.'" Or you can show her the bit about the slow truck and the short straightaway—how you can flip into Low at 10 M.P.H. and squirt on by with a big safety margin. Or sail down a stiff mountain grade and get the braking assist of bottom gear any time you want it. Or shift in the middle of a climbing hairpin turn without losing momentum.

We feel Synchro Low adds a big chunk of pleasure to anybody's three-speed driving. That's a big chunk you don't get in any other standard-shift car—because only Ford takes the trouble.

So trot on down to your Ford dealer and try it; we may wean you away from automatics yet.

TRY TOTAL PERFORMANCE FOR A CHANGE!

FORD

Falcon · Fairlane · Ford · Thunderbird

▲ Ford showed a fresh face for '64, but still found itself fighting an uphill battle in drag racing. Nonetheless, the blue-oval boys were promoting the sportiness of their full-size cars, even claiming that their three-speed's new synchronized first-gear "may wean you away from automatics yet."

▲ Ford was tops in NASCAR, taking 30 Grand National wins to 13 for Dodge, 12 for Plymouth. Ned Jarrett got 15 of them in his No. 11 Galaxie. When NASCAR disallowed its overhead-cam proposal, Ford adopted a high-rev kit that, despite the 410 rating, gave the 427 stock-car motor 550 bhp at 7000 rpm.

▲ Ford's poor power-to-weight ratio was usually its Achilles' heel in quarter-mile competition. But a hot 300-bhp-plus HiPo 289 in a feather-weight AC Cobra body was one place things evened out. Here, Ed Hedrick's "Fuchsia" Dragonsnake does battle with a '62 Pontiac Catalina. This sub-12-second Cobra held the NHRA A, B, and C/Sports national records in 1963 and '64.

▲ Billy Cox's A/SA lightweight 427 Galaxie puts the power down at the '64 Winternationals.

▲ Even with the hottest 427s, big Fords were seldom a match for lighter Mopars and Pontiacs at the drags.

▲ The few Galaxie Lightweights had a fiberglass nose with bubble hood to clear the new manifold.

▲ The Thunderbird 427 Super High Performance big-block was again rated at 425 bhp with dual quads below its pretty, elongated air cleaner. The single-quad version again made 410 bhp. *Motor Trend* ran a 425-bhp 427 with a 4.11:1 axle to 60 mph in 7.4, seconds, and needed 15.4 for the quarter. Not great, but as the Ford ads said, with 480 pounds/feet "those SuperTorque Ford engines climb hills like a homesick Swiss yodeler." Ford's purpose-built drag-racing 427 used a highrise manifold that lifted the air cleaner above the stock hood line, requiring a teardrop-shape bubble hood that later became a popular street-warrior accessory.

▲ New lower-body sculpturing gave Ford's sleek Galaxie 500XL a fresh base for its semi-fastback roofline. Wheelbase was unchanged at 119 inches. About 265,000 Galaxie hardtops were sold, but not too many carried either of the 427 engines. The 300-bhp 390-cid four-barrel or even the 250-bhp 352 four-barrel were more popular to buyers with sporting inclinations.

▲ Nonessentials were taboo: sunvisors, mirror, sound-deadener, armrests—even the jack and lug wrench. The back seat stayed, but lightweight front buckets were borrowed from Ford's police package. An oil pressure gauge went into the dash, and a tach was strapped to the steering column.

▲ Other factory stockers sold to pro drivers were stripped for dragstrip action, but few were starker than a Ford Fairlane Thunderbolt. A trunk-mounted 95-pound bus battery was one of dozens of modifications to the mid-size. With fiberglass doors, front body panels, and bumpers, and Plexiglass windows, a T-Bolt weighed just over the NHRA's 3205-pound minimum.

▲ Stuffing the high-riser 427 into a Fairlane was a battle requiring considerable modification of the front suspension. Then the eight equal-length exhaust headers had to be routed through the suspension components. Two trannies were offered: a Hurst-shifted T-10 four-speed with 4.44:1 axle, or PCA-F automatic with 4.58:1. Huge traction bars and asymmetrical rear springs helped get the power to the pavement. "Officially" rated 425 bhp at 6000 rpm, the engine actually produced at least 500 bhp.

▲ With the strong 427 burdened by too much weight in the Galaxie, the solution was obvious: Put the mill in a lighter car. Tempting as the mid-size Fairlane was, its engine bay just couldn't hold a big-block. Or could it? The job wasn't easy, but with help from Dearborn Steel Tubing, a contract car builder, Ford concocted a handful of race-ready and street-legal, if not exactly streetable, Thunderbolts.

▲ Georgia racer Phil Bonner at the wheel of a Thunderbolt strains to catch Al Eckstrand's "Lawman" Plymouth in the first round of eliminations at the '64 Winternationals. T-Bolts fared well in Super/Stock class. Gas Ronda turned an 11.60 at 124.38 mph at the Winternationals, helping Ford win the Manufacturer's Cup.

▼ Butch Leal dropped his "California Flash" moniker for "Mr. 427" in 1964, and the name fit as he piloted his T-Bolt to the S/S title at the NHRA Nationals in Indianapolis. His ET was 11.76 seconds at 122.78 mph. Here, Leal gets the drop on the Dana Brothers Dodge at the '64 Winternationals.

▲ Ford sold one lucky group of racers T-Bolts for $1, but the usual price was $3900 ($100 more for automatic), double the cost of a regular Fairlane. Few non-racers took the plunge. *Hot Rod* warned that the brutal machine was "not suitable for driving to and from the strip, let alone on the street."

▲ Ford planned to build just 50 Thunderbolts as A/FX cars, but constructed 127, enough to qualify for Super/Stock, where they were very hot. The thick hose visible here is one of the flexible ducts that fed the carbs through screened ram-air intakes installed in place of the inner headlamps.

▲ Mercury's Comet was basically a stretched Falcon, but Ford extended the corporate Total Performance push to include an A/FX Comet version of the Thunderbolt. Here they are in action at the '64 Winternationals.

▲ The lightweight 427 Comet was built as a wagon as well as a hardtop. It hauled. Don Nicholson's "Marauder" wagon turned ETs of around 11.5 at 121 mph at the NHRA's '64 Winternationals.

▲ Ronnie Sox's 427 Comet hardtop turned an 11.49 at 123.45 mph to beat Nicholson's wagon for the A/FX prize at the '64 Winternationals.

▲ When veteran dragger Jack Chrisman put a blown and injected, nitro-burning SOHC 427-cid Ford V-8 into a '64 Comet to run mid-nines at 150 mph, he not only turned heads, he virtually invented a new class of racer. His Sachs & Sons Comet is recognized as the first "funny car." It was a term of amusement at first, but would come to describe the radical "stock" bodied, tube-frame dragsters that evolved from this effort.

1964 MERCURY HIGH-PERFORMANCE ENGINES

TYPE	CID	BORE× STROKE	BHP @ RPM	TORQUE @ RPM	FUEL SYSTEM	COMP. RATIO	AVAIL.
ohv V-8	390	4.05× 3.78	330 @ 5000	427 @ 3200	1×4bbl.	10.0:1	full size
ohv V-8	427	4.23× 3.78	410 @ 5600	476 @ 3400	1×4bbl.	11.5:1	full size
ohv V-8	427	4.23× 3.78	425 @ 6000	480 @ 3700	2×4bbl.	11.5:1	full size (race)
ohv V-8	430	4.30× 3.70	320 @ 4600	465 @ 2600	1×4bbl.	10.1:1	full size

▲ Oldsmobile could claim the first "muscle car" with its Rocket 88 of 1949. But it didn't return to the formula until mid-1964. That's when it massaged its Police Apprehender Pursuit package into the 4-4-2 option for its new F-85/Cutlass series, which had moved from a compact to mid-sized. The 4-4-2 package was optional in any F-85 or Cutlass except the wagon, though it was poorly promoted and only 2999 buyers ordered it.

◄ In its first season, 4-4-2 stood for four-barrel carb, four-speed manual transmission, and dual exhausts. The $136 package included a 330-cid V-8, beefed-up suspension with rear stabilizer, and Red-Line tires.

▲ The 4-4-2's V-8 made 310 bhp, 20 more than the regular four-barrel, thanks to a higher-lift cam, heavy-duty bearings, and dual-snorkel air cleaner. It turned 0-60 times of 7.5 seconds and 15.5 quarter-miles.

Hurst *Dual Gate*

complete control for beefed-up "hydros"

Now complete instructions for beefing "hydro" transmissions are included in every Dual Gate kit. Leading transmission experts tell you how to convert your "hydro" to a neck-snapping screamer. It's a job you can easily do yourself for peanuts. And you really control that power with a Dual Gate. You thrill to jet-fast getaways . . . enjoy dragstrip performance with the Competition Gate. The other gate? A mild-mannered automatic setup that's just for "her." For 2-car performance on a 1-car budget, get a Hurst Dual Gate from your speed shop today. And if you are thinking new car . . . the Dual Gate is designed for many fine 64s, like Pontiac and Olds, as standard equipment.

HURST

HURST PERFORMANCE PRODUCTS, INC., GLENSIDE, PA.

TYPE	CID	BORE×STROKE	BHP @ RPM	TORQUE @ RPM	FUEL SYSTEM	COMP. RATIO	AVAIL.

1964 OLDSMOBILE HIGH-PERFORMANCE ENGINES

TYPE	CID	BORE×STROKE	BHP @ RPM	TORQUE @ RPM	FUEL SYSTEM	COMP. RATIO	AVAIL.
ohv V-8	330	3.94× 3.39	290 @ 4800	355 @ 2800	1×4bbl.	10.25:1	1
ohv V-8	394	4.13× 3.69	330 @ 4600	440 @ 2800	1×4bbl.	10.25:1	2
ohv V-8	394	4.13× 3.69	345 @ 4800	440 @ 3200	1×4bbl.	10.5:1	3

1. F-85, Cutlass 442, Jetfire. 2. 88, S-88, 98. 3. S-88, 98, Starfire, Jetstar I.

▲ Big Plymouths got a cleaner nose and handsome V-shaped rear-roof pillars. The 426-cid V-8 was back, but a new Street Wedge version made things easier for Plymouth drivers on the road. Reintroduction of the killer Hemi, meanwhile, made things much tougher for Plymouth rivals on the track.

▼ Bill Shirey in "Golden Commando #4" and Bill Hanyon aboard the Milne Brothers Plymouth charge the Pomona strip at the '64 Winternationals. These wedges ran mid-11s at 115-118 mph. In NASCAR, Plymouth Hemis swept the Daytona 500 1-2-3.

1964 PLYMOUTH HIGH-PERFORMANCE ENGINES

TYPE	CID	BORE× STROKE	BHP @ RPM	TORQUE @ RPM	FUEL SYSTEM	COMP. RATIO	AVAIL.
ohv V-8	383	4.24× 3.38	330 @ 4600	425 @ 2800	1×4bbl.	10.0:1	full size
ohv V-8	426	4.25× 3.75	365 @ 4800	470 @ 3200	1×4bbl.	10.3:1	full size
ohv V-8	426	4.25× 3.75	415 @ 5600	470 @ 4400	2×4bbl.	11.0:1	full size
ohv V-8	426	4.25× 3.75	425 @ 5600	480 @ 4400	2×4bbl.	12.5:1	full size
ohv V-8	426*	4.25× 3.75	415 @ 6000	470 @ 4600	2×4bbl.	11.0:1	full size
ohv V-8	426*	4.25× 3.75	425 @ 6000	480 @ 4600	2×4bbl.	12.5:1	full size

* Hemi.

◀ The 425-bhp 426 Stage III still topped the wedge tower of power, but the owner of this Sport Fury ordered the new 365-bhp Street Wedge, which Plymouth billed as the Commando 426. It was more streetable, but still tough. *Motor Trend* saw 0-60 mph in 6.3 seconds and ran the quarter in 15.2 at 95.5 mph with the Street Wedge and a 3.91:1 axle.

▶ Whether tucked under the hood of this Plymouth Sport Fury or a subtler Belvedere or Savoy, the new hydraulic-lifter Street Wedge whipped up 365 bhp at 4800 rpm and 470 lbs/ft of torque at 3200. The engine was treated to high-performance valve springs, pistons and cam, plus a dual-point distributor, unsilenced air cleaner, dual exhaust, and heavy-duty clutch.

◀ Unlike the wilder wedges, the street version had a provision to heat the intake manifold for cold startups, and its 10.3:1 compression would suit ordinary fuel. A single four-barrel replaced dual quads and a conventional exhaust manifold supplanted the tuff ram's-head headers.

▶ Bucket seats and a console again graced the Sport Fury, but the driver faced a fresh dashboard with four gauges in a brushed-metal panel. And a four-speed manual gearbox could now be ordered. Handling got a boost as rear track width grew 2.5 inches.

▼ It's a clash of altered-wheelbase A/FX Mopars at the '64 Nationals. Jim Thornton's Ramchargers Dodge clocked an 11.32 ET, but it wasn't enough to beat the searing 11.04 at 127.47 turned in by Tom Grove in his Melrose Missile VI Plymouth.

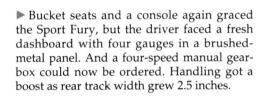

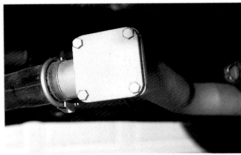

▲ Norman Thatcher drove this stock-bodied '64 Sport Fury to 205.55 mph in the flying mile at the Bonneville Salt Flats. He became the first person to top 200 mph in a supercharged production sedan. Thatcher was a 67-year-old grandfather at the time.

▲ Mopar's high performance big-blocks came with header cut-outs that were simple to remove for the strip or serious street action.

▼ Cars with the 415-bhp wedge got a stock hood sans scoop, though sharp aftermarket wheels were common.

▲ Still available was the potent 415-bhp Super Stock III wedge with dual quads and upswept headers.

▲ This is it. The 1964 Pontiac Tempest GTO was the first modern mass-production automobile to put big-cube power in a mid-size body—the formula that defined the true muscle car. Pontiac circumvented a GM rule prohibiting intermediates from having V-8s over 330 cid by making its 389-cid V-8 part of an option package for the new Tempest, a ploy that didn't require corporate approval. The name *Gran Turismo Omologato* was borrowed from the Ferrari 250 GTO. It stands for a production grand touring machine homologated, or sanctioned, to race.

◄ A Hurst-stirred Muncie four-speed sends 348 bhp at 4800 rpm from this GTO's Tri-Power 389 to a 3.55:1 Positraction rear axle. With a single four-barrel, output was 325 bhp. Both versions ran on 10.75:1 compression and developed 428 lbs/ft of torque. GTOs came in pillared sport coupe, hardtop coupe, and convertible form. All had bucket seats and a simulated engine-turned instrument surround. A three-speed floor shift was standard, two-speed automatic optional.

◄ Credit for the GTO concept generally goes to Pontiac ad exec Jim Wangers, himself a racer, though some cite engineers John DeLorean and Bill Collins. Regardless, it was a grand slam. Pontiac hoped to sell a modest 5000 '64 GTOs; final production was 32,450.

▶ Affectionately tagged the Goat, the GTO was the first factory hot rod with its own identity. It developed a cult following and influenced other makers to create similar machines.

1964 PONTIAC HIGH-PERFORMANCE ENGINES

TYPE	CID	BORE × STROKE	BHP @ RPM	TORQUE @ RPM	FUEL SYSTEM	COMP. RATIO	AVAIL.
ohv V-8	389	4.06×3.75	325@4800	428@3200	1×4bbl.	10.75:1	Tempest GTO
ohv V-8	389	4.06×3.75	348@4800	428@3600	3×2bbl.	10.75:1	Tempest GTO
ohv V-8	421	4.09×3.75	320@4400	455@2800	1×4bbl.	10.5:1	full size
ohv V-8	421	4.09×4.00	350@4600	454@3200	3×2bbl.	10.75:1	full size
ohv V-8	421	4.09×3.75	370@5200	460@3800	3×2bbl.	10.75:1	full size

▲ Only 6644 GTO convertibles were built for '64, including this Marimba Red ragtop. The 389-cid engine was just one part of the GTO package. An extra-tough suspension used a thicker ($^{15}/_{16}$-inch) front sway bar, heavy-duty Delco shocks, and stiffer springs. Red-line high-speed 7.50×14 tires rode 6JK wide-rim wheels.

◀ For the GTO, the 389 got high-output heads from the 421 V-8, a high-lift cam, and a Carter AFB four-barrel. Tri-Power setups like this used three Rochester two-barrels and were ordered on 8245 '64 Goats. Axle ratios from 3.08:1 to 3.90:1 were offered. The GTO package added $296 to the price of a LeMans. The pillared coupe cost $2852, the hardtop $2963, and the convertible $3081.

▲ Finned drum brakes were standard on GTOs, but a $75 "roadability group" added sintered metallic linings, a heavy-duty radiator, and Safe-T-Track differential. Twin hood scoops looked good, but weren't functional.

◀ *Road & Track*'s four-barrel GTO with a 3.23:1 axle did 0-60 in 6.9 seconds and the quarter in 15.0 at 91.5 mph. With Tri-Power, *R&T*'s numbers were 5.7 seconds 0-60 and 14.1 at 104.2 in the quarter.

▲ Buyers could tailor GTOs to taste. Extras included transistorized ignition, a Rally wood steering wheel, and in-dash tachometer. Dealers could install side-exit exhaust splitters.

▲ Part of the GTO's magic was that it was first to integrate all the best performance cues in a single package. It had style, and muscle to back it up. *Motor Trend* turned a 15.8 ET at 93 mph with a four-barrel four-speed.

Get in, turn on,   leave abruptly.

This is where you aim a Catalina 2+2 from. Bucket seats, nylon-blend carpeting, custom steering wheel, the whole bit, all color-coordinated, in either sports coupe or convertible form.

The standard 389-cubic inch engine puts out 283 bhp when coupled to a 4-speed box*, 267 bhp with 3-speed Hydra-Matic*. (The 2+2 comes only with one of these two trans-

missions.) Both shifters are mounted in the standard console. Much automobile.

If you want to make even more automobile of it, there's nothing to stop you from huddling with a Pontiac salesman and a list of performance options and doing wild things with an order form.   *Optional at extra cost.

the 2+2 makers – Pontiac

PONTIAC MOTOR DIVISION • GENERAL MOTORS CORPORATION

▲ Though overshadowed by the new mid-size GTO, Pontiac's Catalina had something new this year: a 2+2 option package with bucket seats, console, and special interior. It was available for $291 on hardtops and convertibles.

▼ The pillared coupe was the lightest and cheapest GTO; 7384 were made. Pontiac was out of "factory" racing, but had a high profile on the street.

▲ Like other full-size models, Catalinas wore slightly more rounded bodies for '64. The 2+2 package was ordered on 7998 of them. A lowly 389-cid two-barrel was standard, but an ad explained that customers could do "wild things with an order form" if extra performance was a priority.

▲ The 2+2 option was Pontiac's first performance package on a full-size model. "Considering the range of options and accessories we've got, no two 2+2s need be alike," said one Pontiac ad.

▲ Optional 2+2 engines included this 330-bhp Tri-Power 389, as well as three 421s, up to the 370-bhp Tri-Power 421, which was capable of 7.2-seconds 0-60 mph and a 16.1-second quarter-mile. The Super Duty engines were gone.

▲ A Studebaker Daytona convertible with the rare R2 supercharged V-8 races at the '64 Winternationals. Only 703 of these Studes were built.

▲ One of the winningest teams on Southern California 'strips was Gordon Williams and his '63 R1 unsupercharged 289-cid, 240-bhp Studebaker Lark.

107

1965

Top horsepower rating remains 425...Ford's 427-cid is the largest engine ● Sanctioned drag racing more popular than ever, now has five major national events...action on the street also picks up ● Chevy's hallowed 409 departs, but is replaced by future-great 396 ● Buick joins muscle-car melee, stuffing 400-cid V-8 into mid-size Skylark to create Gran Sport ● Olds unveils 4-4-2 option ● Chevelle turns up heat with rare 375-bhp SS 396 Z-16 ● Nova available with 327-cid ● Mustang enters first full season, adds 2+2... fiery Shelby GT-350 bows ● Mopar escalates factory-backed drag wars with radical altered-wheelbase intermediates ● Ford counterpunches with overhead-cam 427 Mustangs ● GTO sales more than double ● Chrysler retires letter-series cars...turns attention to mid-size muscle ● Wild wheelie exhibitions by the Little Red Wagon and Hemi Under Glass thrill drag crowds ● Don Garlits goes 206.88 mph and Art Malone turns a 7.56-second ET ● NASCAR disallows Mopar Hemi; Chrysler returns when Hemi is reinstated...too late: Fords rule NASCAR with 48 wins

▲ When GM raised the engine limit for mid-size cars to 400 cid, Buick renamed its 401-cid V-8 the "400" and jammed it into the Skylark. The resultant midyear Gran Sport was Buick's first modern muscle car. Its 325 bhp was less than that of the GTO or 4-4-2, but it had more torque. All Gran Sports got a reinforced convertible frame, dual exhausts, huskier suspension, and bucket seats.

▲ Gran Sports cost about $460 more than Skylarks, with the ragtop at $3299; hardtop and pillared coupe also were offered. *Motor Trend* got 0-60 mph in 7.8 seconds, the quarter in 16.6 at 86 mph.

TYPE	CID	BORE × STROKE	BHP @ RPM	TORQUE @ RPM	FUEL SYSTEM	COMP. RATIO	AVAIL.
ohv V-8	300	3.75 × 3.40	250 @ 4800	335 @ 3000	1 × 4bbl.	10.25:1	Special, Skylark
ohv V-8	401	4.19 × 3.64	325 @ 4400	445 @ 2800	1 × 4bbl.	10.25:1	1
ohv V-8	425	4.31 × 3.64	340 @ 4400	465 @ 2800	1 × 4bbl.	10.25:1	Wildcat, Electra 225
ohv V-8	425	4.31 × 3.64	360 @ 4400	465 @ 2800	2 × 4bbl.	10.25:1	Wildcat, Electra 225

1965 BUICK HIGH-PERFORMANCE ENGINES

1. Skylark, Gran Sport, Wildcat, Electra 225

1965 CHEVROLET HIGH-PERFORMANCE ENGINES							
TYPE	CID	BORE × STROKE	BHP @ RPM	TORQUE @ RPM	FUEL SYSTEM	COMP. RATIO	AVAIL.
ohv V-8	327	4.00 × 3.25	300 @ 5000	360 @ 3200	1 × 4bbl.	10.5:1	1
ohv V-8	327	4.00 × 3.25	350 @ 5800	360 @ 3600	1 × 4bbl.	11.0:1	Chevelle
ohv V-8	396	4.09 × 3.76	325 @ 4800	410 @ 3200	1 × 4bbl.	10.25:1	full size
ohv V-8	396	4.09 × 3.76	425 @ 6400	415 @ 4000	1 × 4bbl.	11.0:1	full size
ohv V-8	396	4.09 × 3.76	375 @ 5600	420 @ 3600	1 × 4bbl.	11.0:1	2
ohv V-8	409	4.31 × 3.50	340 @ 5000	420 @ 3200	1 × 4bbl.	10.0:1	full size
ohv V-8	409	4.31 × 3.50	400 @ 5800	425 @ 3600	1 × 4bbl.	11.0:1	full size

1. Full size, Chevelle, Chevy II. 2. Chevelle SS 396.

▲ Wild match races between stock-bodied cars with altered wheelbases and cross-bred engines were the drag-strip rage in '65, and Chevrolet was well represented. The compact Chevy II (rear) hosted Corvette 327s and even the occasional 427. Here, a '64 goes up against a '65 Plymouth Barracuda, itself far from production with Mopar's devilish 426 Hemi.

◄ Chevy had offered a 220-bhp four-barrel 283 in its compact '64 Nova. For '65, the bowtie boys dropped in the 327-cid small-block. The four-barrel 327 had either 250 or 300 bhp. Its most stylish application was the Nova Super Sport (shown), which came only as a $2433 hardtop. The 327 could also be ordered in a no-frills Chevy II two-door sedan. Powerglide and a Muncie four-speed were optional along with Positraction, tach, and sintered metallic brake linings.

◀ Chevy's mid-size Chevelle was making the best of its 327-cid V-8s, but it couldn't match the big-block GTO and 4-4-2. That changed at midyear with the Z-16, a 375-bhp 396-cid avenger. It was fitted to just 201 Malibu SS models, which got special trim, heavy-duty suspension, and a 160-mph speedometer. It added $1501.05 to the $2647 base Malibu SS hardtop.

▶ The Z-16 Turbo-Jet 396 was basically a hydraulic-lifter version of the 375-bhp 396 offered in the 'Vette. The Malibu's had a Holley four-barrel and 11.0:1 compression. A Muncie four-speed was mandatory, with axle ratios of up to 4.56:1 available. Mid-14-second quarters at around 100 mph were no sweat.

▶ The '65 Chevelle also could have the 300-bhp 327. At midyear, regular and Super Sport Malibus were available with the L79 327, a 350-bhp screamer that essentially was a hydraulic-lifter version of the solid-lifter 365-bhp 327 in the Corvette. Automatic wasn't offered, but with a four-speed, Positraction, and standard 3.31:1 gear, an L79 Malibu could easily turn high 14s.

▼ Malibu SS models with the Z-16 got a fortified convertible-type frame, strengthened front suspension, front and rear anti-roll bars, bigger brakes, and faster power steering. Still, handling was poor with nearly 58 percent of the weight on the front tires. Tamer SS models were far more common, and Super Sport output set a record: 101,577 out of 326,977 Chevelles.

▶ GT trim sharpened Dodge's milquetoast Dart. The hardtop and convertible compacts rode a 111-inch wheelbase. The GT was available for '64 with a two-barrel 273 V-8 at a modest 180 bhp. For '65, it had a 235-bhp version of the 273 twisting a standard three-speed gearbox, optional four-speed, or TorqueFlite. The basic 3.23:1 axle could be replaced by a 2.93:1 or 3.55:1 cog. *Car and Driver* managed 8.2 seconds to 60 mph and a 16.9-second quarter at 87 mph with a GT hardtop. For serious dragstrip work, Fibercraft made Darts with fiberglass body panels, slashing some 400 pounds.

▲ Dart GT touches included full-length racing stripes and rocker-panel vents. Real Cragar mags were a Dart GT option this year.

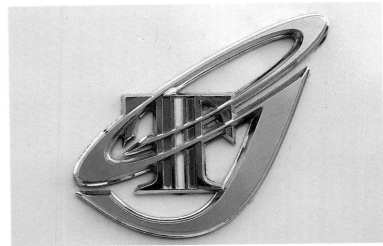

▲ On the surface, the GT was a dressed-for-success Dart 270 with bucket seats, extra chrome, and a stylized badge.

▶ Dart GT's free-revving, short-stroke, hydraulic-lifter 273 used a Carter AFB four-barrel and 10.5:1 compression. The engine cost only $99.40 extra. The GT hardtop started at $2372; ragtop, $2591. A four-speed may have been the choice of stoplight strokers, but *Car and Driver* said TorqueFlite was "one automatic transmission that can actually be shifted," giving it "overwhelming superiority over manual units in super stock drag racing."

▲ Bill "Maverick" Golden's "Little Red Wagon" had a fuel-injected 426 Hemi mounted amidships in a lightened A-100 van. It could turn 10.55 quarters at 127 mph, but its claim to fame was the crowd-pleasing wheelstand, which could be sustained for hundreds of feet.

▲ Performance was focusing on mid-size models, and at Dodge that meant the new 117-inch wheelbase Coronet. A hot street setup was Mopar's 426 RB-Wedge "civilized" to 10.3:1 compression and 365 bhp.

▲ The 426 Street Wedge package added $513.60 to a $2674 Coronet 500 hardtop. *Motor Trend* saw 60 mph in 7.7 seconds and a 15.7 ET at 89 mph. Four-speed or TorqueFlite (shown) were offered.

▲ Factory-built drag Super/Stock Hemi Coronets for '65 had to use all-metal bodies but got two inches trimmed from the stock 117-inch wheelbase.

▲ Drag-race Hemis had dual quads on a ram-tuned magnesium manifold with new aluminum heads. Rating was 425 bhp; actual output was over 550 bhp.

▲ NASCAR said the Hemi wasn't a production engine and banned it in early '65. But it thrived under the NHRA's multi-class rules.

▲ The exciting "Bounty Hunters" Coronet was among the Mopars that fell between the nearly stock class and the profoundly altered factory-racer categories.

▲ Ed Knezevich piloted the "Mister Ed" Coronet. Dodges took plenty of Super/Stock wins, including NHRA Nationals. Bob Harrop topped SS/A class.

▲ This "funny" Hemi-Charger Coronet, lined up against a '56 Pontiac, advertises its achievements: a 10.45-second ET and 138.46 mph trap speed.

▲ This Dick Landy Hemi Dodge fit the A/FX class, for factory-experimentals with 7.50 to 8.99 pounds of curb weight per cubic-inch engine displacement.

▲ Street Dodges wouldn't have the Hemi until '66, but drag racers took full advantage of the engine's superior ability to breath at high rpm.

▲ Tangled tubing tips off twin turbochargers. One of "Bud" Faubel's 426 Dodges used two water-cooled AiResearch turbos and fuel injection.

▲ Super/Stock Automatic tag is misleading; the turbo Honker was primarily an unlimited-class racer. Said *Hot Rod* of one Bud run: "... about 400 feet out of the chute there was an audible increase in the engine revs, almost to 'scream' pitch, tire smoke appeared [generous amounts of it] and there was some evidence of skating as if the increased power, as a result of the 'chargers kicking in, was trying to cut loose."

▲ "Candymatic" meant automatic transmission. Dodge dropped its pushbuttons for '65, and race engineers modified the column-mount shifter to a P-R-N-1-2-D sequence so drivers could upshift from Neutral simply by pulling the lever down as speed increased.

▲ Responding to the popularity of ultra-stock bracket exhibitions in '65, factory-backed racers ventured beyond the frontiers of Super/Stock, to where altered wheelbases, fuel injection, and few restrictions on weight lurked. The Hodges Dodges Coronet was there, waiting.

▲ Chrysler revamped a Hilborn fuel-injection system to suit its Hemis and shipped the modifications to its corps of factory-supported altered-wheelbase racers. The 14-inch velocity stacks gave a ram effect, helping the basic race 426 engine to over 600 bhp on gasoline.

▲ The Yankee Peddler did battle in the "Run-What-Ya-Brung" match races, where mid-9-second ETs ruled. Note the relocated fuel tank. Running nitromethane, these cars had an estimated 700 bhp. The Peddler was among the '65 Chrysler altered-wheelbase factory-supported cars.

1965 DODGE HIGH-PERFORMANCE ENGINES

TYPE	CID	BORE × STROKE	BHP @ RPM	TORQUE @ RPM	FUEL SYSTEM	COMP. RATIO	AVAIL.
ohv V-8	273	3.63 × 3.31	235 @ 5200	280 @ 4000	1 × 4bbl.	10.5:1	Dart
ohv V-8	383	4.25 × 3.75	330 @ 4600	425 @ 2800	1 × 4bbl.	10.0:1	Coronet
ohv V-8	383	4.25 × 3.75	340 @ 4600	470 @ 2800	1 × 4bbl.	10.1:1	full size
ohv V-8	426	4.25 × 3.75	365 @ 4800	470 @ 3200	1 × 4bbl.	10.3:1	1
ohv V-8	426*	4.25 × 3.75	425 @ 6000	480 @ 4600	2 × 4bbl.	12.5:1	Coronet

* Hemi. 1. Coronet, full size.

▲ "Bud" Faubel was among the Mopar-backed drivers to get one of six Coronets with the wheels moved forward—the rears by 15 inches, the fronts by 10—to relocate weight for unlimited-class wars.

▲ The fiberglass hood, front bumper, front fenders and doors, instrument panel and deck lid totaled only 80 pounds. Lighter Dart spindles and brakes saved another 50 pounds for factory racers.

▲ Chrysler's run of altered-wheelbase '65 intermediates bridged the gap between door-slammers and future full-blown funny cars. "Dandy" Dick Landy's, like the others, had a wheelbase of about 110 inches and weighed around 2700 pounds. Canvas straps helped hold hood at 140 mph.

▲ Landy suits up for work in his Coronet "funny" car. The burly Californian liked push-button shift controls and re-engineered them into this car. *Hot Rod* called his "the most controversial stocker ever built [and] the quickest and the fastest in the land."

▲ NHRA banned these Mopars, so they ran in AHRA and match-race competition. Relocated axles and trunk-mounted battery helped achieve a 44/56 percent weight distribution for good dig off the line.

▲ Landy's Dodge started '65 with a dual-quad Hemi, good for 10.2s at 138 mph. Fuel-injection added in the spring got ETs into the mid-9s and made this the first stock-body racer to exceed 140 mph in the quarter. Chicago's "Mr. Norm," meanwhile, ran a blown version to an 8.63.

▲ Ford's big cars shed 100 pounds, but gained new styling and a NASCAR-inspired front-suspension so strong that stock-car racers of all makes used it through the 1970s. The new nine-inch differential also became a legend. This Galaxie 500XL convertible went for $3498.

▲ Midyear brought a new 427-cid block with more efficient lubrication. The "side-oiler" 427 had dual Holley quads and 11.1:1 compression, but kept the 425-bhp rating. A rare Galaxie option, it helped Ford to its best NASCAR year with 48 wins in 55 events. This is Dan Gurney at the wheel.

▲ A 300-bhp 390 V-8 added $137.60 to the $3233 price of this Galaxie 500XL hardtop. The 330-bhp "Interceptor" 390 cost $225.30. And the 425-bhp 427 was advertised as "competitively priced." A 427 hardtop

could do 14.93-second quarter-miles at 101.69 mph. Not bad for a heavyweight. Ford ads called the 427 Galaxie "The Velvet Brute."

▲ Few '65 Galaxies drag raced, so '64s like this lightweight battled the 1965 rivals. Dearborn stayed performance-focused, however, and during the year unleashed an astonishing 427-cid side-oiler with both hemi combustion chambers and single overhead cams. With 616 bhp, or 654

with dual quads, the SOHC 427 was a $2500 dealer-installed option for racing only. NASCAR said it wasn't a true production engine and banned it, but the SOHC 427 went on to become a major force in drag racing.

▲ Carroll Shelby followed his AC Cobra with a super-Mustang, the GT-350. A 306-bhp HiPo 289 GT-350 listed for $4547. About 30 of the 562 GT-350s were racing GT-350Rs with a 360 bhp 289 and $6950 price. Most were road racers, but a few, like this one, hit the strips.

▲ Street Falcons had at most a 200-bhp 289. But this A/FX version with fiberglass fenders and doors had a 427 High-Riser. It was built for drag racer Dick Brannan and turned 11-second ETs.

▲ AC Cobras started '65 with the HiPo 289, but got the 427 at midyear. Street Cobras actually used a 428-cid V-8 of about 410 bhp; racers had true 427s with more than 500 bhp. Both could turn sub-13-second ETs.

▲ High-compression V-8s demanded super-premium gasoline. Sunoco and other brands offered a broad selection of blends, and stickers touting fuel were added to other decals on both street and strip cars.

1965 FORD HIGH-PERFORMANCE ENGINES

TYPE	CID	BORE × STROKE	BHP @ RPM	TORQUE @ RPM	FUEL SYSTEM	COMP. RATIO	AVAIL.
ohv V-8	289	4.00×2.87	271 @ 6000	312 @ 3400	1×4bbl.	10.5:1	1
ohv V-8	289	4.00×2.87	340 @ 6500	331 @ 3750	2×4bbl.	10.8:1	Cobra
ohv V-8	289	4.00×2.87	306 @ 6800	329 @ 4000	1×4bbl.	10.0:1	2
ohv V-8	289	4.00×2.87	390 @ 6600	345 @ 4000	4×2bbl.	10.8:1	3
ohv V-8	390	4.05×3.78	330 @ 5000	427 @ 3200	1×4bbl.	10.0:1	full size
ohv V-8	427	4.23×3.78	425 @ 6000	480 @ 3700	2×4bbl.	11.2:1	4
sohc V-8	427	4.23×3.78	616 @ 7000	696 @ 4400	1×4bbl.	12.0:1	race
sohc V-8	427	4.23×3.78	654 @ 7000	739 @ 4400	2×4bbl.	12.0:1	race

1. full size, Mustang. 2. Shelby GT-350. 3. Cobra (race). 4. full size (race).

If you see this on the window

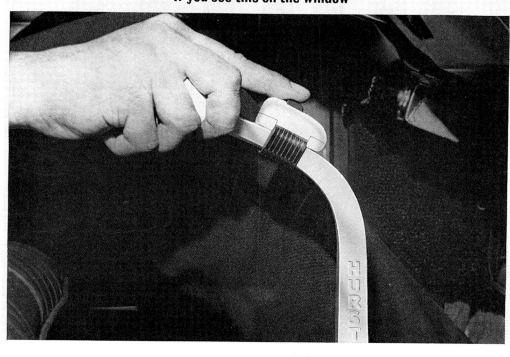

◀ Hurst Performance Products had been marketing slick aftermarket transmission linkages to rodders for years and by the mid-'60s they were also part of "factory" performance packages. Hurst helpers let automatic transmissions be shifted manually in hard acceleration. For manuals, its Line/Loc allowed the driver to rest at the starting line without holding down the brake pedal. An electric switch on the shifter activated the brakes while the driver revved to the engine's sweet spot without creeping. As the start-up tree flashed its last filament, the driver released the switch to catapult out of the hole.

and this on the stick, you're about to get beat.

The name of the game is "How not to get hole shot." And the way to assure it is with Hurst's new line-holding LINE/LOC system.

Line/Loc is an electrically operated control that hooks into the brake system—front and/or rear, but ideally just into the front system. The switch mounts on your shifter with an off-on warning light on the dash.

When you come to the line you brake, press down the Line/Loc switch, hold it, get off the brake pedal and onto the accelerator and work your R.P.M. up to where you want it. There's no chance of creeping because the

front brakes hold you precisely on the line as long as you hold down the switch. Now watch the lights flash down the tree and when it's time to go, lift your finger off the switch and you're *gone*—out of the hole on the split part of a second, with hardly a chance of a false start. Naturally the Line/Loc, like all Hurst products, has been tested unmercifully. And proved in action, too, by people like Gas Ronda, Ronnie Sox and Don Nicholson.

Stop by your local speed shop for details. Or write direct to Hurst Performance Products, Glenside, Pennsylvania 19038.

HURST

▼ One of history's most popular and influential cars, Mustang bowed in April 1964 with a six or a 260-cid (later 289-cid) V-8. The solid-lifter 271-bhp HiPo came in June, and 2+2 fastbacks were added in fall, 1965. Even the HiPo was little threat to true muscle cars: *Sports Car Graphic* ran one with a 4:11.1 gear to 60 mph in 7.5 seconds and turned a middling 15.7 at 89 mph in the quarter. Mustangs had better success at the strip, especially in A/FX classes, where larger engines could be used. Les Ritchey ran one of the best with Weber carbs on a SOCH 427. He was '65 NHRA Nationals A/FX champ, burning Indianapolis with a 10.67 ET.

▲ Bill Lawton took Factory Stock Eliminator and A/FX honors at the '65 NHRA Winternationals. His best ET was a 10.92 at 128.20 mph. Lawton's was part of a small fleet of factory-prepped and supported A/FX Mustangs modified to run the SOHC 427. They had a fiberglass front clip with bubble hood and 'glass doors. Most used dual quads.

▶ Paul Norris cuts loose in the "Fugitive" at the '65 U.S. Nationals. On the street, meanwhile, Mustangs had the 210-bhp 289 two-barrel or the 271-bhp HiPo with headers and solid lifters ($334.60). A Cobra kit brought four Webers for 343 bhp—at a whopping $1232.30. A four-speed added $188, Cruise-O-Matic $189.60, special camshaft $75.10, and heavy-duty distributor $49.80.

▶ The mean A/FX Mustangs shut down a fleet of Mopars and Mercury Comets at a classic Winternationals brawl in Pomona. Gas Ronda, Bill Lawton, Len Richter, and Phil Bonner were among the Ford drivers. Richter turned a 10.91 in the early rounds, but twisted an axle and sat out the final, which went to Lawton. These Mustangs had highly modified front suspensions to clear the 427. Narrowed rear axles allowed 10-inch slicks. Unlike the '64 Fairlane Thunderbolts, the A/FX Mustangs were race-only and not sold to the public.

▲ Mercury's Comet Cyclone could be special-ordered with the HiPo 289. On the strip, it was another host to the SOHC 427. A/FX Comets were driven by some big names, including Arnie "The Farmer" Beswick and Hayden Proffitt. "Dyno" Don Nicholson ran one to a 10.60 at 131.72. Ed Schartman was a Super Stock Eliminator with 10.70-10.80 ETs. And Doug Nash's B/FX 289 Comets ran in the 11.30s. Finally, Jack Chrisman, in the Sachs & Son blown "funny" Comet, turned a 10.13 at a startling 156.25 mph in B/Fuel.

1965 MERCURY HIGH-PERFORMANCE ENGINES

TYPE	CID	BORE× STROKE	BHP @ RPM	TORQUE @ RPM	FUEL SYSTEM	COMP. RATIO	AVAIL.
ohv V-8	289	4.00×2.87	271 @ 6000	312 @ 3400	1×4bbl.	10.5:1	Comet
ohv V-8	390	4.05×3.78	330 @ 5000	427 @ 3200	1×4bbl.	10.0:1	full size
ohv V-8	427	4.23×3.78	425 @ 6000	480 @ 3700	2×4bbl.	11.5:1	full size
ohv V-8	430	4.30×3.70	320 @ 4600	465 @ 2600	1×4bbl.	10.1:1	full size

◄ After a season of 330-cid propulsion, Oldsmobile's 4-4-2 coupe moved up to 400 cubes. So 4-4-2 now meant 400 cid, four-barrel, and dual exhausts. On a 10.25:1 squeeze, the V-8 got 345 bhp, and 440 lbs/ft of torque (up 85). *Car Life* did 0-60 in 7.8 seconds, the quarter-mile in 15.5 at 84 mph.

1965 OLDSMOBILE HIGH-PERFORMANCE ENGINES

TYPE	CID	BORE× STROKE	BHP @ RPM	TORQUE @ RPM	FUEL SYSTEM	COMP. RATIO	AVAIL.
ohv V-8	400	4.00× 3.98	345 @ 4800	440 @ 3200	1×4bbl.	10.25:1	1
ohv V-8	425	4.12× 3.98	360 @ 4800	470 @ 2800	1×4bbl.	10.25:1	98, 88
ohv V-8	425	4.12× 3.98	370 @ 4800	470 @ 3200	1×4bbl.	10.5:1	2

1. Cutlass 4-4-2, F-85.   2. Starfire, Jetstar I, 88, 98.

▲ Chrysler didn't forget Plymouth when it came to purpose-built "unlimited" cars. This particular '65 "Melrose Missile" Belvedere, being launched by Tom Grove, was one of a few assembled without an altered wheelbase, however. It was therefore legal in the NHRA's A/FX class, where it ran a dual-quad 426 Hemi. It had an acid-dipped steel unibody with fiberglass hood, fenders, doors, and bumper. Drag competition was growing more complex each year, with a bewildering proliferation of NHRA classes and categories; four were added for '65, for a total of 75. Stockers alone split into 27 classes, depending on pounds per horsepower.

◀Junior muscle cars were increasingly popular, and Plymouth had one for '65. Based on the compact Valiant, the bubble-back Barracuda bowed as a 1964½ model and by '65 was the best-selling Plymouth. The '65 Formula S package brought a 235-bhp 273-cid "Commando" V-8, plus heavy-duty springs/shocks and sway bar, fatter Goodyear Blue Streak tires on 14-inch rims, and a 6000-rpm tach. *Car and Driver* did 0-60 in 9.1 seconds, the quarter in 17.5 at 88.5 mph with a 3.23:1 gear. *Hot Rod* turned a 16.43 at 89. Some Barracudas ran in sports-car rallies.

▶ In the Formula S, the 273 featured a hotter cam, Carter four-barrel, and 10.5:1 compression with hydraulic lifters. A three-speed was standard; four-speed or TorqueFlite was optional. Front disc brakes could be dealer-installed. With its "throaty, quick-tempo exhaust," a Formula S "was indeed a force to be reckoned with," claimed *Hot Rod*.

▼NASCAR "outlawed" Chrysler's Hemi for the first half of the '65 season, so Richard Petty stuffed one into a Super/Stock Barracuda and headed for the strip. "43 Jr." managed a 10.46 ET in an AHRA event. When NASCAR reinstated the Hemi, Petty returned to win four NASCAR races in Plymouths.

▲ Plymouth moved the Sport Fury onto a 119-inch wheelbase and toward luxury for '65. Taking its place as the top sporty model was the new Satellite (shown), built on a 116-inch wheelbase.

▶ While 426 Wedges made the thunder, far more Satellite buyers opted for the more-sedate but still-strong 383-cid Commando V-8. The reliable four-barrel mill's 330 bhp and surplus of usable torque made it an excellent street choice.

▲ "Drag-On-Lady" Shirley Shahan, a 27-year-old California clerical worker, took up drag racing while dating her husband-to-be, racer H.L. Shahan. She set a National S/SA record of 127.30 mph and turned an 11.21-second ET in her stock-wheelbase Hemi Belvedere.

▲ NASCAR relented and reinstated the Hemi in mid '65. On tracks of over one mile, it could run in full-size Dodges and Plymouths. On tracks of one mile or less and on road courses, it could be used in Dodge Coronets and in Plymouth Belvederes, like this one.

▲ Of 25,201 '65 Satellites, just 1860 were convertibles. The ragtop cost $2869, $220 more than the hardtop coupe.

▲ Ronnie Sox came over from Mercury in '65 to team with Buddy Martin for a long and successful career racing Chrysler products. This is Sox at the wheel of the '65 "Paper Tiger" Hemi Belvedere.

▲ Satellite came standard with bucket seats, center storage console, and custom wheel covers with spinner hubs. This one has the optional console-mounted tachometer and TorqueFlite automatic. Manuals of three- and four-speeds also were available. V-8s of 273-, 318-, and 361-cid were offered. The 383 came in 270- and 330-bhp tune, and the 426 Street Wedge made 365. Late in the year, a few Satellites and Belvederes were built with the 426 race Hemi, rated at 425 bhp.

1965 PLYMOUTH HIGH-PERFORMANCE ENGINES

TYPE	CID	BORE×STROKE	BHP @ RPM	TORQUE @ RPM	FUEL SYSTEM	COMP. RATIO	AVAIL.
ohv V-8	273	3.63×3.31	235 @ 5200	280 @ 4000	1×4bbl.	10.5:1	Dart
ohv V-8	383	4.24×3.38	330 @ 4600	425 @ 2800	1×4bbl.	10.0:1	Satellite, Fury
ohv V-8	426	4.25×3.75	365 @ 4800	470 @ 3200	1×4bbl.	10.3:1	Satellite, Sport Fury
ohv V-8	426*	4.25×3.75	425 @ 6000	480 @ 4600	2×4bbl.	12.5:1	Satellite
* Hemi.							

▲ Chrysler built six altered-wheelbase Plymouths as companions to the six altered-wheelbase Dodges. One went to the Golden Commandos, the Plymouth-supported race team that was the counterpart to the Dodge-sponsored Ramchargers.

▼ Al Eckstrand, a corporate lawyer, pilots the Commandos' fuel-injected Hemi. These cars turned low-9s at more than 140 mph. This one is actually a hardtop; sedan door frames were used to hold in the Plexiglas windows, which didn't roll down. At the Pomona Winternationals, Bill "Grumpy" Jenkins was Top Stock Eliminator in the more-conventional Hemi-powered "Black Arrow" Plymouth with an 11.39 ET at 126.05.

▲ After running with a stock wheelbase in the NHRA's A/FX class (see page 122), the Melrose Missile was reconstructed with the altered wheelbase for work in match races. Note the packed drogue chute: Stock-bodied cars were getting fast enough to need them after the run.

▲ The '65 Hemi was lightened with aluminum heads and intake manifold. These motors were hand assembled by selected Chrysler technicians, who stamped their names on the finished engine. A total of 380 Dodge/Plymouth race Hemis were built this year. Meanwhile, the 426 Wedge would be dropped after '65, to evolve later into the 440.

▲ Pontiac redesigned its big cars for '65. Wheelbase was up one inch on Catalina and Grand Prix, to 121, and new sheetmetal made them look even larger. The 2+2 Catalina option package continued, with new louvers on the front fenders and "2+2" tags on the rears. Some 11,521 were sold.

▼ The 421-cid V-8 was now standard on the 2+2. Three were available. A Carter four-barrel yielded 338 bhp. Next up: a Tri-Power with 356. Top dog was the 421 HO with Tri-Power, higher-lift cam, and long-branch headers for 376 ponies. A three-speed with Hurst shifter and Safe-T-Track diff were standard; four-speed and Turbo-Hydra-Matic were options.

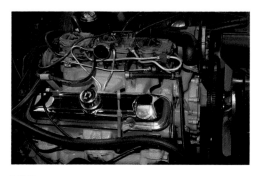

▲ Priced at a modest $244, the 2+2 option could be ordered for Catalina convertibles as well as hardtops. Bucket seats and tachometer were part of the package, and 5316 had a floor-shifted manual gearbox. Transistorized ignition, extra-stiff springs, alloy wheels, and 17.5:1 power steering finished the package.

◄ A good 2+2 with the base 338-bhp 421 could turn a 7.4-second 0-60 and a 15.8 quarter; with 376 bhp, 7.2 and 15.5 were possible. *Car and Driver* later admitted its recorded 3.9-second 0-60 time was "rather preposterous," but its 2+2 had been super-tuned by the Bobcat boys from Royal Pontiac in Michigan.

▼ Pontiac described the 2+2 as "A flying machine for people who can't stand heights."

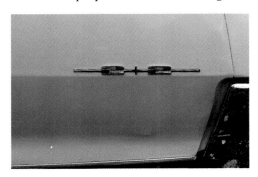

▲ GTOs got a reskin with stacked headlamps for '65. This one is famous as the Goat given away in a contest to name the number of times "tiger" was heard in the song "GeeToTiger."

▲ A Wisconsin 19-year-old won the Hurst-sponsored contest and the GTO, which was stock except for special gold paint and Hurst wheels. GTO production more than doubled, to 75,352, for '65.

▲ GTO kept its 389, but the base version gained 10 bhp, to 335, and the Tri-Power (shown) added 12, to 360, thanks to a revised induction system and improved camshaft profile.

▲ GTO was again a $290 Tempest option. The hood scoop still was just for show, but about 200 cars were fitted by dealers with an optional "Ram Air" setup that made the scoop functional.

▲ *Car Life* reported that its Tri-Power with a 4.11:1 gear did 0-60 mph in 5.8 seconds, the quarter in 14.5 at 100 mph. A 335-bhp convertible could do 0-60 in 7.2. Aluminum front brake drums were new options.

1965 PONTIAC HIGH-PERFORMANCE ENGINES

TYPE	CID	BORE × STROKE	BHP @ RPM	TORQUE @ RPM	FUEL SYSTEM	COMP. RATIO	AVAIL.
ohv V-8	326	3.72×3.75	285 @ 5000	359 @ 3200	1×4bbl.	10.5:1	1
ohv V-8	389	4.06×3.75	333 @ 5000	429 @ 3200	1×4bbl.	10.5:1	full size
ohv V-8	389	4.06×3.75	335 @ 5000	431 @ 3200	1×4bbl.	10.75:1	GTO
ohv V-8	389	4.06×3.75	338 @ 4800	433 @ 3600	1×4bbl.	10.75:1	full size
ohv V-8	389	4.06×3.75	360 @ 5200	424 @ 3600	3×2bbl.	10.75:1	GTO
ohv V-8	421	4.09×3.75	338 @ 3600	459 @ 2800	1×4bbl.	10.5:1	full size
ohv V-8	421	4.09×4.00	356 @ 4600	459 @ 3200	3×2bbl.	10.75:1	full size
ohv V-8	421	4.09×3.75	376 @ 5000	461 @ 3600	3×2bbl.	10.75:1	full size

1. Tempest, LeMans

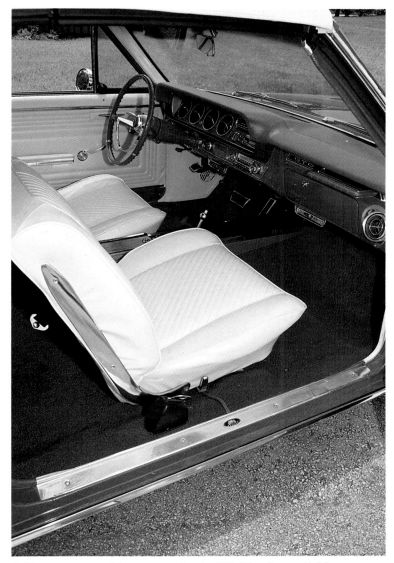

▲ No supercar cabin was cooler in '65. Newly available were an AM/FM radio and a Rally Cluster with an 8000-rpm tach. The standard Hurst-shifted three-speed could be replaced by a heavy-duty three-speed, close- or wide-ratio Hurst-shifted Muncie four-speed, or two-speed automatic. Six axle ratios were offered, from 3.08:1 to 4.33:1.

1966

Horsepower race stands pat with Chrysler Hemis and Ford side-oiler 427 atop the heap at 425 bhp... Ford's "7-Liter" 428 is the biggest stock block ● Mopar unleashes the Street Hemi in Plymouth Satellite and in Dodge's Coronet and striking new Charger fastback ● Chevrolet Nova is a giant-killer with its newly available 350-bhp 327 ● All Chevelle Super Sports become SS 396s after 396 is made standard ● Big Chevys add 427-cid V-8 option ● Ford builds 57 Fairlane drag specials with 427 V-8...but too few to make an impact on the street ● Hertz puts a handful of Shelby GT-350 Mustangs into its rental fleet ● Mercury launches Comet Cyclone GT ...paces Indy 500 and comes on strong in NASCAR ● Olds issues rare W-30 drag option for 4-4-2 ● Pontiac elevates the GTO to a series of its own, still with 389-cid V-8 ● Emergence of the true funny car led by the flip-top Comets of Don Nicholson and Ed Schartman...these cars point the way to some of the wildest wheeled vehicles ever ● Gas Ronda's SOHC 427 Mustang is the first unblown, full-bodied car to run a sub-8-second ET ● Rail dragsters dip into 7.30s

▲ Fresh sheetmetal gave Buick's Skylark Gran Sport a new look. Rear-facing hood scoops were non-functional. Little changed beneath the skin, though there was a 340-bhp upgrade from the 325-bhp V-8.

▲ New roofline with sail-panel rear pillars looked sharp, but GS option accounted for only 13,816 of 106,217 Skylarks built for '66. The pillared coupe cost $2956; the Sport Coupe, $3019 (shown); and the convertible, $3167.

◄ GS emblems were on blacked-out grille and rear fenders. Dual exhausts and heavy-duty suspension were standard. Options included metallic brake linings and a rear stabilizer bar.

1966 BUICK HIGH-PERFORMANCE ENGINES

TYPE	CID	BORE × STROKE	BHP @ RPM	TORQUE @ RPM	FUEL SYSTEM	COMP. RATIO	AVAIL.
ohv V-8	340	3.75×3.85	260 @ 4200	365 @ 2800	1×4bbl.	10.25:1	1
ohv V-8	401	4.19×3.64	325 @ 4400	445 @ 2800	1×4bbl.	10.25:1	2
ohv V-8	425	4.31×3.64	340 @ 4400	465 @ 2800	1×4bbl.	10.25:1	3

1. Skylark, Sportwagon, LeSabre. 2. Skylark Gran Sport, Wildcat, Electra 225. 3. Riviera, Wildcat, Electra 225.

◄ The GS leaned toward luxury, but was no slouch. *Car and Driver*'s 340-bhp GS with the 3.36:1 axle went to 60 mph in 6.8 seconds and turned a 14.92 quarter-mile at 95 mph. *Motor Trend* managed 7.6 seconds to 60 and 15.47 at 90.54 mph on the strip.

▲ With the base engine and automatic in its Buick GS, *Car Life* needed 7.4 seconds to reach 60 mph, and 15.3 for the quarter. Hardtops sold best. Only 1835 pillared coupes and 2047 convertibles were built.

▲ Half-a-dozen axle ratios, from 2.78:1 to 4.30:1, could kick a Gran Sport off the line. The performance cogs, at $42 extra, incorporated a Positive Traction axle. Fender vents, like hood scoops, were fake.

◄ In standard form, Buick's 401-cid "Wildcat 445" four-barrel V-8 was rated at 325 bhp, but a 340-bhp version also was available. A three-speed manual came with either; a four-speed added $184, and Super Turbine automatic cost $205. Power steering ($95), power brakes ($42), and chrome-plated wheels ($73) were other options, while the heater/defroster could be deleted for a $71 credit. Buick promised that its lively GS "would rattle your faith in the established order of sporting machinery."

▲ Bill "Grumpy" Jenkins storms off the line at the '66 Winternationals in defense of his Mr. Stock Eliminator title earned in the previous year's event. This 327 Chevy II ran a 12.09 at 118.42. Jenkins was a Pennsylvanian who became a Chevy hero, but oddly enough, won his '65 Winternationals crown in a Plymouth.

▲ Nova got new skin and a 275-bhp, 327-cid V-8 to replace the 250- and 300-bhp variants. It turned ETs in the low 16s. Big news was availability of the 350-bhp L79 327 first seen in '65 Chevelles. It got a Nova into the low 15s at 93 mph, to the surprise of bigger super-cars. Super Sport package added $159.

▶ All Malibu Super Sports got the 396-cid V-8 for '66, thus earning the SS 396 designation. The base Turbo-Jet had 325 bhp with a Holley four-barrel. The 360-bhp L34 upgrade used a four-bolt-main block and bigger four-barrel. Both had 10.25:1 compression. About 100 cars had a solid-lifter L78, basically an upgrade of the '65 Z-16. It had 375 bhp, 11.0:1 compression, and an 800cfm Holley. A three-speed was standard; four-speed and Powerglide were available. Wheels on this car are aftermarket items.

▲ The departure from stock was nearly complete. Racers were now using fiberglass body shells over tube-frame chassis instead of the factory-altered production platforms of just a year earlier. Bobby Wood's supercharged "Palomino II" Chevelle was an example of a real "funny car." The best were turning mid-8s at around 160 mph. Masks protected drivers from nitro-fuel fumes.

◀ Like the NASCAR-bred 427-cid V-8 from which it was derived, the 396 in the Chevelle SS had "porcupine," or canted-valve, heads for improved airflow. *Car and Driver*'s L34 with a 3.65:1 axle turned a very serious 14.66 at 99.8 mph, with an estimated 0-60 time of 6 seconds flat. The SS hardtop listed for $2776, the ragtop for $2984. Wheels on this car are from a later model year.

135

▲ Chevy rebored its 396 V-8 at midyear, restoring it to 427-cid size. In street tune, the Mark IV big-block had 390 bhp; a "special performance" solid-lifter version with a four-bolt main block gave 425. The 427 was offered only in the Corvette and in the full-size models. This Impala ragtop has Super Sport mag-type wheelcovers.

▲ Mid-size muscle was hot, and SS Impala sales fell sharply for '66. But a plain Biscayne with the rare 425-bhp 427 was still a street threat, and a B/S Biscayne was NHRA Winternationals Junior Stock champ. Both 427s could have a three-speed, the M21 close-ratio four-speed, or the new-but-noisy M22 "Rock Crusher." Turbo Hydra-Matic came only with the 390-bhp version.

1966 CHEVROLET HIGH-PERFORMANCE ENGINES

TYPE	CID	BORE × STROKE	BHP @ RPM	TORQUE @ RPM	FUEL SYSTEM	COMP. RATIO	AVAIL.
ohv V-8	283	3.88 × 3.00	220 @ 4800	295 @ 3200	1 × 4bbl.	9.25:1	1
ohv V-8	327	4.00 × 3.25	275 @ 4800	355 @ 3200	1 × 4bbl.	10.25:1	1
ohv V-8	327	4.00 × 3.25	350 @ 5800	360 @ 3600	1 × 4bbl.	11.0:1	Chevy II
ohv V-8	396	4.09 × 3.76	325 @ 4800	410 @ 3200	1 × 4bbl.	10.25:1	Chevelle, full size
ohv V-8	396	4.09 × 3.76	360 @ 5200	420 @ 3600	1 × 4bbl.	10.25:1	2
ohv V-8	396	4.09 × 3.76	375 @ 5600	415 @ 3600	1 × 4bbl.	11.0:1	2
ohv V-8	427	4.25 × 3.76	390 @ 5200	460 @ 3600	1 × 4bbl.	10.25:1	full size
ohv V-8	427	4.25 × 3.76	425 @ 5600	460 @ 4000	1 × 4bbl.	11.0:1	full size

1. Chevelle, Chevy II, full size.   2. Chevelle SS 396 and El Camino.

▲ This was the year of the Street Hemi. At Dodge, the new detuned version of the '65 race Hemi went in the Coronet and the new Charger. The 425-bhp 426 added $1000 to a $2705 Coronet 500 hardtop. It was big-league quick. *Car and Driver*'s did 0-60 mph in 5.3 seconds and the quarter in 13.8 at 104 mph. *Motor Trend* called its acceleration "absolutely shattering."

▲ Chicago's Dodge dealers took the reasonable course and based their Coronet drag car on the pillared coupe, which at 3215 pounds was the lightest body style available with the hot Hemi. Dodge built 250,842 Coronets and 37,344 Chargers for '66, but the Street Hemi was ordered in fewer than 1000 of them.

1966 DODGE HIGH-PERFORMANCE ENGINES							
TYPE	CID	BORE×STROKE	BHP @ RPM	TORQUE @ RPM	FUEL SYSTEM	COMP. RATIO	AVAIL.
ohv V-8	273	3.63×3.31	235 @ 5200	280 @ 4000	1×4bbl.	10.5:1	Dart GT
ohv V-8	361	4.12×3.88	265 @ 4400	380 @ 2400	1×4bbl.	9.0:1	Coronet
ohv V-8	383	4.25×3.75	270 @ 4400	390 @ 2800	1×4bbl.	9.2:1	full size
ohv V-8	383	4.25×3.75	325 @ 4800	425 @ 2800	1×4bbl.	10.0:1	Coronet, full size
ohv V-8	426*	4.25×3.75	425 @ 5000	490 @ 4000	2×4bbl.	10.25:1**	Charger
ohv V-8	440	4.32×3.75	350 @ 4400	480 @ 2800	1×4bbl.	10.1:1	full size

* Hemi. ** Std. comp. ratio: 10.2:1.

▲ A couple of good 'ol Mopar NASCAR boys, Cotton Owens and David Pearson, backed the "Cotton Picker," a match-race drag car that ran just for the '66 season. It had a fiberglass Dart wagon body and a rear-mounted race Hemi.

▶ Actual horsepower was near 500, but Dodge advertised its Street Hemi at 425 bhp on a 10.25:1 compression. A detuned version of the 12.5:1-squeeze race Hemi, the solid-lifter 426-cid V-8 had a milder camshaft for smoother low-rpm running and a heat chamber so it could warm up properly. Coronets and Chargers ordered with the Hemi got stiffer springs and bigger (11-inch) brakes. Front discs were optional. And instead of the usual five-year/50,000-mile coverage, Hemi buyers got a year and 12,000. Chrysler warned that even that would be voided if the car was "subjected to any extreme operation [i.e., drag racing]."

▶ Roger Lindamood's popular "Color Me Gone" Charger had a nitro-burning, fuel-injected Hemi and ran 8.50s at 160-170 mph. Despite the highly altered wheelbase and use of fiberglass body panels, this car retained the near-stock driving position.

▲ Charger bowed for '66 on the Coronet's 117-inch platform, but added a fastback roofline, hidden headlamps, and full-width taillights.

▲ "Beauty and the beast" was how Dodge described a Charger with the 426. "The Hemi was never in better shape," it crowed.

▲ Given a good launch, a Hemi Charger would rocket to 60 mph in about 5.3 seconds and devour the quarter-mile in around 13.8 at 104 mph. Its inline dual Carter four-barrels sat atop an aluminum intake manifold.

▲ A Street Hemi added $877.55 to Charger's $3122 base price and included heavy-duty suspension, four-ply nylon Blue Streak tires, and 11-inch brakes. But it was still too wild for most buyers. Of 37,344 Chargers built for '66, only 468 had the Hemi.

◄ Charger cost $417 more than a Coronet 500 hardtop, and part of the deal was a state-of-the-art '60s interior. It had lots of chrome, four bucket seats, available center consoles front and rear, and full instrumentation that included a 150-mph speedometer and 6000-rpm tach. A 318-cid V-8 with three-on-the-tree was standard. Chargers with the 361- or 383-cid V-8, or the Hemi, got the four-speed manual or TorqueFlite automatic programmed for full-throttle shifts at 5500 rpm. *Hot Rod* ran the 325-bhp 383 to a 16.28-second ET at 85 mph.

▲ This is no garden-variety Charger, but one of 85 delivered with a NASCAR-replica package that included a rear lip spoiler. The tires were stock, but they were mounted on deep-offset steel wheels that were the same as those on the race cars.

▲ NASCAR replicas had a stock Street Hemi, but added a special cowl-induction air cleaner, Mallory ignition, and an extra NASCAR-style motor mount.

▲ Hemis powered Dodge to the '66 NASCAR manufacturer's title. This is David Pearson, who won the driver's championship with 15 wins.

▲ Charger's rear buckets folded to create a cargo bay four feet wide and seven-and-a-half-feet long.

▲ "The hot new leader of the Dodge Rebellion....looks like a pampered thoroughbred, comes on like Genghis Khan," Dodge said of its '66 Charger.

▲ Fairlane's side-oiler 427 had 410 bhp with a single four-barrel, 425 with dual quads (shown). Both had 11.1:1 compression and solid lifters. Fitting the 427 required bigger front springs and relocated shock towers. Also included: A four-speed 'box, handling package, and front disc brakes. Interior was stock except for 9000-rpm tachometer.

▲ Ford's Thunderbolt drag car had set the stage for the emergence of a streetable 427-cid V-8 in the reskinned '66 Fairlane. The limited-edition package was available in specially built two-door hardtops and sedans.

▲ The 427 Fairlane's lift-off fiberglass hood was held by four NASCAR tie-down pins and had a functional air scoop. A production run of at least 50 was needed to qualify the car for the NHRA's A/S Super Stock class, and Ford is believed to have built just 57. Box-stock, they'd turn 14.5-second quarter miles at 100 mph. But most went to professional drag teams, where they were super-tuned and not really road-worthy. Thus, Ford street racers were denied a potent weapon against the big-block GM and Mopar intermediates.

1966 FORD HIGH-PERFORMANCE ENGINES

TYPE	CID	BORE × STROKE	BHP @ RPM	TORQUE @ RPM	FUEL SYSTEM	COMP. RATIO	AVAIL.
ohv V-8	289	4.00×2.87	271 @ 6000	312 @ 3400	1×4bbl.	10.5:1	1
ohv V-8	289	4.00×2.87	340 @ 6500	331 @ 3750	2×4bbl.	10.8:1	Cobra
ohv V-8	289	4.00×2.87	306 @ 6800	329 @ 4000	1×4bbl.	10.0:1	Shelby GT-350
ohv V-8	289	4.00×2.87	390 @ 6600	345 @ 4000	4×2bbl.	10.8:1	Cobra
ohv V-8	390	4.05×3.78	335 @ 4800	427 @ 3200	1×4bbl.	11.0:1	Fairlane
ohv V-8	427	4.23×3.78	410 @ 5600	476 @ 3400	1×4bbl.	11.1:1	Fairlane, full size
ohv V-8	427	4.23×3.78	425 @ 6000	480 @ 3700	2×4bbl.	11.1:1	Fairlane, full size
sohc V-8	427*	4.23×3.78	700 @ 6500	754 @ 4400	8V FI	12.0:1	race
ohc V-8	428	4.23×3.78	360 @ 5400	459 @ 3200	1×4bbl.	10.5:1	full size

*Hemi.
1. Falcon, Fairlane, Mustang, full size.

▲ Street Mustangs were taking it on the chin with their 289-cid small blocks, but with the single-overhead-cam 427, highly modified examples were dragstrip terrors. Hubert Platt's turned 8.50s at 161 mph.

▶ The "Cammer" 427 Mustangs were a step beyond A/FX, competing head-to-head with Mopar and Mercury "ultra-stock" cars. This is Bill Lawton's at the '66 AHRA Winter-nationals.

▶ Gas Ronda's 427 Mustang was the first unblown, full-bodied car to break into the 8-second range. He did it in '66 at Bakersfield, California, beating Tom "Mongoose" McEwen's Hemi Barracuda in a match race. Ronda's historic run was an 8.96 at 155 mph. Here, he's battling a Sox and Martin 'Cuda at the '66 NHRA Winter-nationals in Pomona.

▲ The 427 Fairlane initially ran in A/Stock against the Street Hemis. The Ford was down some 50 bhp to the Mopars, but it weighed about 200 pounds less, so the better ones held their own. The Lafayette Ford-sponsored ride driven by Bob Spears was a regional Stock Eliminator champ in '65 and '66. *Hot Rod* tried a showroom-fresh 427 Fairlane, complete with full wheelcovers and whitewall tires. "Even with the shift not working as slick as we like, it's almost like child's play to make a good run," wrote *Hot Rod*. "Bring the revs up to about a grand....Let the clutch out. Easy on the gas until you're underway and then pin the pedal to the mat. Ahhhhh! All those eight butterflies are flapping open and the sleek Fairlane body is twisting its way to the right, fighting the torque. The tach touches six grand and—wham!—second gear. The body rocks back momentarily before you catch your breath...then through third and fourth...all the way through the lights and beyond. No sweat."

▲ All Fairlanes but the GT could get the 427. All were white hardtops with GT-level suspensions and de-baffled stock mufflers.

▲ Big Fords could have a dual-quad "7-Liter" 425-bhp 427, though they were not often winners on street or strip. An exception was Mike Schmitt's Galaxie. Its 11.85 at 119.6 won the '66 NHRA Winternationals Street class.

▼ The NHRA didn't quite know what to make of these nitromethane, or "fuel," burning cars, so for a time it classified them as C/FD, for "fuel dragster." Holman and Moody built the chassis for Ronda's car, which located the engine about 18 inches behind the stock placement. Race weight was around 2100 pounds.

▲ The funny car as we know it debuted in January 1966. It was Don Nicholson's Eliminator I Comet, the first full "flip-top" body on a chromemoly tube-frame. This also was the first sub-8-second funny car, running a 7.94 on September 14 at Martin, Michigan.

Don Nicholson discovers Mercury Comet!

Mercury Comet Match Race Car has fiberglass body, weighs 1800 lbs, tops 160 mph. Covers the quarter in 8.7 sec. 427 CID SOHC engine puts out up to 900 hp. Other Cyclone GT's are running in C/Stock with standard 335 hp engine and are expected to top 110 mph.

Now discover how Cyclone GT puts you in the drag picture!

Apart from the all-out drag exhibition Comet campaigned by Atlanta's Don Nicholson, Mercury Cyclone GT's can be equipped with a special drag package. Used with the 390 4-barrel engine, it puts you into C/Stock with a vengeance. See your Mercury dealer for information on how to order this special equipment. Ask him how you, too, can enjoy one of America's most exciting, fastest-growing sports! Exotic performance parts lists also available. For booklet "What Makes Drag Racing?" write Frank E. Zimmerman, Jr. General Marketing Manager, Lincoln-Mercury Division, Ford Motor Company, 2550 East Grand Blvd., Detroit, Michigan 48211.

"Performance Car of the Year"

Mercury COMET

Ford LINCOLN-MERCURY DIVISION

Have **you** driven a Mercury Comet lately? Take a discovery ride!

▲ "Dyno" Don Nicholson took his nickname from the "Dyno-tuned" prep work of his early mounts.

◄ A classic example of the link between success on the track and sales promotion was this Mercury ad from the July '66 issue of *Hot Rod*. It touted the drag-pack option for the street Comet's 390-cid V-8, noting that "it puts you into C/Stock with a vengeance." Nicholson's fiberglass flip-top Eliminator I, on the other hand, used an injected SOHC 427 with 900 bhp in an 1800-pound car. Ed Shartman's similar funny Comet was the only other racer at Nicholson's level during the '66 season. Both were running 7.80s at 175 mph; other "funny cars" were in the 8.30s.

▲ Jack Chrisman's blown and injected Comet was set up for top speed and hit 188 mph before being destroyed by an engine fire.

▲ With a 335-bhp 390, a good Comet Cyclone GT could turn a 15.2 at 92 mph, but the going was tough on the street against Mopars.

1966 MERCURY HIGH-PERFORMANCE ENGINES

TYPE	CID	BORE × STROKE	BHP @ RPM	TORQUE @ RPM	FUEL SYSTEM	COMP. RATIO	AVAIL.
ohv V-8	390	4.05×3.78	335 @ 4800	427 @ 3200	1×4bbl.	11.0:1	Cyclone GT
ohv V-8	410	4.05×3.78	330 @ 4600	444 @ 2800	1×4bbl.	10.5:1	full size
ohv V-8	428	4.13×3.98	360 @ 5400	459 @ 3200	1×4bbl.	10.5:1	S-55, full size

▼ New sheetmetal and a slightly wider track distinguished the '66 Olds 4-4-2. Still an option, the 4-4-2 package added only $185 to the price of an F-85, $151 to a Cutlass. 4-4-2s gained their own grille and taillamps and a fake front-fender scoop this year. A trifling compression hike brought five extra horses to the standard 400-cid V-8. Olds built 21,997 4-4-2s for '66; this is one of about 2750 convertibles.

► Comet graduated to the Fairlane platform for '66, in hardtop and convertible form. The $2700 base version had a 289. The $2891 GT had the 390. A four-speed was optional at $183; the Sport Shift three-speed automatic cost $184.

► Super Stock 4-4-2s could benefit from the new W-30 option, a drag-racing package available through dealers. It added fiberglass inner fenders, trunk-mounted battery, cold-air induction, and radical cam. Only 54 were built.

▲ Base 4-4-2 V-8 four-barrel (shown) had 350 bhp, but a new triple-two-barrel option ($114) bumped output to 360. *Motor Trend*'s tri-carb four-speed hit 60 mph in 7.2 seconds and did the quarter in 15.2 at 96.6 mph.

▲ Best-selling 4-4-2 was the Holiday hardtop, going to 10,053 customers. Not many ordered the extra-cost factory tachometer. Bucket seats with console were an option, too.

▲ The rare W-30 forced-air option slashed 0-60 times to 6.3 seconds and quarter-mile ETs to 14.8 at 97 mph. True to the Oldsmobile ethic, however, most 4-4-2s had a softer nature. *Car Life* called even the tri-carb model a "Civilized Supercar....[that] lacks, or perhaps one should say masks, the brutal nature which is apparent in some of the others."

▲ Bold insignia identified the sportiest Olds. *Car Life* lauded the 4-4-2's road manners, saying it had a softer ride, yet better handling and steering control than the Chevelle SS and GTO, GM's two other A-body intermediates. Part of the credit went to the rear anti-roll bar standard on the 4-4-2 (Chevelle got one for '66, also). Estimated fuel economy with the tri-power was 10-13 mph.

1966 OLDSMOBILE HIGH-PERFORMANCE ENGINES

TYPE	CID	BORE × STROKE	BHP @ RPM	TORQUE @ RPM	FUEL SYSTEM	COMP. RATIO	AVAIL.
ohv V-8	330	3.94 × 3.38	320 @ 3600	360 @ 3600	1 × 4bbl.	10.25:1	1
ohv V-8	400	4.00 × 3.98	350 @ 3600	440 @ 3600	1 × 4bbl.	10.5:1	4-4-2
ohv V-8	425	4.12 × 3.98	300 @ 4400	430 @ 2400	1 × 2bbl.	9.0:1	2
ohv V-8	425	4.12 × 3.98	365 @ 4800	470 @ 3200	1 × 4bbl.	10.25:1	3
ohv V-8	425	4.12 × 3.98	375 @ 4800	470 @ 3200	1 × 4bbl.	10.5:1	4
ohv V-8	425	4.12 × 3.98	385 @ 4800	480 @ 3200	1 × 4bbl.	10.5:1	Toronado

1. Cutlass, Jetstar 88, F-85, Vista Cruiser. 2. Delta 88, Dynamic 88. 3. 98, Delta 88, Dynamic 88. 4. Starfire, 98, Delta 88.

▲ Billows of smoke from *all four wheels* erased most doubt that this twin-engine four-wheel-drive 4-4-2 was, as Hurst Performance Products billed it, "drag racing's wildest exhibition vehicle." Its supercharged 425-cid Toronado V-8s burned a nitro-alcohol blend.

◀ "Gentleman Joe" Schubeck launches the Hairy Olds. The car had two Hurst shifters, double instrumentation, and dual fuel throttles. Eleven-inch racing slicks rode all four corners. Its trap speeds were around 170 mph.

▲ A/S class champ Jere Stahl accepts the trophy for his performance at the NHRA Nationals.

▲ Jere Stahl, of Stahl exhaust-header fame, on his way to Top Stock Eliminator at the '66 U.S. Nationals at Indy. Stahl's Hemi-powered '66 Plymouth Belvedere turned a best ET of 11.73 at 119.68 mph.

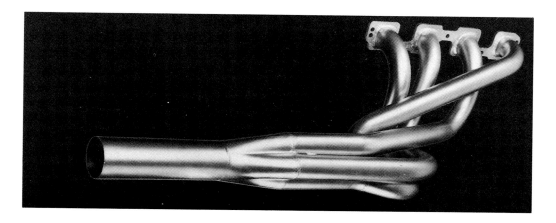

◀ Stahl Engineering of York, Pennsylvania, was one of the best-known fabricators of specialty exhaust systems in the 1960s. Pictured here is a set of "Total Tuned" four-into-one Stahl headers for Mopar's Street Hemi. Jere Stahl was one of many dragstrip aces who blended engineering expertise, an aftermarket company connection, and skill behind the wheel. A competitor was Los Angeles-based Doug's Headers, which advertised "individualized headers for all V-8s," including a Street Hemi system priced at $150.

▲ Like its Dodge Coronet cousin, the Plymouth Satellite could get a Street Hemi this year. It added $907.60 to the $2695 price of a hardtop.

▲ *Car and Driver* said the Satellite Hemi had "the best combination of brute performance and tractable street manners we've ever driven."

▶ The Street Hemi had cast-iron instead of aluminum heads and an aluminum intake manifold instead of a ram-type magnesium unit. Compression slipped from 12.5:1 to 10.25:1. Alloy heads and a wilder cam were factory options, however. A Sure-Grip axle was mandatory with both the four-speed and TorqueFlite. A tachometer added another $48.35.

▲ *Car and Driver*'s Hemi Plymouth hit 60 mph in 5.3 seconds and turned an ET of 13.8 at 104 mph. *Car Life* took 7.1 seconds to 60, with an ET of 14.5 at 95 mph. Front discs were unavailable, but police-grade 11-inch drums landed the Satellite.

▲ *Car Life*'s Hemi Satellite listed for a hefty $4360, with options. The editors praised its balance of power and civility, but reported that brisk cornering brought copious body lean and tire howl, the power steering was without road feel, and early rear-brake lock induced skidding. Normal fuel economy was estimated at 10-13 mpg, but would be less during acceleration runs, when the TorqueFlite automatically shifted to second at 4900 rpm and to third at 5200. "Wide-open throttle from rest induces noisy, unproductive wheelspin and a great amount of tire smoke," *Car Life* noted.

1966 PLYMOUTH HIGH-PERFORMANCE ENGINES

TYPE	CID	BORE × STROKE	BHP @ RPM	TORQUE @ RPM	FUEL SYSTEM	COMP. RATIO	AVAIL.
ohv V-8	273	3.63×3.31	235 @ 5200	280 @ 4000	1×4bbl.	10.5:1	1
ohv V-8	361	4.12×3.88	265 @ 4400	380 @ 2400	1×4bbl.	9.0:1	Belvedere
ohv V-8	383	4.24×3.38	270 @ 4400	390 @ 2800	1×4bbl.	9.2:1	Belvedere
ohv V-8	383	4.24×3.38	325 @ 4800	425 @ 2800	1×4bbl.	10.0:1	2
ohv V-8	426*	4.25×3.75	425 @ 5000	490 @ 4000	2×4bbl.	10.25:1	Satellite
ohv V-8	440	4.32×3.75	365 @ 4600	480 @ 3200	1×4bbl.	10.1:1	Sport Fury

* Hemi.
1. Valiant, Barracuda. 2. Satellite, Fury, VIP

Ken Heinemann blasts off in the "Brand X Eliminator" Belvedere at Bristol, Tennessee. Heinemann's Hemi was a consistent 12-second, 120-mph car, but was shut down by Shirley Shahan in her "Drag-On-Lady" Plymouth with an 11.26 at 126.7 for A-Stock/Automatic honors at the '66 Winternationals. The Hemi invited hyperbolae. Here's how *Hot Rod* began its preview: "Pow! For '66, Plymouth will offer 426 inches of 'street hemi,' a fire-breathing, dual-four-throat version of the hottest stocker in drag strip hollow."

▲ Adding a "Formula S" package to the bucket-seat Barracuda brought an upgraded suspension, blue-streak tires, and 150-mph speedometer.

▲ Front-disc brakes were a new $82 option on the '66 Barracuda. The 273-cid V-8 with a four-barrel had 235-bhp and 8-second 0-60 ability.

▼ With Sox at the wheel, the Sox & Martin '65 Plymouth was the first gasoline-powered "funny car" to run in the 10s. They turned 8.40s at 165 with their nitro-burning A/XS '66 Hemi Barracuda. But even that wasn't enough to beat the Nicholson and Shartman Comets. After this season, Sox and Martin would apply their talents to the stock classes, where their success translated into a long-time partnership with Plymouth and a thriving high-performance parts business of their own.

▶ North Carolinians Buddy Martin (left) and Ronnie Sox formed the Sox & Martin racing venture in 1962 and won their first NHRA title with a '64 Comet. They switched to Plymouth for '65, and in '67 began to concentrate on the stock classes. They became one of the muscle era's winningest teams and were priceless promoters of Plymouth performance.

▲ Pontiac signaled its continued interest in the big-muscle market by making the 2+2 a separate model for '66. It was still based on the Catalina, which, along with the Grand Prix, lost two inches of body length while keeping the 121-inch wheelbase.

▼ Production of the 2+2 dropped by nearly half for '66, to 6383, as enthusiasts focused on mid-size muscle. The big Ponchos, however, were unmatched at blending luxury with performance. The convertible started at $3602; the hardtop coupe at $3298.

▲ Buckets and console were 2+2 standards, but a tach and auxillary gauges cost extra. All came with a Hurst-shifted three-speed floor shift, but a four-speed or Turbo Hydra-Matic were optional. Pontiac told buyers to ask for the "GTO/2+2 performance catalog—and go-go-go."

▲ Only the full-size Pontiacs could get the 421-cid V-8, and only on the 2+2 was it standard. The base four-barrel had 338 bhp; optional Tri-Power 421s like this one had 356 or 376 bhp. Axle ratios from 3.08 to 4.11 were available, as was the aluminum wheel/hub combo.

▲ Private teams bore the brunt of converting GM cars for the radically modified classes. One that did was Gay Pontiac of Texas. Here's teenager Don Gay in the altered-wheelbase 421 "Infinity" GTO. The blown fuelie had a steel center body section and fiberglass front and rear clips. At the Winternationals, the rose-colored Goat "funny car" turned a 9.40 at 151.77 mph.

▲ The GTO was still Tempest-based, but became a series all its own for '66. Hood scoops looked hot, but were functional only when optional Ram Air induction was installed. Checking that item gave the Tri-Power 389 the benefit of cold-air entry, even though output was the same 360-bhp as the "ordinary" tri-carb mill. The GTO's plastic grille was an industry first. This blue hardtop wears the rare red plastic inner fender liners. Axle ratios spanned 3.08:1 to 4.33:1.

▶ GTO's four-barrel 389 again made 335 bhp. Tri-Power (shown) cost $112.51 extra. *Car and Driver's* Tri-Power with a 3.55:1 gear took 6.5 seconds to 60 mph and turned the quarter in a quick 14.05 at 105 mph. *Car Life's* four-speed four-barrel with the 3.08 axle and air conditioning needed 6.8 seconds to 60 and 15.4 at 92 for the quarter. It averaged 12.4 mpg. This was the factory Tri-Power's last season; at midyear, GM banned all multi-carb packages.

▲ Twin '66 GTOs joust for C/S honors at the NHRA Nationals: Ace Wilson's Royal (foreground), versus the "Tin Tiger." Royal Pontiac, a Michigan dealer, turned out savagely modified "Royal Bobcat" GTOs.

▲ Standard GTO gear included a three-speed column shift, heavy-duty springs/shocks, and front stabilizer bar. A wood-trimmed dash was standard, but a gauge cluster with tach cost extra.

▲ Voluptuous new Coke-bottle contours and continued strong performance resulted in sales of 96,946 '66 GTOs, the highest-ever one-year production total for a true muscle car. Styling highlights included the recessed backlight and cool fluted taillamps.

▲ This is one of 12,798 GTO ragtops built for '66. It cost $3082 and weighed 3555 pounds. The $2847 hardtop weighed 3465; 73,785 were built. The $2783 pillared coupe weighed 3445 pounds, and 10,363 were built.

▲ *Car Life* said the lightly loaded rear wheels of its nose-heavy GTO "skitter and skip on anything but the driest pavement." Braking power was poor, but the shifter was sweet, the motor willing, and assembly quality high.

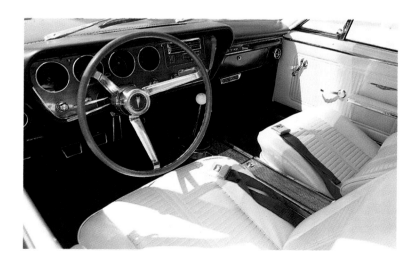

1966 PONTIAC HIGH-PERFORMANCE ENGINES							
TYPE	CID	BORE × STROKE	BHP @ RPM	TORQUE @ RPM	FUEL SYSTEM	COMP. RATIO	AVAIL.
ohv V-8	326	3.72 × 3.75	285 @ 5000	359 @ 3200	1 × 4bbl.	10.5:1	1
ohv V-8	389	4.06 × 3.75	290 @ 4600	418 @ 2400	1 × 4bbl.	10.5:1	full size
ohv V-8	389	4.06 × 3.75	325 @ 4800	429 @ 2800	1 × 4bbl.	10.5:1	2
ohv V-8	389	4.06 × 3.75	333 @ 5000	429 @ 3200	1 × 4bbl.	10.75:1	2
ohv V-8	389	4.06 × 3.75	335 @ 5000	431 @ 3200	1 × 4bbl.	10.75:1	GTO
ohv V-8	389	4.06 × 3.75	360 @ 5200	424 @ 3600	3 × 2bbl.	10.75:1	GTO
ohv V-8	421	4.09 × 3.75	338 @ 4600	459 @ 2800	1 × 4bbl.	10.5:1	full size
ohv V-8	421	4.09 × 4.00	356 @ 4600	459 @ 3200	3 × 2bbl.	10.75:1	full size
ohv V-8	421	4.09 × 3.75	376 @ 5000	461 @ 3600	3 × 2bbl.	10.75:1	full size
1. Tempest, LeMans 2. Grand Prix, full size							

◀ With its standard bucket seats and dashboard covered in genuine wood veneer, the GTO set the standard for sporty interiors.

153

1967

Corvette has top advertised horsepower, 435 ... Hemi is right behind at 425... Mopar's 440-cid V-8 is biggest muscle engine ● Several General Motors models actually lose horsepower after GM dictates that only Corvette can have more than one bhp per 10 pounds of car weight ● Camaro launched as rival to Ford's Mustang ... SS 396 and Z-28 versions show Chevy is serious about this ● Pontiac goes ponycar with Firebird and available 400-cid V-8 ● Ford answers with second-generation Mustang with available 390-cid V-8...Shelby GT-500 gets 428-cid V-8 ● 427-equipped Camaros modified by Don Yenko are quickest Chevys on the street ● Inspired by GTO, Chrysler intermediates finally get some sporting individuality with debut of Dodge Coronet R/T and Plymouth GTX...440 Magnum or 426 Hemi are underhood ● Mopar plays big-block catch-up, squeezing 383 V-8 into Dart and Barracuda ● Super Stockers break into the 10-second range ● Chuck Kurzawa's "Ramchargers" rail dragster turns a 6.76 at 223.88 mph—quickest ET to date

▲ Buick renamed its Gran Sport the GS400 to denote its new 400-cid V-8, which replaced the old 401-cid design. Transmission choices included a three-speed, Muncie four-speed, or Super Turbine automatic.

▲ Buick said GS400 was the "epitome" of the big, fast, American sporting car. Sales stayed around 14,000: 2140 convertibles, 10,659 hardtops, 1014 pillared coupes. All had red- or white-stripe F70×14 Wide-Oval tires.

▶ Hot fun in the summertime was just a turn of the key away in a GS400 ragtop. This one has the optional Strato buckets, $184 four-speed manual, and tachometer. A 3.36:1 final drive was standard with the four-speed, but ratios up to 4.30:1 were available on special order. With a list price of $3167, the convertible was the most expensive GS.

1967 BUICK HIGH-PERFORMANCE ENGINES

TYPE	CID	BORE×STROKE	BHP @ RPM	TORQUE @ RPM	FUEL SYSTEM	COMP. RATIO	AVAIL.
ohv V-8	340	3.75×3.85	260 @ 4200	365 @ 2800	1×4bbl.	10.25:1	1
ohv V-8	400	4.04×3.90	340 @ 5000	440 @ 3200	1×4bbl.	10.25:1	GS400
ohv V-8	430	4.19×3.90	360 @ 5000	475 @ 3200	1×4bbl.	10.25:1	2

1. GS340, Special Skylark, Sportwagon, LeSabre. 2. Riviera, Wildcat, Electra 225.

▲ Buick broadened the GS's appeal with the new GS340. All were hardtops with a 260-bhp, 340-cid four-barrel and three-speed or automatic. All had white or silver paint with a red side stripe and fake hood scoops.

▲ "Your father never told you there'd be Buicks like this," said the ads. Hood scoops on the GS400 now faced forward, but still weren't functional. The ragtop started at $3167, the hardtop at $3019, the coupe at $2956. Bucket seats and a Positive Traction limited-slip axle were options.

▲ The GS340 listed for just $2845. Only 3692 were built, but other junior muscle cars would follow.

▲ The GS400 helped shake up Buick's staid image, but never had the following of the Chevy SS or GTO.

▲ The new 400 had a futuristic plastic air cleaner. Like its 401-cid predecessor, it had a 10.25:1 compression, hydraulic lifters, and made the same 340 bhp as the top 401. But the smoother, more-modern V-8 could rev higher and was easier to keep in tune.

▲ Zero-60 claims varied widely for the GS400. *Car and Driver* said it took 6 seconds with automatic, 6.6 with a four-speed. *Car Life* said its 6-second run beat the 6.1 of a Ram Air GTO. More realistic times were 7.8 to 60 and around 15.9 in the quarter.

▲ Bill Jenkins was the '67 NHRA Super Stock Eliminator. "Grumpy's" 427 Camaro ran 11.55 seconds at 115.97 mph at Indy.

▲ The Z-28 was torrid right out of the box. Ben Wenzel's was B/Stock champ at the '67 Nationals with a 12.33 ET at 113.92 mph.

▲ SS Camaros got 350- or 396-cid V-8s, but Z-28s had this solid-lifter 302. It was rated 290 bhp. True output was likely closer to 400 bhp.

▲ Chevy's counterpunch to the Mustang in SCCA Trans Am battle was the Z-28. To make the SCCA's 305-cid limit, its 302 was a 327 with the 283's forged crankshaft. It had big-port heads from the Corvette L-69, a hot cam, and a Holley quad on an aluminum manifold. The peaky 302 was lethargic below 3000 rpm, a gun above.

▼ The Z-28 option added $400 to Camaro's $2466 base price; mandatory Muncie four-speed and power front discs brought the total near $3150. Only 602 were built. *Car and Driver*'s did 14.9 at 97 mph in the quarter.

▲ Chevy created the SS 427 Impala for '67, but the 385-bhp big-block could still be ordered in plainer Impalas like this base hardtop.

▲ Any full-size Chevy could be ordered with the 427, though most big-car bow tie enthusiasts were content with the 396's 325 bhp.

▲ For '67, the 427 officially came only in 385-bhp tune, but the 425-bhp L72 was still available. The four-speed's 3.73:1 was the hottest axle.

▲ On SS Impalas, bucket seats, console, and full instrumentation were moved to the options list. SS models could be ordered with any engine.

1967 CHEVROLET HIGH-PERFORMANCE ENGINES

TYPE	CID	BORE × STROKE	BHP @ RPM	TORQUE @ RPM	FUEL SYSTEM	COMP. RATIO	AVAIL.
ohv V-8	302	4.00×3.00	290 @ 5800	290 @ 4200	1×4bbl.	11.0:1	Camaro Z-28
ohv V-8	327	4.00×3.25	275 @ 4800	335 @ 3200	1×4bbl.	10.0:1	1
ohv V-8	327	4.00×3.25	325 @ 5600	355 @ 3600	1×4bbl.	11.0:1	2
ohv V-8	350	4.00×3.48	295 @ 4800	380 @ 3200	1×4bbl.	10.25:1	3
ohv V-8	396	4.09×3.76	325 @ 4800	410 @ 3200	1×4bbl.	10.25:1	4
ohv V-8	396	4.09×3.76	350 @ 5200	415 @ 3400	1×4bbl.	10.25:1	5
ohv V-8	396	4.09×3.76	375 @ 5600	420 @ 3600	1×4bbl.	11.0:1	5
ohv V-8	427	4.25×3.76	385 @ 5200	460 @ 3400	1×4bbl.	10.25:1	full size
ohv V-8	427	4.25×3.76	425 @ 5600	460 @ 2000	1×4bbl.	11.0:1	full size

1. full size, Chevelle, Chevy II, Camaro. 2. Chevelle, Chevy II. 3. Camaro SS 350. 4. full size, Camaro SS, Chevelle SS 396. 5. Camaro SS 396, Chevelle SS 396.

▲ "For the man who'd buy a sports car if it had this much room," was how Chevy promoted the new SS 427 Impala. It came with stiffer springs and shocks, a front stabilizer bar, and 8.24×14 red-stripe tires. *Car Life*'s 427 Impala hit 60 in 8.4 seconds and turned a 15.75 at 86.5 in the quarter.

▲ Mildly facelifted Chevelle SS 396 kept the prior year's non-functional hood blisters. Underhood changes also were modest. At $2825 for the coupe and $3033 for the ragtop, the Super Sports cost about $285 more than comparable Malibu models.

▶ A 325-bhp version of the 396 was standard in the Chevelle SS, while the $105 L34 upgrade (shown) dropped from 360 bhp to 350 because of GM's new edict against any car but Corvette having more than one bhp per 10 pounds of car weight.

▼ Ordering the new $121 power front-disc brake option brought Rally-style 14-inch slotted wheels to replace the usual small hubcaps or SS covers. Three-speed Turbo Hydra-Matic joined two-speed Powerglide as an option in place of the three- or four-speed sticks.

▲ "If you have a taste for action, here's the satisfier," Chevy said of the SS 396. A heavy-duty suspension and F70×14 red- or white-stripe tires were part of the package. Options included Strato bucket seats and a tach.

▲ This is the 325-bhp 396. The 375-bhp L78 was officially killed, but a few were installed and made it into the media's hands. *Motor Trend's* L78 four-speed coupe turned a 14.9 at 96.5 and managed 8.8 mpg.

▲ Nova Super Sport fans mourned the passing of the 350-bhp 327 V-8, though a few of those L79 mills probably were installed on special order. That left the capable but ho-hum 275-horse 327 as the top V-8.

Other changes to Chevy's compact were minimal. With Camaro's arrival, output of the Nova SS skidded to 10,100 out of 106,000 Chevy IIs built.

▲ About 8200 of the Nova SS hardtops got the 327 V-8. They started at $2590, $103 more than a six-cylinder version. Mainly an appearance package, the Nova SS did include bucket seats.

▲ Even though the 350-bhp 327 was no longer officially available in the Nova SS, this hardtop's license suggests that it's one of the rare few. Transmissions were the same as in '66, but axle ratios got a shuffling.

▶ Coronet changed little for '67, but Dodge did add the R/T—for "Road and Track"—as the new muscle model. Standard were fake hood vents, a Charger-inspired grille with exposed headlamps, and the biggest displacement V-8 of the day, Mopar's 440. The Hemi was the only engine option. Only 628 R/T ragtops were built for '67.

▲ The 440 was limited to full-size cars before the Magnum was fitted to the R/T. A four-speed was standard; TorqueFlite and $111 front disc brakes were optional. All R/Ts got a Sure-Grip diff and beefed suspension.

▲ At 375 bhp, the 440 Magnum four-barrel was the ideal street-racer's engine. It was more flexible, easier to maintain, and cheaper than a Hemi, yet had nearly as much torque and at lower rpm. A good 440 could stay with the mighty 426 Hemi up to 70-80 mph.

▲▼ A 440 R/T automatic like the one above turned a 15.4 quarter at 94 mph for *Motor Trend*, while *Hot Rod*'s TorqueFlite 440 did the quarter in 14.91 at 93.16. Just 283 of the 10,181 Coronet R/Ts built for '67 got the $907.50 Hemi option (below). *Motor Trend*'s Hemi automatic turned a lukewarm 15.0 at 96 mph. Dodge ads warned that a Coronet R/T was "not for the timid."

▼ At $3199 for the hardtop and $3438 for the convertible, the 440 R/T was, according to *Super Stock* magazine, "one of the best all-around performance packages being offered."

▲ Charger got only minor alterations for '67. Big news was availability of the 440 Magnum engine. Sales, however, dropped by more than half, to 15,788. A vinyl roof, in white or black, was a new option.

▲ A rear lip spoiler was added for '67. Charger's shape should have been a boon on NASCAR superspeedways, but the car never was a major NASCAR force. Don White drove his '67 Charger to the championship in USAC, where shorter tracks prevailed.

▲ Charger's center console became an option and no longer extended to the rear seat. Standard was a front center cushion with fold-down armrest, permitting seating for five instead of four. Both the four-speed and TorqueFlite came with Sure-Grip. Extinguisher was not stock.

1967 DODGE HIGH-PERFORMANCE ENGINES

TYPE	CID	BORE × STROKE	BHP @ RPM	TORQUE @ RPM	FUEL SYSTEM	COMP. RATIO	AVAIL.
ohv V-8	383	4.25 × 3.75	280 @ 4200	400 @ 2400	1 × 4bbl.	10.0:1	Dart GT
ohv V-8	383	4.25 × 3.75	325 @ 4800	425 @ 2800	1 × 4bbl.	10.0:1	1
ohv V-8	440	4.32 × 3.75	350 @ 4400	480 @ 2800	1 × 4bbl.	10.1:1	full size
ohv V-8	440	4.32 × 3.75	375 @ 4600	480 @ 3200	1 × 4bbl.	10.1:1	2
ohv V-8	426*	4.25 × 3.75	425 @ 5000	480 @ 4000	2 × 4bbl.	10.25:1	3

* Hemi.
1. Coronet, Charger, full size. 2. Coronet R/T, Charger, full size. 3. Coronet, Charger.

◄ Just 118 '67 Chargers got the Hemi, again conservatively rated at 425 bhp. *Car Life* ran one to 60 in 6.4 seconds, and to an ET of 14.16 at 96.15 mph on the standard 3.23:1 axle. With the 375-bhp 440, most testers saw 0-60 times of around 8.0 and ETs of around 15.0.

▲ Tom "The Mongoose" McEwen (center) drove Ford's SOHC 427 exhibition racer on its one and only run, an 8.28 at 171 mph at the '67 Winternationals in Pomona.

▲ The 427 Fairlanes were back, including one driven by NASCAR veteran Lee Roy Yarbrough (top left). The Paul Harvey rig was among the best, running in the low 10.9s at 127 mph, but competition was tougher than ever, and the Fairlanes didn't win a single national championship.

▶ NHRA switched the 427 Fairlanes among several classes during the '66 season, forcing them to run against all manner of purpose-built machinery, including the sub-9-second "ultra-stock" SOHC Mustangs. By '67, the rules anchored Fairlanes like this one in the Super Stock/B category, where Mopars were giving everyone a rough time.

▼ The professionally campaigned Super Stock Fairlane shared much inside with its cousin down at the showroom. But there were differences, including the big tach and supplementary engine gauges. Note the special drag-racing automatic-transmission gearshift, the competition safety harness and roll cage, and the seatback braces to support the driver in high-g-load acceleration.

▲ The 427 became a Fairlane regular-production option for '67. The solid-lifter mill had 410 bhp with a single four-barrel or 425 with dual quads. Super-tuned drag versions like this one could expect over 500 bhp. The big impact was in NASCAR, where 427 Fairlanes ran non-stock tunnel-port heads and Galaxie front suspensions. Mario Andretti won the Daytona 500 in one. It was one of 10 Ford victories, but again, Plymouth dominated.

◀ This quarter-miler's frame was modified by Holman and Moody of Charlotte, North Carolina, which also built Fairlane's NASCAR underpinnings. Its fuel tank was shortened to make way for the Ford nine-inch differential with 5.67:1 gearing. A ladder-bar rear suspension works with the massive slicks to put a tornado's worth of torque on the pavement.

▲ The stock steel hood was available this year on 427 Fairlanes; the cop-baiting fiberglass version with the air scoop was made optional.

▲ Even though the 427 engine was now a regular production option, fewer than 200 are thought to have been ordered. Chrome valve covers were standard.

▲ Only a base, 500, or 500XL Fairlane could get a 427 engine. GTs stuck with two- and four-barrel 390 V-8s, the latter down by 15 bhp, to 320.

▲ Fairlane 500XL blended pleasant accommodations with decent go: *Motor Trend*'s 390 GTA (for Automatic) did the quarter in 16.2 at 89 mph and got between 10.8 and 12.5 mpg. XL hardtops started at $2724; convertibles at $2950. GT models added another $115 and came with front disc brakes.

▲ Big Fords had given up most performance pretensions; Blue Oval boosters had turned to Fairlanes and Mustangs for drag duty. Fresh sheetmetal gave the '67s a rounded profile, as seen on this XL convertible. Engine choices ranged from a 200-bhp 289 V-8 to 427- and 428-cid big-blocks.

▲ The biggest engine in the Ford stable was the "7-Litre" 428, a quiet, long-stroke V-8 with the low-rpm power needed to move full-size cars. It was rated at 345 bhp, and had 462 pounds/feet of torque at just 2800 rpm with a single four-barrel carburetor. The hotter 427 was available for its final year, and even the SOHC 427 was offered as a special factory option. But the bloom was off big-car muscle.

165

▲ GT-350s again used the 306-bhp solid-lifter 289 with a 715cfm Holley and aluminum high-rise manifold. Headers were no longer standard.

▲ Shelby Mustangs broke into big-blocks for '67 with introduction of the GT-500. It used Ford's 428-cid "Police Interceptor" V-8 rated at 360 bhp.

▲ New factory options like air conditioning and power steering signaled the GT-350 Shelby Mustang's transition from racer to Grand Touring machine. Shelby installed a roll bar, 8000-rpm tach, and 140-mph speedo.

▲ *Motor Trend's* GT-500 did 0-60 in 6.2 seconds and the quarter in 14.52 at 101.35 mph on 3.50:1 gears. The standard heavy-duty suspension was similar to the '67 Mustang GT/GTA's, though adjustable Gabriel shocks replaced the previous Shelby's Konis. Tires grew to E70×15. Wheel options were these Kelsey-Hayes MagStars or cast-aluminum Shelby 10-spokes.

1967 FORD HIGH-PERFORMANCE ENGINES

TYPE	CID	BORE× STROKE	BHP @ RPM	TORQUE @ RPM	FUEL SYSTEM	COMP. RATIO	AVAIL.
ohv V-8	289	4.00×2.87	271 @ 6000	312 @ 3400	1×4bbl.	10.5:1	Mustang
ohv V-8	289	4.00×2.87	306 @ 6800	329 @ 4000	1×4bbl.	10.0:1	1
ohv V-8	390	4.05×3.78	320 @ 4800	427 @ 3200	1×4bbl.	10.5:1	2
ohv V-8	427	4.23×3.78	410 @ 5600	476 @ 3400	1×4bbl.	11.0:1	Fairlane, full
ohv V-8	427	4.23×3.38	425 @ 6000	480 @ 3700	1×4bbl.	11.0:1	3
ohv V-8	428	4.13×3.98	345 @ 4600	462 @ 2800	1×4bbl.	10.5:1	full size
ohv V-8	428	4.13×3.98	360 @ 5400	459 @ 3200	1×4bbl.	10.5:1	4
sohc V-8	427*	4.23×3.78	700 @ 6500	754 @ 4400	2×4bbl.**	12.0:1	Race

*Hemi. **Some had fuel injection.
1. Shelby GT-350. 2. Mustang, Fairlane 3. Fairlane, full size 4. Shelby GT-350, full size.

◄ The 428 had an aluminum "427" medium-riser manifold with twin 600cfm Holleys, an oval alloy air cleaner, and aluminum valve covers. A Toploader four-speed or C-6 automatic mated with axles ranging from 3.50:1 to 4.11:1. A few GT-500s got the 427-cid medium-riser V-8.

◀ Fairlane's Mercury cousin, the Comet, wasn't officially offered with the 427 engine, though 50 or so were built. The top official choice was the 320-bhp, 390-cid four-barrel Cyclone GT. The hardtop listed for $3034, the convertible for $3294. Both came with the twin-scoop fiberglass hood and front disc brakes. This car has aftermarket mags instead of the standard wheelcovers, which looked like chrome wheels.

▲ Mercury dressed the '67 Cyclone in checkered-flag badges and body-side stripes, but still didn't ignite much sales interest. Just 3797 were built; Pontiac, by contrast, assembled nearly 82,000 GTOs. Arrival of the new Cougar helped divert what interest there was in Mercury sportiness.

▲ The exhibition-racer, fiberglass-shell, tube-frame dragsters had been called funny cars for several seasons, but it wasn't until '67 that the NHRA established an official Funny Car class. Jack Chrisman switched to an enclosed body for his '66 Cyclone and went to work.

▲ Chrisman's flip-top GT-1 Funny Car used a Cyclone-replica fiberglass body, but about the only thing the same as on the production car was the wheelbase, which retained the stock 116-inch span. His SOHC 427 used a supercharger, which made it a better top-speed machine than non-blown rivals. Chrisman usually lagged behind for the first 300-400 feet, however, until the boost was up; then he surged forward as if an afterburner had kicked in. A competitor had to have a good lead by then to stay ahead of the GT-1's 180-mph-plus charge. What performance image Mercury had in the mid-'60s was nurtured by its Cyclone-bodied Funny Cars.

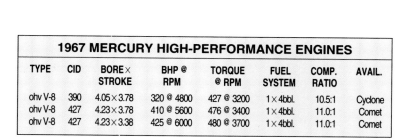

TYPE	CID	BORE × STROKE	BHP @ RPM	TORQUE @ RPM	FUEL SYSTEM	COMP. RATIO	AVAIL.
ohv V-8	390	4.05 × 3.78	320 @ 4800	427 @ 3200	1 × 4bbl.	10.5:1	Cyclone
ohv V-8	427	4.23 × 3.78	410 @ 5600	476 @ 3400	1 × 4bbl.	11.0:1	Comet
ohv V-8	427	4.23 × 3.38	425 @ 6000	480 @ 3700	1 × 4bbl.	11.0:1	Comet

1967 MERCURY HIGH-PERFORMANCE ENGINES

▲ Don Nicholson's Eliminator II was among the most successful Funny Cars. He scored 135 NHRA victories in a 10-month span, for a 90.6 winning percentage. Near-stock driver's position is thought to have been a bow to the Mercury public-relations effort.

▲ Nicholson poses with the injected SOHC 427, which made more than 900 bhp. Dyno Don blasted the Eliminator II to a record 7.6-second ET, while Jack Chrisman drove it to 184.42 mph at Riverside. *Drag Racing* magazine named it "Performance Car of the Year."

▲ "Sedate it ain't," was Oldsmobile's tag line for the '67 4-4-2. Priced at $184.31, the performance package now included functional hood louvers and made available such options as transistorized ignition and front disc brakes.

▲ The 4-4-2's 400-cid four-barrel was again rated at 350 bhp. The tri-power option died, but the W-30 setup with its air-induction and radical camshaft was back. *Car and Driver* hit 60 in 7.5 seconds and ran the quarter in 15.8 at 91 mph with a regular 350-bhp version. *Hot Rod's* W-30 turned a 13.9 with the four-speed, 14.5 with automatic.

1967 OLDSMOBILE HIGH-PERFORMANCE ENGINES

TYPE	CID	BORE × STROKE	BHP @ RPM	TORQUE @ RPM	FUEL SYSTEM	COMP. RATIO	AVAIL.
ohv V-8	330	3.94 × 3.39	310 @ 5200	340 @ 3600	1×4bbl.	9.0:1	1
ohv V-8	330	3.94 × 3.39	320 @ 5200	360 @ 3600	1×4bbl.	10.25:1	1
ohv V-8	400	4.00 × 3.98	300 @ 4600	425 @ 2600	1×2bbl.	10.5:1	Supreme
ohv V-8	400	4.00 × 3.98	350 @ 5000	440 @ 3600	1×4bbl.	10.5:1	2

1. Supreme, Cutlas, F-85, Vista Cruiser. 2. 4-4-2, Supreme.

▲ Plymouth finally took an encompassing approach to mid-size performance, creating an executive-class hot rod for '67 with the Belvedere GTX. It used the Super Commando 440 or 426 Street Hemi.

▲ This badge added $546 to the $3178 GTX coupe or $3418 convertible. Of course, you got a legendary 425-bhp engine in the bargain.

▲ Hemi engines were specially built at Chrysler's Marine/Industrial Division plant. Quality was extremely high, and they ran with surprising smoothness. *Car and Driver*'s Hemi GTX shot to 60 in 4.8 seconds and ran the quarter in 13.5 at 105 mph. "They don't call it King Kong for nothing," said one Plymouth advertisement.

▲ Plymouth built 12,500 GTXs for '67. Of the 720 ordered with the Hemi, 407 had the TorqueFlite and 313 had the four-speed.

▲ A 150-mph speedometer and bucket seats were standard on the GTX; a console floor shift was optional with the automatic.

▲ This special-order A/Stock Belvedere drag car carried a blueprinted and ultra-tuned Street Hemi. All sound insulation was deleted, lightweight van seats were used, and the battery was moved to the trunk. With street tires, these cars were reportedly legal for road use. At the NHRA Springnationals, "The Boss" Plymouth Hemi GTX campaigned by Sox & Martin in Super Stock turned an 11.34-second ET at 123.45 mph with Ronnie Sox at the wheel. The Plymouth public-relations machine was in high gear, and fans were encouraged to attend Sox & Martin Supercar Clinics held at dragstrips prior to the actual runs.

1967 PLYMOUTH HIGH-PERFORMANCE ENGINES							
TYPE	CID	BORE × STROKE	BHP @ RPM	TORQUE @ RPM	FUEL SYSTEM	COMP. RATIO	AVAIL.
ohv V-8	383	4.24×3.38	280 @ 4200	400 @ 2400	1×4bbl.	10.0:1	Barracuda
ohv V-8	383	4.24×3.38	325 @ 4800	425 @ 2800	1×4bbl.	10.0:1	Satellite, Fury
ohv V-8	426*	4.25×3.75	425 @ 5000	490 @ 4000	2×4bbl.	10.25:1	GTX
ohv V-8	440	4.32×3.75	350 @ 4400	480 @ 2800	1×4bbl.	10.1:1	Sport Fury
ohv V-8	440	4.32×3.75	375 @ 4600	480 @ 3200	1×4bbl.	10.1:1	GTX, Fury VIP
* Hemi.							

▲ The big hood scoop on the A/Stock Belvedere fed the Street Hemi's dual quads. Actual horsepower may have been as high as 550. NASCAR versions used a single four-barrel and powered Richard Petty to the most remarkable one-year record in stock-car-racing history. Petty started 48 Grand National races in his "Petty Blue" No. 43 GTX and won 27 of them. Plymouth took 31 checkered flags in all to dominate the series.

▲ Plymouth assembled 75 of these special drag Belvederes. The survivors still win in classes that correspond to those for which they were designed. This one has wheels and tires that represent present-day technology.

▲ Stripes and (non-functioning) scoops erased any notion of the GTX as a sleeper. TorqueFlite with modified upshift points was standard; a four-speed was optional. Heavy-duty suspension and upgraded 11-inch drum brakes were standard; front discs were optional.

◄ The 440 retained the 10.1:1 compression it had in the full-size models, but for Super Commando duty got a revised camshaft, free-flowing exhaust system, and an unsilenced air cleaner. It made 375 bhp, 25 more than the other 440s. *Car Life*'s automatic with 3.23:1 gears did 0-60 in 6.6 seconds, the quarter in 15.2 at 97, and averaged 12.3 mpg.

▲ Plymouth officially listed the 325-bhp, 383-cid four-barrel as the top Satellite engine, but as this photo shows, some evidently were powered by the 426 Hemi. The 440 was not available.

▲ Satellite shared the GTX's interior, but got a satin-silver Aluma-Plate lower-body finish. The hardtop cost $2747. The convertible, which this year gained a glass backlight, cost $2986.

▲ Plymouth's 383 V-8 was one of the era's most durable engines, doing duty in a variety of models and holding its own when tuned for performance applications, as is this four-barrel variant.

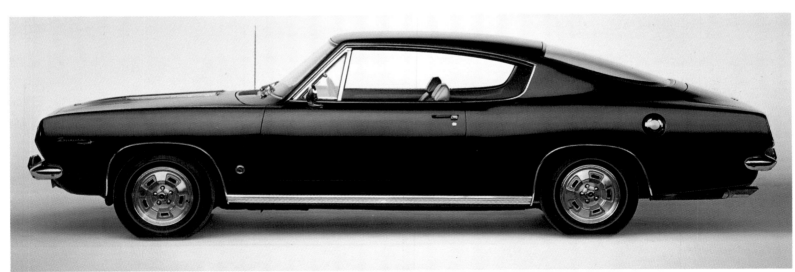

▲ Barracuda gained two inches of wheelbase, to 108, and two inches in engine bay width—enough to hold the 383. The four-barrel mill was optional on the top-of-the-line Formula S fastback. At 280 bhp, it was good for mid-15-second ETs at 92 mph, but left no room in the nose-heavy car for a power steering pump.

▲ Mopar versus Pontiac was a classic mid-'60s tussle. Here, Dick Landy's '67 Coronet R/T hardtop gets the drop on a '67 GTO in B/SA class action. A Royal "Bobcat" modified GTO with Ram Air turned a 13.09-second ET at 106.5 mph in the hands of *Motor Trend*, hitting 60 in just 4.9 seconds. *Hot Rod*'s automatic Bobcat turned a 13.89.

▲ GTO was back, stylish as ever, but the 389 had been bored to become the newly standard 400-cid V-8. Three versions were offered, all with 10.75:1 compression. In base trim, the 400 had 335 bhp via a Quadrajet carb; the High Output had a long-duration cam, improved exhaust manifolds, and 360 bhp at 5100 rpm. Ram Air with a functional hood scoop rated the same 360 horses, but at 5400 rpm. Ram Air cost $76.89 and came only with a 4.33:1 axle.

1967 PONTIAC HIGH-PERFORMANCE ENGINES

TYPE	CID	BORE × STROKE	BHP @ RPM	TORQUE @ RPM	FUEL SYSTEM	COMP. RATIO	AVAIL.
ohv V-8	326	3.72 × 3.75	285 @ 5000	359 @ 3200	1 × 4bbl.	10.5:1	1
ohv V-8	400	4.12 × 3.75	290 @ 4600	428 @ 2500	1 × 4bbl.	10.5:1	Catalina, full size
ohv V-8	400	4.12 × 3.75	325 @ 4800	410 @ 3400	1 × 4bbl.	10.75:1	Firebird Formula 400
ohv V-8	400	4.12 × 3.75	325 @ 5200	410 @ 3600	1 × 4bbl.	10.75:1	Firebird Formula 400
ohv V-8	400	4.12 × 3.75	325 @ 4800	445 @ 2900	1 × 4bbl.	10.5:1	Bonneville, full size
ohv V-8	400	4.12 × 3.75	333 @ 5000	445 @ 3000	1 × 4bbl.	10.5:1	Bonneville, full size
ohv V-8	400	4.12 × 3.75	335 @ 5000	441 @ 3400	1 × 4bbl.	10.75:1	GTO
ohv V-8	400	4.12 × 3.75	350 @ 5000	440 @ 3200	1 × 4bbl.	10.5:1	Grand Prix
ohv V-8	400	4.12 × 3.75	360 @ 5100	438 @ 3600	1 × 4bbl.	10.75:1	GTO
ohv V-8	400	4.12 × 3.75	360 @ 5400	438 @ 3800	1 × 4bbl.	10.75:1	GTO
ohv V-8	428	4.12 × 4.00	360 @ 4600	472 @ 3200	1 × 4bbl.	10.5:1	full size
ohv V-8	428	4.12 × 4.00	376 @ 5100	462 @ 3200	1 × 4bbl.	10.75:1	full size

1. Tempest, LeMans, Firebird H.O.

▲ This Goat's slightly elevated stance was a typical modification, though its tires are not of the period. Cross-hatch grille and "lid-less" taillamps help identify the '67s. Power front discs were a $105 option.

▲ A three-speed manual was standard; a Muncie four-speed a $184 option. A Hurst Dual Gate shifter was a factory-order item with the $226 Turbo Hydra-Matic. Eight axle choices ranged from 2.78:1 to 4.33:1.

▼ Competition ate into GTO sales. Production slipped to 81,722, (including 9517 convertibles), but nearly half had stick shift. The pillared Sports Coupe started at $2871, the hardtop $2935, and the ragtop $3165.

▲ *Motor Trend* tried two Ram Air Goats, both with Royal "Bobcat Kits," open headers, 3.90:1 gears, Hurst linkages, and 8.50×14 M&H Super Stock rear tires. The four-speed's best ET was 13.09 at 106.5; the Turbo Hydra-Matic's was 13.36 at 105. With stock tires, the ETs were slower by .75 to 1.12 seconds. The cars averaged 13.5 mpg highway, 11.5 around town.

▲Firebird alighted a few months after the comparable Camaro. Choices ranged from a base hard-top with an OHC six-cylinder, to 326-cid V-8s, to the 325-bhp Firebird 400 (Ram Air $616 extra). *Hot Rod* turned a 15.4 at 92 with a regular 400 ragtop. It had automatic, 3.08:1 gears, and a test weight of 3855 pounds.

▼Pontiac's big 2+2 returned with a new base engine: a 428-cid four-barrel with 360 bhp. A high-output edition had 376 bhp. The 2+2 reverted to a $400 Catalina option, however, and sales were so low that it was dropped after this year. It went out with bucket seats, floor-shifted three-speed, dual exhaust, and heavy-duty suspension. Gauges and a hood-mounted tach could be ordered, too.

1968

Plymouth debuts the Road Runner...its blend of fun, power, and affordibility is widely influential ● American Motors saddles up for the ponycar wars with the Javelin and its two-seat AMX derivative ● General Motors redesigns its intermediates on shorter wheelbases, all get rounded new bodies and stay aggressive toward performance ● Chevy IIs can get big-block 396 with 375 bhp ● Dodge groups its hot cars under the "Scat Pack" umbrella...highlight is the dramatically restyled Charger ● Coronet Super Bee answers Road Runner ● Special Hemi Darts and Barracudas go dragging ● Ford reaches the upper-echelon of production-car power with the new 428 Cobra Jet V-8...it goes first into a troop of Mustangs that quickly dominate their NHRA Super Stock classes with ETs in the 11s ● Hurst/Olds 4-4-2 gets a 455-cid Toronado V-8 ● Bill "Grumpy" Jenkins's 427 Camaro breaks into the 9-second range ● Top Fuel car hits 6.87 at 230.76 ● Cale Yarborough and Lee Roy Yarbrough finish Daytona 500 1-2 in new Mercury fastbacks...Ford gets 20 NASCAR wins; Plymouth is second with 16

▲ Hardly known for high performance, AMC scored with the AMX. Based on the new Javelin fastback, the AMX was shorter by a foot and had just two seats. Its 97-inch wheelbase was one inch less than Corvette's, and its $3245 base price with the standard 225-bhp 290-cid V-8 was $1100 below that of a 'Vette.

▲ AMXs had balanced handling, as well as good straight-line kick. A 280-bhp, 343-cid V-8 could replace the 290, but most buyers opted for the 315-bhp 390. A Borg-Warner four-speed was standard; three-speed automatic optional. A "Go" package added power front discs, E70×14 tires, Twin-Grip limited slip, and racing stripes.

▲ Derived from the 343, AMX's 390 V-8 had the same 10.2:1 compression, but a stronger block, forged rods and crank, and bigger bearings. All AMX mills used a single four-barrel. Factory-order axles ranged from 2.87:1 to 3.54:1; dealers could install 4.10:1 or 5.00:1 gearing.

◄ Pete's Patriot was the first significant AMC drag car. It was a Street Eliminator champion and is shown here with Loren Downing at the wheel at the '68 NHRA U.S. Nationals. As for the customer AMXs, *Car and Driver* said the four-speed's shift linkage was "an abomination....a long, wobbly business with lots of play in every direction," yet its 390 still took just 6.6 seconds to 60 mph and turned a 14.8 ET at 95 mph. The editors said the AMX couldn't match a Corvette's road manners, but that it "will get you down the road and around the corners in admirable fashion." Just 6275 '68 AMXs were built.

▼ General Motors redesigned its intermediates on a shorter 112-inch wheelbase for '68, and that spelled big styling changes for the Chevrolet Chevelle, Olds 4-4-2, Pontiac GTO, and Buick's Gran Sport. The Buick shed its sedan proportions for the fashionable long-hood, short-deck look. Replacing the GS340 as the junior partner to the 400-cid GS400 was this GS350 hardtop. It had a 280-bhp four-barrel 350-cid V-8.

1968 AMC HIGH-PERFORMANCE ENGINES							
TYPE	CID	BORE×STROKE	BHP @ RPM	TORQUE @ RPM	FUEL SYSTEM	COMP. RATIO	AVAIL.
ohv V-8	343	4.08 × 3.28	280 @ 4800	365 @ 3000	1 × 4bbl.	10.2:1	1
ohv V-8	390	4.17 × 3.57	315 @ 4600	425 @ 3200	1 × 4bbl.	10.2:1	1
1. Javelin, AMX, Ambassador Rebel.							

◄ Most GS Buicks were hardtops or convertibles, though some dealers stocked a pillared coupe known as the California GS; it came with the 350-cid engine. Transmission choices continued from '67, along with the Positraction option. Prices were up only $100 from '67, and GS production nearly doubled, to a record 21,514, with 8317 of them GS350s.

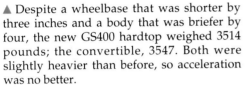

▲ Despite a wheelbase that was shorter by three inches and a body that was briefer by four, the new GS400 hardtop weighed 3514 pounds; the convertible, 3547. Both were slightly heavier than before, so acceleration was no better.

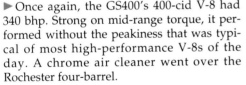

▶ Once again, the GS400's 400-cid V-8 had 340 bhp. Strong on mid-range torque, it performed without the peakiness that was typical of most high-performance V-8s of the day. A chrome air cleaner went over the Rochester four-barrel.

1968 BUICK HIGH-PERFORMANCE ENGINES							
TYPE	CID	BORE×STROKE	BHP @ RPM	TORQUE @ RPM	FUEL SYSTEM	COMP. RATIO	AVAIL.
ohv V-8	340	3.80×3.85	280 @ 4600	375 @ 3200	1×4bbl.	10.25:1	1
ohv V-8	400	4.04×3.90	340 @ 5000	440 @ 3200	1×4bbl.	10.25:1	GS400, Sportwagon
ohv V-8	430	4.19×3.90	360 @ 5000	475 @ 3200	1×4bbl.	10.25:1	2
1. GS340, California GS, Special, Skylark, Sportwagon, LeSabre. 2. Wildcat, Electra 225, Riviera.							

▲ Though a good GS400's mid-15-second ETs were no quicker than in '67, the shorter wheelbase, widened 59-inch front track, heavy-duty springs and shocks, and stabilizer bar gave it better handling and a less-floaty ride. In the Buick tradition, these were solid, stylish cars, and they blended power with poise in a mix that appealed to the more mature driving enthusiast. Base price of the GS350 was $2926; the GS400 started at $3127 for the hardtop and $3271 for the convertible.

◀ Camaro's $400 Z-28 package was little changed, though now it had fender emblems. Chevy made heavier-duty four-speeds available, and four-wheel disc brakes were a midyear "service option." When ordered with the Rally Sport package (note RS grille badge), any Camaro got hidden headlamps.

▲ Camaro was coming on strong at the strip, as well as on road courses. In the Trans Am sedan series, Chevy finally accomplished what it had set out to do with the Z-28. Mark Donohue's dark blue No. 6 Sunoco Camaro won 10 of the 11 races in the series to capture the championship in the over-two-liter class.

▲ Z-28's solid-lifter 302 was again rated at 290 bhp with the standard 800cfm Holley four-barrel. Newly available was a special manifold with twin 600cfm Holley quads at $500, plus dealer installation. *Hi Performance Cars* magazine tried a dual-quad Z-28 and turned the quarter in 13.75 at 107 mph. Though omitted from sales brochures for the second year running, Chevy did advertise the Z-28 as "closest thing to a Corvette yet," and production jumped to 7198.

1968 CHEVROLET HIGH-PERFORMANCE ENGINES

TYPE	CID	BORE × STROKE	BHP @ RPM	TORQUE @ RPM	FUEL SYSTEM	COMP. RATIO	AVAIL.
ohv V-8	302	4.00×3.00	290 @ 5800	290 @ 4200	1×4bbl.	11.0:1	Camaro Z-28
ohv V-8	327	4.00×3.25	275 @ 4800	355 @ 3200	1×4bbl.	10.0:1	1
ohv V-8	327	4.00×3.25	325 @ 5600	355 @ 3600	1×4bbl.	11.0:1	Chevelle
ohv V-8	350	4.00×3.48	295 @ 4800	380 @ 3200	1×4bbl.	10.25:1	2
ohv V-8	396	4.09×3.76	325 @ 4800	410 @ 3200	1×4bbl.	10.25:1	3
ohv V-8	396	4.09×3.76	350 @ 5200	415 @ 3400	1×4bbl.	10.25:1	4
ohv V-8	396	4.09×3.76	375 @ 5600	420 @ 3600	1×4bbl.	11.0:1	4
ohv V-8	396*	4.09×3.76	375 @ 5600	420 @ 3600	1×4bbl.	11.0:1	5
ohv V-8	427	4.25×3.76	385 @ 5600	460 @ 3400	1×4bbl.	10.25:1	full size
ohv V-8	427	4.25×3.76	425 @ 5600	460 @ 2000	1×4bbl.	11.0:1	full size

* RPO L89, aluminum heads, available 12/67.
1. full size, Chevelle, Chevy II, Camaro. 2. Camaro SS 350, Chevy II SS 350. 3. full size, Camaro SS 396, Chevelle SS 396.
4. Camaro SS, Chevelle SS 396, Chevy II SS 396. 5. Chevelle SS 396, Camaro SS 396.

▲ Camaros lost their wing windows with the advent of the flow-through Astro-Ventilation system. Side marker lights also identified a '68. Of 235,147 Camaros built for this year, 27,844 got the SS package.

▲ Performance models, such as this SS 396, gained five-leaf rear springs and staggered shocks to minimize axle tramp. SS models also got a blacked-out tail panel and gained front disc brakes as standard.

▶ The SS Camaro's four-barrel V-8s again began with a 295-bhp, 350-cid unit. The 396-cid big-block (shown) gained a 350-bhp edition to go along with the carryover 325- and 375-bhp versions. About 270 of the 396 engines received special-order aluminum cylinder heads, but their 375-bhp rating was unchanged.

▲ Turbo Hydra-Matic Camaros gained a stirrup-shaped shifter, and the optional rev counter and clock could be combined into a single gauge Chevy tabbed the "Tick-Tock Tach."

▲ A distinctive band around the nose helped SS Camaros stand out. For '68, SS 396 models also got their own hood with dual banks of four non-functional ports.

▼ Downsized and restyled, the 1968 Super Sport Chevelle began the best-selling four-year run of any big-block intermediate. Now a distinct series, the SS 396 was muscle for the common man.

▼ SS 396 Chevelles got a black-out grille and rear panel and light-colored cars got a dark lower body treatment. The double-dome hood was carried over and F70×14 tires were made standard. Front disc brakes were a $100 option.

▲ SS 396 hardtops started at $2899; Chevy built 60,499 of them. Ragtops began at $3102; 2286 were built. For the first time, the pickup truck-like El Camino could be ordered as an SS 396.

► A 325-bhp Turbo-Jet was standard. The 350-bhp L-34 cost $105. Top dog was this solid-lifter 375-bhp L-78. Just 4751 were ordered. Gear ratios ranged from 2.73:1 with automatic or 3.07:1 with air conditioning to a dealer-installed 4.88:1 with the hotter engines and four-speed.

▲ *Motor Trend*'s 3922-pound base-engine SS 396 coupe with automatic and A/C turned a 15.8 at 90 mph. Its rough-running L-34 was slower, but *MT* said a few "performance preparations" would get a good L-34 stick into the high 13s.

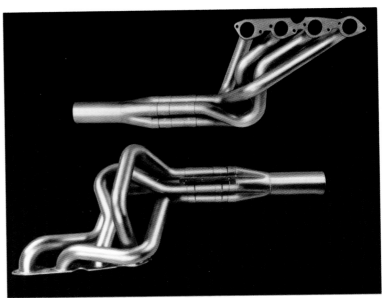

▲ As usual, the aftermarket delivered an alluring selection of high-performance components for big-block Chevelles. These Stahl exhaust headers fit 1968-72 models. Hooker, Doug's, and Jardine were other header brand names.

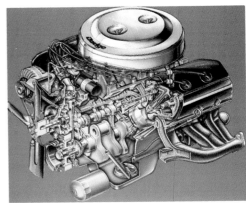

▲ The 426 Hemi still was rated at 425 bhp. At Dodge, it added $605 to the Coronet R/T and Charger R/T, and nearly $1000 to the new Coronet Super Bee. Air conditioning was unavailable with the Hemi.

▲ Charter members of Dodge's "Scat Pack" performance team for '68 were (from top) the Dart GTS, Coronet R/T, and Charger R/T. Audiences of the hit film *Bullitt* thrilled as the new 440 Magnum-equipped Charger R/T tore about hilly San Francisco in a classic duel with Steve McQueen's 390 Mustang. Would McQueen have caught a Hemi?

1968 DODGE HIGH-PERFORMANCE ENGINES

TYPE	CID	BORE × STROKE	BHP @ RPM	TORQUE @ RPM	FUEL SYSTEM	COMP. RATIO	AVAIL.
ohv V-8	340	4.04 × 3.31	275 @ 5000	340 @ 3200	1 × 4bbl.	10.5:1	Dart GT
ohv V-8	383	4.25 × 3.75	300 @ 4400	400 @ 2400	1x4bbl.	9.2:1	Dart GT
ohv V-8	383	4.25 × 3.75	290 @ 4400	390 @ 2800	1 × 4bbl.	9.2:1	1
ohv V-8	383	4.25 × 3.75	330 @ 5000	425 @ 3200	1 × 4bbl.	10.0:1	1
ohv V-8	383	4.25 × 3.75	335 @ 5200	425 @ 3400	1 × 4bbl.	10.0:1	Dart 383 GTS
ohv V-8	426*	4.25 × 3.75	425 @ 5000	490 @ 4000	2 × 4bbl.	10.25:1	2
ohv V-8	440	4.32 × 3.75	350 @ 4400	480 @ 2800	1 × 4bbl.	10.1:1	full size
ohv V-8	440	4.32 × 3.75	375 @ 4600	480 @ 3200	1 × 4bbl.	10.1:1	2

* Hemi.
1. Coronet, Charger, full size. 2. Coronet R/T, Charger R/T.

▲ Super Bee, a midyear offshoot of the Coronet, was Dodge's response to Plymouth's Road Runner. A "stripper" performance car, its $3037 base price included a 335-bhp, 383-cid V-8, four-speed with Hurst Competition-Plus shifter, heavy-duty suspension, and Charger instrumentation. Pillared coupe was the only Super Bee body for '68.

▶ Tongue-in-cheek icons and wild graphics were part of late-'60s culture, and Dodge was right there with the "Scat Pack" bumblebee. Dodge promoted its hot models as "The cars with the bumblebee stripes."

▲ Standard in the Coronet R/T and Charger R/T was Mopar's fine 375-bhp, 440-cid Magnum four-barrel. It was a smooth runner with root-rousing torque.

▲ Coronet R/T wrapped new sheetmetal around its carryover platform. The convertible cost $3630; the coupe, $3530.

▲ R/T instrumentation was stock Coronet unless the optional round-gauge Rallye cluster was ordered. *Car Life*'s Coronet R/T ragtop hit 60 in 6.6 seconds and did the quarter in 14.69 at 97.4 mph.

▶ The 440 in *Motor Trend*'s Coronet R/T hardtop would "wind easily to 6000 rpm," but *MT* got its best times by manually shifting the TorqueFlite at 5300 rpm. With 3.54:1 gears, the car took 6.9 seconds to 60 mph and turned 15.1 at 95 mph in the quarter. Massive wheelspin was a problem, and the R/T averaged only 11 mpg around town, but *MT* said the optional $73 front disc brakes did their job. The standard heavy-duty suspension gave the nose-heavy car adequate handling, but the $95 optional power steering was numb. Assembly quality was high. Only 230 Coronet R/T buyers picked the Hemi over the Magnum.

▲ "Dandy" Dick Landy gave the new Charger some of its most successful exposure. His Hemi was set up for the AHRA's new Super Stock category, a forerunner of the NHRA's Pro Stock class. His 426 used the stock Carter dual AFB four-barrels, but added an eight-quart deep-sump oil pan, Isky cam, and 30-inch Doug's headers. A Hurst Competition Plus shifter worked the four-speed to a stock Sure-Grip with a 4.88:1 final drive.

▲ The second-generation Charger was one of the '60's handsomest muscle cars, aptly described by *Car and Driver* as "all guts and purpose." At $3480, the R/T included the 440 Magnum, heavy duty brakes, R/T handling package, and F70×14 Red Streak or white sidewall tires. The bumblebee stripes could be deleted from the order form. Divided front-bench "bucket" seats were standard, but a tach was a $49 option.

◄ Just 475 '68 Charger R/Ts were ordered with the 426 Hemi, and only 211 of those had the four-speed. With TorqueFlite and standard 3.23:1 gears, *Car and Driver*'s Hemi Charger got to 60 mph in 6.0 seconds and turned a killer 13.5 at 105 in the quarter. For most buyers, the standard 440 Magnum was enough. It gained a high-flow unsilenced air cleaner for '68, and *Motor Trend* said it breathed much better. Manually shifting the TorqueFlite, *MT* got its 440 Charger to 60 mph in 6.5 seconds and through the quarter in 14.85 at 95.5 mph.

▲ Landy's 3650-pound Hemi Charger turned a 10.86 at 127 mph. Cragar wheels and 10.50×15 Goodyear slicks got the power down. Dick's brother Mike ran a 3550-pound Super Stock 440 Coronet R/T to an ET of 11.99 at 118.

▲ A full-width hidden-headlamp grille, flying-buttress rear roof, and race-inspired fender-top gas cap were Charger trademarks and helped increase production sixfold over 1967, to 96,100. "...You wouldn't change a line of it if you could," boasted Dodge.

▲ The Dart GTS got Mopar's fine 340- or 383-cid V-8s, but about 48 were fitted with a 440 Magnum by Hurst-Campbell Inc., of Michigan.

▲ The 440 Darts were sold by "Mr. Norm's" Grand Spaulding Dodge in Chicago, which also stuffed some Hemis into the lightweight compacts.

▲ Shirley Shahan's Hemi Dart wasn't one of her more successful "Drag-On-Lady" rides, but its high-10- low-11-second capability gave this big-block 'Cuda a run for its Winternationals money. On the street, a GTS with the 275-bhp 340 was as quick as one with the optional 383; the big-block's extra weight in the nose hurt traction off the line, offsetting its 60 more bhp.

► The GTS came with a Rallye Suspension, buckets, tail stripes, fake hood vents, and E70×14 tires. The 340 hardtop cost $3163, the convertible, $3383. *Car and Driver*'s 340 GTS turned a 14.4 at 99 mph with a 3.91:1 rear axle.

▲ Fairlane retained its previous chassis, but gained new styling, including a fastback body that gave Ford's intermediates an edge on NASCAR ovals. The 427-powered Fords took 20 checkered flags, and David Pearson won the driver's title in a Holman-Moody fastback. The 427 also powered Fairlane drag cars, including Hubert Platt's Super Stock/F Automatic runner, here in action at the '68 NHRA U.S. Nationals. This was an 11.9-12.0-second car.

◄ Ford's new fastback came in Fairlane 500 form and as the new Torino and Torino GT (shown). The 390-bhp 427 was phased out during the model year, and for a time, the 335-bhp, 390-cid four-barrel was top dog. *Motor Trend* left the Cruise-O-Matic in D and ran its 390 GT to an ET of 15.1 at 91 mph. Phased in during '68 was the new 335-bhp, 428-cid Cobra Jet, which made its biggest impact in Mustangs.

1968 FORD HIGH-PERFORMANCE ENGINES							
TYPE	CID	BORE×STROKE	BHP @ RPM	TORQUE @ RPM	FUEL SYSTEM	COMP. RATIO	AVAIL.
ohv V-8	390	4.05×3.78	265 @ 4400	390 @ 2600	1×2bbl.	9.5:1	Fairlane, Torino
ohv V-8	390	4.05×3.78	280 @ 4400	403 @ 2600	1×2bbl.	10.5:1	Mustang
ohv V-8	390	4.05×3.78	315 @ 4600	427 @ 4800	1×4bbl.	10.5:1	1
ohv V-8	390	4.05×3.78	335 @ 4800	427 @ 3200	1×4bbl.	10.5:1	Fairlane
ohv V-8	427*	4.23×3.78	390 @ 5600	460 @ 3200	1×4bbl.	10.9:1	2
ohv V-8	428	4.13×3.98	335 @ 5400	440 @ 3400	1×4bbl.	10.6:1	3
ohv V-8	428	4.13×3.98	360 @ 5400	460 @ 3200	1×4bbl.	10.5:1	3

* Discontinued at midyear.
1. Fairlane, Torino, Falcon, Thunderbird. 2. Fairlane, Torino, Mustang. 3. Fairlane, Mustang, Shelby.

▲ Trounced by the Z-28 in Trans Am, Ford responded with this "tunnel-port" head version of Mustang's new 302-cid V-8. The race mill never made it to production and its power was unspecified, but *Car and Driver* burned a 13.9 ET at 106 mph with a four-speed prototype.

▲ Mustang started '68 with the 427 V-8 as an official option, but few were built. Instead, Ford made 50 special lightweights to show-case the new 428 Cobra Jet that became a midyear Mustang option. All were white fastbacks (above and opposite, top). The factory took eight of them to the '68 Winter-nationals, where they dominated their Super Stock class.

▶ The 428 CJ was based on the staid 428 big-car motor, but had larger-valve heads and the race-brewed 427 intake manifold. Strip versions used a wilder cam than the street engine, with solid tappets and even bigger valves. Both ran a 735cfm Holley quad and were rated by the factory at 335 bhp; the more realistic figure was closer to 410 bhp. The optional Ram Air "shaker" hood-scoop setup was called Super Cobra Jet, but carried the same 335-bhp rating.

▲ The first 20 Super Stock 428 CJ Mustangs built by Ford for racing shifted weight to the rear and deleted radio and heater. Holman & Moody built two others, and all eliminated sound deadener.

▲ SS/E at the '68 Winternationals was an all-Cobra Jet final as Al Joniec shut down Hubert Platt with an ET of 11.49 at 120.6 mph. Joniec then snared SS Eliminator with a 12.5 at 97.9 mph on the Pomona track.

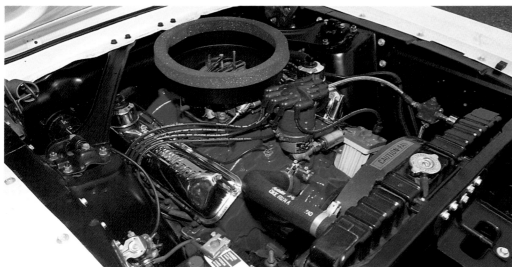

▲ The 428 CJ was offered to the public in 2+2s with the GT package and added $393—$526 for the Ram Air version. The latter was good for ETs in the mid-13-second range at 100-105 mph. The Equa-Loc diff ($79) and the Competition Handling Package ($62) were wise options.

▲ The $54 8000-rpm tachometer (with no redline indicated) helped keep tabs on a GT's V-8. A four-speed and Cruise-O-Matic were other options.

▲ Blown SOHC 427 Mustangs continued hot in the flip-top Funny Car ranks. Bill Lawton's was named "Mystery 7" for the ET range it inhabited.

▲ Most '68 performance Mustangs were fastbacks with the $147 GT package, which included fog lamps, power front discs, heavy-duty suspension, and F70×14 tires on styled steel wheels. The 390 four-barrel was commonly fitted, but it was not a real threat on the street.

▲ A handful of Shelby Mustang ragtops had been built to order, but for '68, it was "official." Convertible production: 404 GT-350s, 402 GT-500s, and 318 GT-500KRs. Each was about one-third of fastback production.

Carroll Shelby has gone and done it!

Convertible types, rejoice! He's built Shelby COBRA GT performance, handling, style and safety into a Mustang *convertible* complete with the best-looking roll bar in the business. If you don't flip your lid over this, you just don't flip (unless his Mustang-based Cobra GT 2 + 2 fastback gets to you). □ Both styles are available in GT 350 or GT 500 versions. The GT 350 boasts 302 cubic inches of Ford V-8 performance with an optional Cobra supercharger for added zip. The GT 500 really delivers with your choice of two great V-8's . . . 428 cubic inches are standard. A new 427 engine is the ultimate performance option. □ All the Le Mans-winning handling and safety features are better than ever for 1968. They're wrapped up in a fresh new luxury package. And the Mustang base means an exciting price. □ Any questions? Your Shelby Cobra dealer has some great answers!

Shelby COBRA GT 350/500

▲ At midyear, the GT-500's 360-bhp 428 Police Interceptor was replaced by a Cobra Jet with medium-riser heads and a 735cfm Holley. With that, the GT-500KR (King of the Road) tag was adopted. Horsepower was closer to 400 than the rated 335. A GT-500KR convertible cost a princely $4594.

▲ Shelby ragtops got a roll bar, and all '68s gained '65 Thunderbird sequential taillights. Production of Shelby Mustangs moved from California to Michigan, where Ford had more control over them. It was a turning point, and Shelbys began to lose their individuality.

▲ *Hot Rod*'s four-speed GT-500KR fastback turned the quarter in 14.01 at 102.73. For '68, the Shelby Mustangs got a new fiberglass fascia and redesigned hood with air scoops at the leading edge.

▲ This GTE version of Mercury's Cougar has the 390-bhp 427 offered during early '68. All were automatics. *Car Life*'s did the quarter in 15.1 at 93.6 mph, but the 3.50:1 gears lacked a limited-slip, so the launch was hampered by tire spin.

▲ "The entire world will come to recognize this engine—the 428 Cobra Jet—at the pop of a hood," declared *Motor Trend*. The 428 CJ came to Mercury in mid '68, where it was offered in high-performance Cougars and mid-size Cyclones. It had the same 335-bhp rating as at Ford. *Car Life*'s 428 CJ Cyclone automatic ran a 14.4 at 99.4 mph. Its 3.91:1 gears had the 428 turning 5300 rpm through the traps, 300 rpm short of maximum engine speed, "and the strong powerplant was still pulling hard at these lofty speeds," wrote the editors.

1968 MERCURY HIGH-PERFORMANCE ENGINES

TYPE	CID	BORE × STROKE	BHP @ RPM	TORQUE @ RPM	FUEL SYSTEM	COMP. RATIO	AVAIL.
ohv V-8	390	4.05×3.78	265@4400	390@2600	1×2bbl.	9.5:1	Cyclone
ohv V-8	390	4.05×3.78	280@4400	403@2600	1×2bbl.	10.5:1	1
ohv V-8	390	4.05×3.78	325@4800	427@3200	1×4bbl.	10.5:1	2
ohv V-8	390	4.05×3.78	335@4800	427@3200	1×4bbl.	10.5:1	3
ohv V-8	427*	4.23×3.78	390@5600	460@3200	1×4bbl.	10.9:1	4
ohv V-8	428	4.13×3.98	335@5400	440@3400	1×4bbl.	10.6:1	5

* Dicontinued at midyear.

1. Cougar, Montego. 2. Cougar GT, XR7, Cyclone, Montego. 3. Montego, Cyclone. 4. Cougar GTE, Cyclone. 5. Montego, Cyclone, Cougar.

▲ Mercury continued with Don Nicholson's 1000-bhp blown SOHC 427 '68 Cougar Funny Car. It ran 7.30s at 190. After a crash in this car, "Dyno" Don turned to Super Stock and Pro Stock rides.

▲ A new Montego nameplate graced Mercury's intermediates, with the 428 CJ Cyclone GT atop the line. *Motor Trend*'s turned a 13.8 at 101.6 with 4.11:1 gears, automatic, and the Traction-Lok differential.

◄ NHRA's handicapping system allowed cars of very different specification to race each other. Here, the '48 Ford Anglia of Rob Riffle takes on a very special '68 Cougar driven by Darrell Droke. The old ultra-light British Fords were popular choices for installation of American V-8 muscle. The "Top Cat" Cougar, meanwhile, used a 289-cid V-8 with Gurney/Westlake heads. It was a sort of factory secret weapon and was in fact streetable, though never built for production. It ran in the high-10s and low-11s at around 120 mph.

▲ Olds intermediates got new styling for '68 and the 4-4-2's 400-cid V-8 gained a new under-bumper Force-Air induction system good for 360 bhp. The blueprinted W-30 version could turn 13.3s at 103 mph. The most radical '68 4-4-2, however, was the Hurst/Olds. This is one of only 515 built. All had a 455-cid Toronado V-8 with a radical cam, recurved distributor, Rochester Quadrajet, and Force-Air induction for 390 bhp.

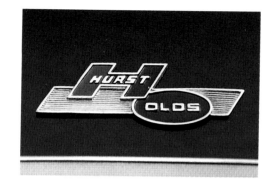

1968 OLDSMOBILE HIGH-PERFORMANCE ENGINES							
TYPE	CID	BORE × STROKE	BHP @ RPM	TORQUE @ RPM	FUEL SYSTEM	COMP. RATIO	AVAIL.
ohv V-8	400	3.87 × 4.25	290 @ 4600	425 @ 2400	1 × 2bbl.	9.0:1	4-4-2
ohv V-8	400	3.87 × 4.25	325 @ 4800	440 @ 3200	1 × 4bbl.	10.5:1	4-4-2
ohv V-8	400	3.87 × 4.25	350 @ 4800	440 @ 3200	1 × 4bbl.	10.5:1	4-4-2
ohv V-8	400	3.87 × 4.25	360 @ 5400	440 @ 3600	1 × 4bbl.	10.5:1	4-4-2
ohv V-8	455	4.13 × 4.25	390 @ 5000	500 @ 4200	1 × 4bbl.	10.25:1	Hurst/Olds

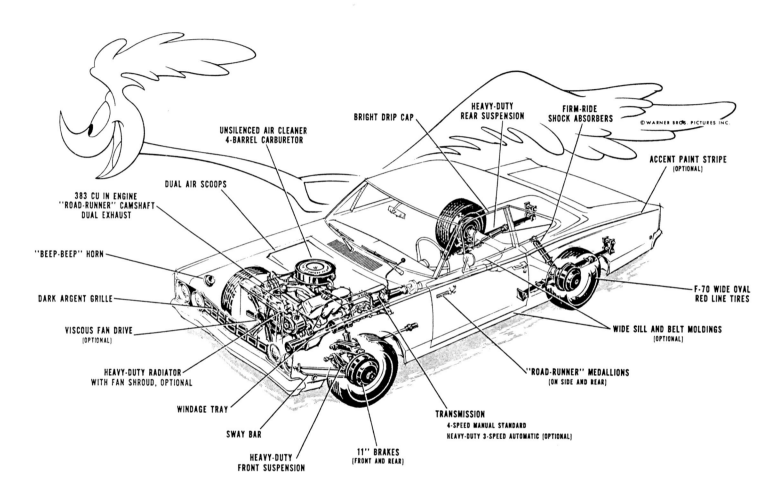

THE PLYMOUTH
road runner

67-2505

▲ One of muscle's most influential cars: the '68 Plymouth Road Runner. It was a $2986 factory hot rod in plain Belvedere skin.

▲ The base V-8 was a 335-bhp 383 four-barrel with heads from the 440. The 425-bhp 426 Hemi (shown) was the sole option, at $714.

▲ Plymouth's Sox & Martin team quickly put a Hemi Road Runner into drag duty. Street versions were turning mid-13s at 105 mph. A $139 SureGrip axle with 3.54:1 cogs was a mandatory Hemi option.

▲ Street 'Runners had F70×14 rubber; F70×15 on the Hemi. *Motor Trend*'s 383 automatic with 3.55:1 SureGrip turned 15.0 at 93 mph. Coupes, hardtops, and convertibles were offered, all with a "beep-beep" horn.

▲ Except for safety equipment and extra gauges, Ronnie Sox's work station wasn't much different from the low-bucks bench-seat cabin of the standard Road Runner, including the available "pistol grip" shift lever.

▲ Road Runner was a hit, with 44,599 built the first year, but just 1019 had the Hemi. This is Sox & Martin's mill, only slightly massaged beyond the showroom item. A Road Runner like this was no cartoon.

▼ GTX continued atop the line of restyled mid-size Plymouths. Like Road Runner, it used the Belvedere/Satellite platform, but again came standard with the 375-bhp, 440-cid four-barrel. GTX sales rose to 18,940 this year.

▲ The GTX ragtop started at $3590; the hardtop at $3355. Just 1026 convertibles were built. *Car Life*'s Hemi convertible with automatic and 3.23:1 gears turned a 14.0 ET at 96.5.

1968 PLYMOUTH HIGH-PERFORMANCE ENGINES							
TYPE	CID	BORE × STROKE	BHP @ RPM	TORQUE @ RPM	FUEL SYSTEM	COMP. RATIO	AVAIL.
ohv V-8	340	4.04×3.31	275 @ 5000	340 @ 3200	1×4bbl.	10.5:1	Barracuda
ohv V-8	383	4.25×3.38	290 @ 4400	390 @ 2800	1×2bbl.	9.2:1	1
ohv V-8	383	4.25×3.38	300 @ 4400	400 @ 2400	1×4bbl.	10.0:1	2
ohv V-8	383	4.25×3.38	330 @ 5200	425 @ 3200	1×4bbl.	10.0:1	1
ohv V-8	383	4.25×3.38	335 @ 5200	425 @ 3400	1×4bbl.	10.0:1	3
ohv V-8	426*	4.25×3.75	425 @ 5000	490 @ 4000	2×4bbl.	10.25:1	GTX
ohv V-8	440	4.32×3.75	350 @ 4400	480 @ 2800	1×4bbl.	10.1:1	Sport Fury
ohv V-8	440	4.32×3.75	375 @ 4600	480 @ 3200	1×4bbl.	10.1:1	4

* Hemi.
1. Satellite, Fury. 2. Barracuda, Fury. 3. Road Runner. 4. GTX, Fury VIP.

▲ Just 450 GTXs got the optional Hemi in '68. With the less-costly and easier-to-maintain 440, a hardtop automatic with 3.23:1 gears turned a 14.6-second ET 95.6 mph for *Car Life*.

▲ GTX used the well-appointed Satellite interior, with bucket seats and console. The TorqueFlite automatic was standard with either engine; a four-speed manual was a no-cost option and included the 3:54:1 SureGrip.

▲ Don Grotheer's Hemi Barracuda turned high-9s at around 135 mph to set NHRA national SS/B and SS/BA speed and ET records.

▲ Plymouth contracted with Hurst Performance for a limited run of '68 Hemi Barracudas for sale to factory-approved drag racers.

▲ NHRA founder Wally Parks bestows the hardware on Vanke for his performance at the '68 NHRA Nationals in Indianapolis.

▲ Arlen Vanke's SS/B Hemi 'Cuda (foreground) caught and beat "Grumpy" Jenkins's 427 SS/C Camaro to win Super Stock Eliminator at the '68 NHRA Nationals. Vanke's winning run was a 10.64 at 118.11 mph.

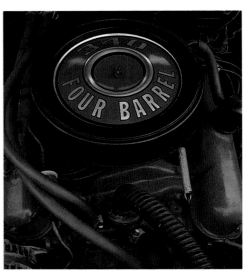

▲ The Sox & Martin Hemi Barracuda took the SS/D class at the '68 Springnationals with an ET of 11.20 at 106.5. Their immaculate red-white-and-blue Mopars were a valuable tool for promoting Chrysler performance.

▲ Hot street Barracudas got this frisky 275-bhp 340 four-barrel or the 383, now with 300 bhp.

◄ Pontiac's redesigned GTO retained its Tiger's temper. The 400-cid V-8 was still the only engine, but power was up. *Motor Trend* smoked a 360-bhp Ram-Air version to a 14.45-second ET at 98.2 mph. Its base 350-bhp model turned a 15.1 at 95 mph.

▲ Hidden headlamps were a GTO option, but most buyers chose them. The optional hood-mounted tach looked boss, but wasn't that practical in poor weather. The new Endura energy-absorbing bumper that formed the nose was an industry first—though a chrome bumper was available. GTO's weight was up, but a three-inch wheelbase cut and G77×14 tires helped improve handling. Of the 87,684 GTOs built for 1968, 9980 were convertibles.

1968 PONTIAC HIGH-PERFORMANCE ENGINES

TYPE	CID	BORE × STROKE	BHP @ RPM	TORQUE @ RPM	FUEL SYSTEM	COMP. RATIO	AVAIL.
ohv V-8	350	3.88 × 3.75	320 @ 5100	380 @ 3200	1 × 4bbl.	10.5:1	Tempest, Firebird HO
ohv V-8	400	4.12 × 3.75	330 @ 4800	430 @ 3300	1 × 4bbl.	10.75:1	Firebird 400
ohv V-8	400	4.12 × 3.75	335 @ 5000	430 @ 3400	1 × 4bbl.	10.75:1	Firebird 400
ohv V-8	400	4.12 × 3.75	340 @ 4800	445 @ 2900	1 × 4bbl.	10.5:1	full size
ohv V-8	400	4.12 × 3.75	350 @ 5000	445 @ 3000	1 × 4bbl.	10.5:1	Grand Prix
ohv V-8	400	4.12 × 3.75	350 @ 5000	445 @ 3000	1 × 4bbl.	10.75:1	GTO
ohv V-8	400*	4.12 × 3.75	360 @ 5100	445 @ 3600	1 × 4bbl.	10.75:1	GTO
ohv V-8	428	4.12 × 4.00	375 @ 4800	472 @ 3200	1 × 4bbl.	10.5:1	full size
ohv V-8	428	4.12 × 4.00	390 @ 5200	462 @ 3400	1 × 4bbl.	10.75:1	full size

* Ram Air, Ram Air II 366 bhp.

▲ For $3101, GTO hardtop buyers got 350 bhp, 15 more than in '67. A two-barrel, 265-bhp economy version cost no more. The H.O. 400 had 360 bhp, same as the Ram-Air 400, but the Ram Air had open hood scoops and higher rpm capability. A Hurst-shifted three-speed, a Muncie M21 close-ratio four-speed, or M40 Turbo Hydra-Matic were offered.

▲ Strong acceleration, good road manners and braking, fine instrumentation: "Our complaints are minor. Our praise is high," said *Motor Trend*. "Pontiac has improved on their GTO—which took some doing."

▲ Compared to the base 400, the H.O. (shown) got a different series four-barrel and, with manual transmission, a hotter cam. Ram Air cost $342 extra, came only with 4.33:1 gears, and not with air conditioning.

▲ The second-generation Goat's curvaceous styling was a triumph and its bucket-seat interior was a study in the art. Front disc brakes remained optional at $63. At midyear, Ram Air II replaced the initial Ram Air. It retained the 360-bhp rating, but gained new heads, forged pistons, and other hop-ups.

▲ The 2+2 survived in spirit in such cars as this Ventura, special-ordered with eight-lug wheels, four-speed, and 375-bhp, 428-cid V-8.

▲ Firebirds did their share of drag-strip duty, but weren't as successful as Camaro and Mustang. This "Tiger" is at the NHRA Nationals.

▼ Like its Camaro cousin, Firebird lost its vent windows for '68, but changed little otherwise. The 400 V-8 added five horses to both base and Ram Air versions (now 330 and 335 bhp).

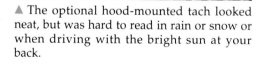

▲ The optional hood-mounted tach looked neat, but was hard to read in rain or snow or when driving with the bright sun at your back.

▲ The 326 was bored to 350 cid as the new base Firebird V-8. It had 265 bhp, 320 with the $181 four-barrel. Rear suspension on the 400 models gained multi-leaf springs and staggered shocks to combat wheel hop. Ram Air versions kept their functional hood scoops and high-output cam. A four-speed Ram Air ragtop with 3.90:1 gears turned a 15.0 at 110 for *Sports Car Graphic*.

▲ Firebird fancied itself a grand touring machine, not merely a pony car, but it nonetheless shared its dash and interior appointments with Camaro.

1969

Muscle nears its peak, with special-edition supercars from all manufacturers • AMC and Hurst create SC/Rambler compact, capable of ETs near 14 seconds • Buick GS 400 bulks up with Stage 1 and 2 engine options • COPO (Central Office Production Order) Camaros and Chevelles unleashed with 427-cid V-8s • Impala SS 427 is last gasp for full-size Chevy muscle • Dodge issues wild street versions of the aero Charger 500 and winged Charger Daytona to qualify them for NASCAR • 440 Six Pack debuts in Dodge Super Bee and Plymouth Road Runner • 'Cuda option for Barracuda can get 383 and 440 V-8s • Ford issues 428 CJ Cobra Fairlanes, plus droop-nosed NASCAR Torino Talladega and Mercury Cyclone Spoiler • Mustangs add limited-edition Boss 302 and Boss 429 • Pontiac GTO "Judge" bows with Ram-Air V-8... Firebird Trans Am arrives at midyear • Quickest Super Stock time at World Finals is 10.23 by Ronnie Sox in '68 'Cuda • Mark Donohue's 170-mph Camaro Z-28 wins second Trans Am crown • Richard Petty moves to Ford, wins 10 NASCAR races

▲ This June 1968 archival shot suggests that American Motors considered producing a 1969 "Rebel Machine." It did introduce such a car, but as a 1970. The production car had stripes and a big hood scoop, not this Machine's menacing dark hues, flat hood, and fab "gear" fender logo. Some AMC aficionados say versions of a '69 Machine did in fact show up outside AMC.

▲ Rambler's compact sedan could get a 290 V-8 from the factory, but this '67 American, shown running at the '69 NHRA Winternationals, has been modified to hold AMC's 390. Tipping the scales at around 2600 pounds, the junior Rambler was a good starting point for modified production.

▲ This '69 Javelin, sponsored by a Southern California dealership, ran mid- to low-11s in Super Stock/Automatic. AMC never had a well-financed drag team and it supported independents in an effort to gain exposure its meager advertising budget couldn't.

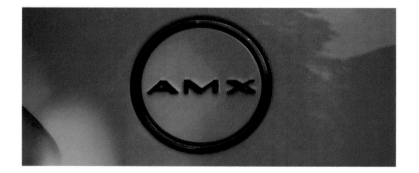

1969 AMC HIGH-PERFORMANCE ENGINES							
TYPE	CID	BORE × STROKE	BHP @ RPM	TORQUE @ RPM	FUEL SYSTEM	COMP. RATIO	AVAIL.
ohv V-8	343	4.08 × 3.28	235 @ 4400	345 @ 2600	1 × 2bbl.	9.0:1	Rebel, Ambassador
ohv V-8	343	4.08 × 3.28	280 @ 4800	365 @ 3000	1 × 4bbl.	10.2:1	1
ohv V-8	390	4.17 × 3.57	315 @ 4600	425 @ 3200	1 × 4bbl.	10.2:1	1
1. AMX, Javelin, Rebel, Ambassador.							

▲ AMC consulted the muscle-car bible, put its biggest engine into a compact body, and got help from Hurst Performance Research to create the Rogue-based Hurst SC/Rambler. It bowed in mid-1969 and sold for that year only. About two-thirds of the 1512 built had this wild paint scheme.

► AMC promised that the 3160-pound SC/Rambler would turn 14.3-second ETs. Some road testers bested that by a tenth or two, and at 100 mph. A $61 AM radio was the sole option on the $2998 hardtop.

▲ Tongue-in-cheek graphics gave the low-down on the SC/Rambler's fiberglass ram-air hood scoop. *Car and Driver* likened the car to a "tri-colored nickelodeon." *Road Test* called it a "drag strip eliminator at a penny pinching price."

◄ SC/Rambler borrowed a 315-bhp 390 V-8 from the AMX and gave it ram-air induction. A Borg-Warner four-speed with T-handle Hurst shifter helped send the power to a Twin-Grip diff with 3.54:1 gears. E70×14 tires, front-disc brakes, and a Sun 8000-rpm tach were also standard.

▲ Good news for the '69 AMX was replacement of AMC's balky shift linkage with a Hurst setup. Also new: a 140-mph speedometer and optional leather upholstery. Production reached 8293 for the year.

▲ AMX's optional 390 (shown) didn't change. But AMC built 52 drag-intended Super Stock AMXs with twin Holley carbs, 12.3:1 heads, and more. AMC said 340 bhp; the NHRA said 420. Best ET: 10.73 at 128.

▲ Buick's GS 400 gained functional hood scoops for '69, but big news was the new Stage 1 and Stage 2 engine options. Both added to the standard 400-cid V-8 a high-lift cam, special Quadrajet carb, and larger exhausts. They earned a 3.64:1 axle with four-speed, 3.42:1 with automatic, both with limited-slip. This is a Stage 1 ragtop with tires from a later period.

▲ The standard 400 four-barrel was rated at 340 bhp at 5000 rpm. Various sources list the Stage 1 version at 345 or 350 bhp at 5800 rpm. The Stage 2 variant used an even higher-lift cam and assorted other performance-enhancers. It is thought to have produced as much as 360 bhp. Both had dual-snorkel air cleaners that mated with the new cool-air induction hood vents.

1969 BUICK HIGH-PERFORMANCE ENGINES							
TYPE	CID	BORE × STROKE	BHP @ RPM	TORQUE @ RPM	FUEL SYSTEM	COMP. RATIO	AVAIL.
ohv V-8	340	3.80 × 3.85	280 @ 4600	375 @ 3200	1×4bbl.	10.25:1	1
ohv V-8	400	4.04 × 3.90	340 @ 5000*	440 @ 3200	1×4bbl.	10.25:1	2
ohv V-8	430	4.19 × 3.90	360 @ 5000	475 @ 3200	1×4bbl.	10.25:1	3

* 350 bhp with Stage 1 pkg, 360 bhp with Stage 2.
1. GS 350, LeSabre, Special Deluxe, Skylark. 2. GS 400, Sportwagon, LeSabre. 3. Riviera, Electra, Wildcat.

▲ Front disc brakes and a heavy-duty Rallye suspension were GS options. Ordering buckets added a console for the Turbo Hydra-Matic shifter. Base price of the GS 400 ragtop was $3325.

▲ GS production rose by nearly 6000, to 2454 GS 400 convertibles, 10,743 GS 400 coupes, 8317 GS 350 coupes, and 4831 California GS coupes. The latter two used a 200-bhp four-barrel 350.

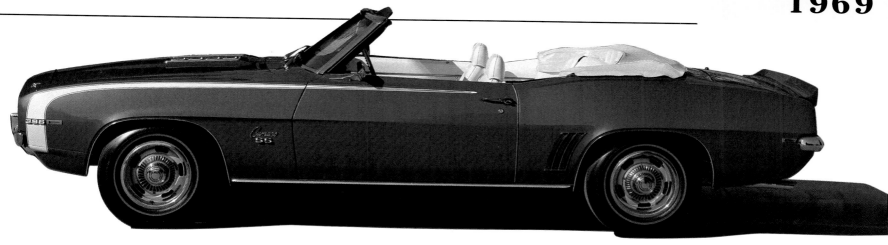

▲ New sheetmetal gave Camaro an angular look, but engine choices didn't change. SS offerings included the 375-bhp 396 at $316 and an aluminum-head 396 for $711. The optional Muncie M21 four-speed gained Hurst linkage, and with 3.73:1 gears, a 396 turned high-14s.

▲ Z-28's solid-lifter 302 was again underrated at 290 bhp. It gained four-bolt main-bearing caps during the year, while a rear-facing scoop was newly available. Axles ranged from 3.07:1 to 4.10:1.

▲ Four-wheel discs were a new Z-28 option at $500, but most went into race models. Tires grew to E70×15s. The Z-28 package was offered only on coupes and tacked $458 onto the $2726 base. RS option added hidden headlamps. Low-15-second ETs were common.

▲ A '69 Camaro paced the Indy 500, but unlike in '67, Chevy issued a Pace Car Replica. Most of the 3675 built had a 300-bhp 350 V-8; about 100 had the 396. All were white with "hugger" orange stripes. The SS package included F70×14 tires, Rally wheels, and power front discs.

▲ Convertibles also got Pace Car trim. A rear lip spoiler was now an SS option. So was the "Super Scoop" force-air induction hood that drew on the high-pressure area at the windshield base. A union strike lengthened the '69 model year, helping boost Camaro output to 243,085.

▲ Chevy built 69 drag-ready ZL-1 Camaros with aluminum-block 430-bhp 427s and sold them though selected dealers for $7300. Another variety of COPO (Central Office Production Order) Camaro was the Yenko/SC (shown). Don Yenko, a performance-oriented Pennsylvania dealer, added unique graphics to his 427 Camaros. This LeMans Blue coupe is one of 201 he built. The 427 Camaros turned high-12s/low-13s at over 110 mph.

▲ Yenko got Chevy to factory-equip Camaros with the iron-block 427; Chevy rated them at 425 bhp, Yenko said 450. Each had a Z-28 suspension, close-ratio four-speed, and 140-mph speedometer.

▲ The Chevelle SS 396 became a $348 Malibu option for '69, but that didn't dim sales, which hit a record 86,307. Car and Driver's 325-bhp coupe with the $222 auto trans and $42 optional 3.55:1 limited-slip did 0-60 mph in 5.8 seconds and ran the quarter in 14.4 at 97.35 mph.

▲ Three 396-cid V-8s again went into SS 396 Chevelles: 325 (shown), 350, or 375 bhp. About 500 cars with the Corvette's L-72 425-bhp aluminum-head 427 went to buyers with connections via the COPO ordering process.

▲ The SS 396 option was offered on the Sport Coupe, convertible, and the Chevelle 300 pillared coupe. It included the 396 engine, power front discs, and seven-inch sport wheels. Car and Driver said its SS 396 coupe was remarkably refined. It praised the heavy-duty suspension, but deemed the brakes "barely acceptable." The editors recommended spending $253 for the 375-bhp engine.

▲▼ This SS 396 four-speed ragtop has the optional $175 buckets and center console. Head restraints cost $17, and a tach and extra gauges added $95. Note the sport steering wheel and eight-track tape player.

▶ The Impala SS was in its final year and went out in style with the 427-cid V-8 as standard (above right). Horsepower was up by five, to 390. The $422 SS package for coupes and convertibles included G70 tires on 15-inch wheels, black-accented grille, and SS badges. Three- and four-speed manuals and the Turbo Hydra-Matic were available. About 10 percent of the 2455 SS Impalas built for '69 were ragtops. Exhaust headers on this one are non-stock.

▲ Once again, Don Yenko had his own idea of power for the Chevy Nova. Underhood went yet another 427-cid V-8, this time rated 425 horsepower. The drivetrain and suspension were beefed up and YSC graphics added, but the humble hubcaps are entry-level Nova.

▲ Those who couldn't find $5000-plus for a Yenko 427 Nova could turn to a fine selection of showroom SS Novas. Chevy built 17,654 of them, most with the base 300-bhp 350. Chevy also offered SS 396 Novas and built 1947 in 350-bhp tune and 5262 in 375-bhp form. *Hot Rod*'s 375-bhp 396 four-speed with 3.55:1 gears turned a 13.87 at 105.14 mph.

▲ Yenko's 427 Nova conversion was ultra-professional. The carefully tuned mills churned out nearly one horsepower per cubic inch. "The car was a beast, almost lethal," writer Jerry Heasley quoted Don Yenko as saying.

1969 CHEVROLET HIGH-PERFORMANCE ENGINES

TYPE	CID	BORE × STROKE	BHP @ RPM	TORQUE @ RPM	FUEL SYSTEM	COMP. RATIO	AVAIL.
ohv V-8	302	4.00 × 3.00	290 @ 5800	290 @ 4800	1 × 4bbl.	11.0:1	Camaro Z-28
ohv V-8	350	4.00 × 3.48	300 @ 4800	380 @ 3200	1 × 4bbl.	10.25:1	1
ohv V-8	396	4.09 × 3.76	325 @ 4800	410 @ 3200	1 × 4bbl.	10.25:1	2
ohv V-8	396	4.09 × 3.76	350 @ 5200	415 @ 3400	1 × 4bbl.	10.25:1	2
ohv V-8	396	4.09 × 3.76	375 @ 5600	420 @ 3600	1 × 4bbl.	11.0:1	2
ohv V-8	396	4.09 × 3.76	375 @ 5600	420 @ 3600	1 × 4bbl.	11.0:1	Camaro, Chevelle
ohv V-8	427	4.25 × 3.76	335 @ 4800	460 @ 3200	1 × 4bbl.	10.25:1	full size
ohv V-8	427	4.25 × 3.76	390 @ 5400	460 @ 3600	1 × 4bbl.	10.25:1	full size
ohv V-8	427	4.25 × 3.76	425 @ 5600	460 @ 4000	1 × 4bbl.	11.0:1	Camaro, full size
ohv V-8	427*	4.25 × 3.76	430 @ 5600	460 @ 4000	1 × 4bbl.	12.5:1	Camaro

* ZL1 engine, aluminum block and heads.
1. Chevelle, Nova, Camaro, full size. 2. Camaro, Chevelle, Nova.

▲ Professionally prepped and heavily modified big-block Darts like this were running in the high-9s and low-10s at 135-140 mph.

▼ This Dart GTS has the optional 335-bhp 383 Magnum in place of the standard 340 four-barrel. A four-speed and 3.91:1 Sure-Grip top it off.

▲ About 600 '69 Darts were fitted with the 440 Magnum engine, most installed by Grand Spaulding Dodge of Chicago. The majority were for sanctioned drag racing, but some showed up on the street.

▲ Dodge also contracted with Hurst to build 80 Hemi Darts for racing. They included the "Lone Star 2," which ran in the modified-production class and had a 4.56:1 axle.

▲ The hardtop GTS started at $3226, the ragtop at $3419. But the "Bumblebee" stripe could also adorn the new Dart Swinger 340 hardtop, which had GTS performance but cost $390 less.

▲ This was the last year for the GTS, but the Swinger 340 continued.

▲ A 383 like this in a Dart seemed like a good idea, but too much weight and resulting tire spin meant that without suspension modification, it was unlikely to beat the mid-14 ETs of a good 340.

▲ Dodge built 6700 GTS Darts and an unspecified number of Swinger 340s for '69. All got heavy-duty suspension.

▲ Rated at 275 bhp, Mopar's 340 may have had 325 or more. To *Car Life*, it was "as cleverly engineered as the 426 Hemi, just not so fussy." *Car and Driver* called its 340 Dart GTS (four-speed, 3.91:1 gears, 14.4 ET at 99 mph) "a giant killer."

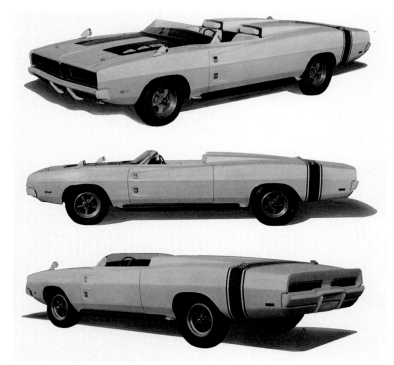

▲ What might a Charger R/T roadster be like? Dodge answered with this exercise for the '69 auto-show circuit. The two-seater had a cut-down windshield, special rear-deck cowls, body-colored bumpers, and non-glare hood panels. Finally, trunk and door handles were deleted.

▲ Experimentation went on outside Dodge, as well. Western Liquid Gas Association and Impco Carburetion sponsored this Hemi Charger 500 modified to run on propane. It turned 11-second ETs at 121 mph.

▲ "You in a heepa trouble, boy," Sheriff Joe Higgins advises Buddy Baker. Higgins was a fictional Dodge pitchman; Baker was a genuine NASCAR star.

▲ Keith Black, renowned builder of Mopar performance engines, put his talent into this promotional Charger Daytona.

▲ Precursor to the winged Daytona was the Charger 500. Dodge built street versions (52 with a Hemi, 340 with the 440) to qualify it for NASCAR. *Car Life*'s Hemi turned a 13.68 at 104.8 mph. This 440 is one of 106 with a four-speed. The 500 wasn't as fast as the new aero Fords and Mercurys on superspeedways.

▲ Charger 500 used a flush-fitted Coronet grille with exposed headlamps and a flush-mounted back window to cut turbulence on the superspeedways.

▲ King Kong returned unchanged and underrated at 425 bhp. Dodge built 20,057 Charger R/Ts for 1969. The majority had the fine 375-bhp four-barrel 440 Magnum. Just 232 were ordered with the 426 Hemi, which was again the only R/T engine option.

▲ Daytonas and Charger 500s got the raves, but most customers were happy with the mainstream models—albeit Hemis like this one were rare. Changes for '69 were few: The grille got a louvered divider; elongated tail-lamps replaced four round ones; and the bucket seats were revised.

▼ When the Charger 500 fell short of expectations, Dodge went all out with the 1969½ Charger Daytona. It was built for NASCAR superspeedways, but street versions looked just as wild. Standard was the 375-bhp 440 Magnum; 70 of the 503 built held a Hemi at $648 above the $3993 base. "You may not like it, but you'll never forget it," said *Road Test*.

▲ The Super Bee coupe was joined by a hard-top for '69, and at midyear, the 440 "Six Pack" joined the standard 383 and optional Hemi.

▲ Of 27,800 Super Bees built for '69, 1907 had the $463 triple-deuce option and 259 got the Hemi. The coupe started at $3076, the hard-top at $3138.

▲ The Six Pack's 1375cfm of triple Holley carburetion was fed by a huge scoop on the pinned-down fiberglass hood. Output was 390 bhp. To the 440 four-barrel, the Six Pack mill added Hemi valve springs, a revised camshaft, magnafluxed rods, and dual-point distributor. Standard was a four-speed and Dana 9¾-inch Sure-Grip axle with 4.10:1 gears. Sinister black-painted wheels with chrome lugs also were standard. *Car Life's* four-speed turned a 13.8 at 104 mph.

1969 DODGE HIGH-PERFORMANCE ENGINES

TYPE	CID	BORE × STROKE	BHP @ RPM	TORQUE @ RPM	FUEL SYSTEM	COMP. RATIO	AVAIL.
ohv V-8	340	4.04 × 3.31	275 @ 5000	340 @ 3200	1 × 4bbl.	10.5:1	1
ohv V-8	383	4.25 × 3.75	290 @ 4400	390 @ 2800	1 × 2bbl.	9.2:1	Coronet, full size
ohv V-8	383	4.25 × 3.75	330 @ 5200	410 @ 3600	1 × 4bbl.	10.0:1	Dart GTS
ohv V-8	383	4.25 × 3.75	330 @ 5000	425 @ 3200	1 × 4bbl.	10.0:1	Charger, full size
ohv V-8	383	4.25 × 3.75	335 @ 5000	425 @ 3200	1 × 4bbl.	10.0:1	Coronet Super Bee
ohv V-8	426*	4.25 × 3.75	425 @ 5000	490 @ 4000	2 × 4bbl.	10.25:1	2
ohv V-8	440	4.32 × 3.75	350 @ 4400	480 @ 2800	1 × 4bbl.	10.1:1	full size
ohv V-8	440	4.32 × 3.75	375 @ 4600	480 @ 3200	1 × 4bbl.	10.1:1	Charger, full size
ohv V-8	440	4.32 × 3.75	390 @ 4700	490 @ 3200	3 × 2bbl.	10.5:1	Super Bee

*Hemi.
1. Dart Swinger 340, Dart GTS.   2. Coronet, Charger, Super Bee.

▲ Coronet R/T returned for '69 with a revised grille and taillamps, but few other alterations. The 375-bhp 440 Magnum continued as standard; the 425-bhp 426 Hemi was again optional.

▲ A Performance Axle Package for the Coronet R/T put 3.55:1 gearing into a Sure-Grip diff and was augmented by Hemi handling components. The Track-Pak option offered a 3.54:1 Dana and four-speed.

▲ *Car and Driver* was delighted when its 383 Super Bee automatic with the $102 3.55:1 limited-slip option turned an ET of 14.04 at 99.55 mph. Then it discovered that the distributor and large-diameter exhaust were non-stock. It estimated a true production example would run a still-laudable 14.2-second quarter-mile at 98.4 mph.

▲ Newly optional for 383 Super Bees and 440 Coronet R/Ts and standard on Hemi R/Ts was a Ramcharger fresh-air induction package with a two-scoop hood. Available axle ratios were as long as 4.10:1.

▲ At $88.55 extra, styled wheels dressed up the Super Bee. Power front discs added $93. *Car and Driver* praised the Super Bee's "exceptionally well-coordinated feel" and the completeness of its instrument panel, which was borrowed from the Charger.

▲ Ford jumped on the budget-muscle bandwagon with the '69 Fairlane Cobra. It was a dressed-down Torino with plain bench seats, fleet-grade hubcaps, and the 428 Cobra Jet engine. This notchback has optional wheels. The SportsRoof fastback was the other Cobra body style.

▲ At under $3200 with standard four-speed, ads touted the Fairlane Cobra as "Bargain day at the muscle works." Early models carried a multi-colored decal of a stylized snake, fangs bared and tires trailing flames. This metal Cobra emblem replaced it on cars made later in the model year.

▲ Cobra's standard 428 CJ breathed through a 735cfm Holley four-barrel and exhaled via new cast-iron headers. Intake and exhaust ports were bigger than in '68, and peak horsepower arrived at 5200 rpm instead of 5400. Ram Air (shown) was a $133 option, but didn't change the 335-bhp rating. C-6 SelectShift Cruise-O-Matic was optional. Axles ranged from 3.25:1 to 4.30:1.

▲ Ram-Air Cobras with automatic and 3.50:1 limited-slip turned a 14.04 at 100.61 mph for Car and Driver, and a 14.5 at 100 for Motor Trend. A four-speed/3.50:1 ran a 14.9 at 95.2 for Car Life. Car and Driver said Ram Air cut the ET by .2 seconds and added 1.4 mph.

▲ Ram Air was dubbed CJ-R and brought a hood scoop with a vacuum flap that opened at full throttle. It required purchase of a tach, buckets, and wide-ovals. A competition suspension with staggered rear shocks, F70×14s on six-inch rims, and hood pins were Cobra standards.

▲ Ford countered the Charger 500 with a droop-snoot Torino and had to offer street versions to qualify the design for NASCAR racing. The modified SportsRoof was named for the Talladega speedway.

▲ NASCAR required that 500 Torino Talladegas be built; Ford made 754, including prototypes. Each had the 335-bhp 428 CJ, C-6 Cruise-O-Matic, 3.25:1 Traction-Lok, and Competition Handling Suspension.

▼ Torino GT returned in SportsRoof, hard-top, and convertible. A hood scoop was new, but functioned only with the 428 CJ-R option.

▲ Standard in Torino GT was a 302-cid V-8, but most buyers went with a 351 or optional 390 four-barrel, and a few for the 428 CJ (shown). Ford ads warned that a 428 CJ-R was "not for the timid soul."

▲ Snake decal identifies this promotional shot as one of an early Cobra. The 428s in both SportsRoofs and Talladegas were successful in stock-car racing, winning the Daytona 500 and the NASCAR crown.

1969 FORD HIGH-PERFORMANCE ENGINES

TYPE	CID	BORE × STROKE	BHP @ RPM	TORQUE @ RPM	FUEL SYSTEM	COMP. RATIO	AVAIL.
ohv V-8*	302	4.00 × 3.00	290 @ 5800	290 @ 4300	1 × 4bbl.	10.5:1	Mustang
ohv V-8	351	4.00 × 3.50	290 @ 4800	380 @ 3400	1 × 4bbl.	11.0:1	1
ohv V-8	390	4.05 × 3.78	320 @ 4600	427 @ 3200	1 × 4bbl.	10.5:1	1
ohv V-8**	428	4.13 × 3.98	335 @ 5200	440 @ 3400	1 × 4bbl.	10.6:1	1
ohv V-8	429	4.36 × 3.59	360 @ 4600	480 @ 2800	1 × 4bbl.	10.5:1	full size
ohv V-8*	429	4.36 × 3.59	375 @ 5200	450 @ 3400	1 × 4bbl.	10.5:1	Mustang

* BOSS ** Cobra Jet.
1. Fairlane, Torino, Mustang, Shelby.

▲ Ford's Camaro Z-28 fighter was the Boss 302. It had a handling suspension, F60×15 tires, quicker steering, and a modified 302-cid four-barrel rated at 290 bhp. With 3.91:1 gears, it turned ETs of 14.8 at 96 mph. It cost $3588, and 1934 were built for '69.

▲ In the late '60s, Ford's racing support ranged from Le Mans sports-racers, to Indy open-wheel cars, to Daytona stockers, to the nation's dragstrips. Here's Hubert Platt's factory-supported 11-second Super Stock Mustang at the NHRA Winternationals.

▲ Mach 1 debuted for '69 as the mainstream high-performance Mustang. Two- and four-barrel 351s were offered, plus the four-barrel 390. Top options were the 428 CJ, or CJ-R with "shaker" hood. Either way, a 428 Mach 1 was the finest Mustang street racer ever. Typical ETs were around 14 seconds at 100 mph.

▲ The "Shelby" link was all but gone, and Ford now built the GT 500 and GT 350 alongside regular Mustangs. The GT 350 gained the new 351-cid Windsor, but sales shrunk. The end neared.

▲ To NASCAR-certify its new 429, Ford put the semi-hemi V-8 into 858 Mustangs. With stock ETs in the low 14s, these 375-bhp Boss 429s never fulfilled their street potential. This is a custom drag car.

▲ The Torino SportsRoof was not a popular shell for a Funny Car, and dapper Phil Bonner's 7.8-second/180-190-mph ride was never a champion.

▲ Cyclone CJ came with the 428 CJ, with the CJ-R optional. Torquey and foolproof with automatic transmission, these were Mercury's finest street racers, with consistent ETs in the high 13s at 100 mph.

▲ A competition handling package was part of the Cyclone CJ's $3224 base price. A Drag Pak option replaced standard 3.50:1 gears with 3.91:1 or 4.30:1, LeMans connecting rods, and an engine oil cooler.

▲ Mercury honored two of its NASCAR drivers with namesake Cyclone Spoilers. The red-on-white "Cale Yarborough Special" (above) was sold by western dealers, while the blue-on-white "Dan Gurney Special" (above right) was sold in the east. Some were built with the aero Torino Talladega nose, and all had a decklid air foil that wasn't used on the race car. Standard was the 290-bhp 351 Windsor V-8 with Cruise-O-Matic and 3.25:1 Traction-Lok.

▲ Adding Ram-Air Induction with hood scoop to a Cyclone CJ cost $138.60. Mercury promised "maximum street get-up-and-go for a modest price."

▼ To qualify for NASCAR, 500 street-going Cyclone Spoilers had to be built and two variations were produced, both for '69 only. As many as 519 were built as the Spoiler fastback (below left) with the conventional Cyclone nose. About 300 were produced as the Spoiler II, with the elongated NASCAR front and a blacked-out grille (below). Both of those pictured are dressed in "Dan Gurney Special" trim.

▲ Mercury answered the Mach 1 Mustang with the Cougar Eliminator. Top engine was the 335-bhp 428 Super Cobra Jet, but choices began with a 290-bhp 351. The facelift retained hidden headlamps.

▲ Eliminator seemed overwhelmed by the 428 CJ. Some got the solid-lifter Boss 302 and were more balanced. They turned 14.8s at 96 mph, but at 3600 pounds, Cougar was more tourer than dragger.

► Eliminator's $3499 base price included a 351 four-barrel. The 290-bhp Boss 302 mill cost $335.50 extra; the 428 Cobra Jet added $283.60; and a 320-bhp 390 also was available. The hood scoop was functional only with the CJ-R. At right is a sample of the over-the-counter hop-ups available through Mercury dealers. They included headers and free-flow exhausts, deep-sump oil pan, special intake manifolds, dual-quads, low-restriction air cleaners, and even a multi-carb Weber setup. Those were the days.

▼ Because the Eliminator was not an XR-7 model, it received the base Cougar's standard vinyl interior, though its instrumentation did include a tachometer. Hurst T-handle lever provided a better grip during power shifts.

1969 MERCURY HIGH-PERFORMANCE ENGINES							
TYPE	CID	BORE × STROKE	BHP @ RPM	TORQUE @ RPM	FUEL SYSTEM	COMP. RATIO	AVAIL.
ohv V-8	302	4.00×3.00	290 @ 5800	290 @ 4300	1×4bbl.	10.5:1	Cougar
ohv V-8	351	4.00×3.50	290 @ 4800	380 @ 3400	1×4bbl.	11.0:1	1
ohv V-8	390	4.05×3.78	320 @ 4600	427 @ 3200	1×4bbl.	10.5:1	1
ohv V-8*	428	4.13×3.98	335 @ 5200	440 @ 3400	1×4bbl.	10.6:1	1
ohv V-8	429	4.36×3.59	360 @ 4600	480 @ 2800	1×4bbl.	10.5:1	full size

*Cobra Jet.
1. Cougar, Comet, Cyclone, full size.

▲ Hurst and Olds were back with another special 4-4-2, and it was bolder than ever with "Firefrost Gold" striping and a dual-scoop hood. The rear spoiler gave a claimed 15 pounds of downward force at 60 mph. Goodyear Polyglas F60×15 tires rode seven-inch Super Stock II rims. This hardtop has a Rocket rally pack and performance 3.91:1 axle ratio.

▲ About 906 Hurst/Olds were built, but only two were convertibles. The W-46 mill wore W-30 heads and a unique intake manifold. Its scoops worked better than under-bumper units on other hot Oldsmobiles.

▲ Olds authorized the Hurst car as a showroom traffic-builder, but it was no slouch. Again wielding a wicked 455-cid V-8, detuned slightly to 380 bhp, the W-46 Hurst/Olds put down 500 lbs/ft of torque. Zero-60 took 5.9 seconds, the quarter-mile just 13.98 at 101.3 mph.

▲ The 360-bhp Force-Air version of the standard 400-cid V-8 was again Olds 4-4-2's top gun. Production slipped to 26,357, including 4295 convertibles, despite a new ad campaign headed by "Dr. Oldsmobile."

▲ With three- or four-speed stick, the base 4-4-2 400 had 350 bhp. Turbo Hydra-Matic cut it to 325, but a new W-32 package blended the stronger 350-bhp V-8 and Force-Air with the M40 automatic.

▲ A Hurst/Olds at the '69 Nationals carries Linda Vaughn, Hurst's most famous Miss Golden Shifter.

1969 OLDSMOBILE HIGH-PERFORMANCE ENGINES							
TYPE	CID	BORE × STROKE	BHP @ RPM	TORQUE @ RPM	FUEL SYSTEM	COMP. RATIO	AVAIL.
ohv V-8	400	3.87 × 4.25	325 @ 4800	440 @ 3000	1 × 4bbl.	10.5:1	4-4-2
ohv V-8	400	3.87 × 4.25	350 @ 4800	440 @ 3200	1 × 4bbl.	10.5:1	4-4-2
ohv V-8	400	3.87 × 4.25	360 @ 5400	440 @ 3600	1 × 4bbl.	10.5:1	4-4-2
ohv V-8	455	4.13 × 4.25	380 @ 5000	500 @ 3200	1 × 4bbl.	10.25:1	Hurst/Olds

▲ Comedian Dick Smothers piloted this Hurst/Olds in SS/F action at the '70 NHRA U.S. Nationals.

▲ Dickie's Hurst/Olds ran in the 12s at 110 mph. The Smothers Brothers also sponsored a Top Fuel car.

▼ Road Runner's budget-bomb feel changed with new options like bucket seats, console, and power windows. But its performance persona was intact. Five new extra-cost axle packages allowed ratios up to 4.10:1.

▲ A 335-bhp 383 was again standard, and the Hemi the top option. But a 390-bhp 440 with triple two-barrel carbs was a midyear addition.

▲ The "440+6" mill got a lift-off fiberglass hood with a huge scoop. This Road Runner has the 383, which could get its own fresh-air hood.

▼ Road Runner production peaked at 84,420, nearly doubling the '68 figure. Only 2128 were the new-for-'69 $3313 convertible.

▲ The standard 383 (shown) again delivered 15-second ETs. The 440+6 cost $463 more and included a 4.10:1 Sure-Grip and Hurst shifter. It was nearly as quick as the $813 Hemi, which could turn mid-13s at 105 mph. Hemis went into 788 Road Runners, including 10 ragtops.

▲ Plymouth had the muscle era's most evocative artwork. This one promotes '69's new cool-air induction system option for 383s, 440s, and Hemis.

▲ *Motor Trend* ran three '69 Road Runners. Its 383 automatic with 3.23:1 gears turned an ET of 14.7 at 94.6. Its 383 four-speed/4.10:1 turned a 14.3 at 101.5. Its Hemi automatic/4.10:1 cooked a 13.5 at 105.3.

▲ Plymouth's new "Coyote Duster" cool-air induction system was standard with the Hemi and optional with the 383 and 440+6. The driver could open vents in the standard hood slots to direct air through underhood cowling.

▲ "The Hemi Road Runner has more pure mechanical presence than any other American automobile," said *Car and Driver*. It liked the Hemi's taut suspension, but bemoaned the unavailability of an oil-pressure gauge.

▼ GTX got Plymouth's cartoon treatment, too. Axle-ratio choices expanded to 3.54:1 and 4.10:1 for '69, and the new "Air Grabber" hood was available for the standard Super Commando 440 four-barrel and was included with the $701 Hemi. (The new 440+6 was not a GTX offering.) The GTX hardtop started at $3416 and weighed 3465 pounds, the ragtop based at $3635 and weighed 3590.

▲ GTX four-speeds now had a standard Hurst linkage. TorqueFlite was a no-cost item. GTX ads recommended the Hemi only "if you're serious about sanctioned racing...otherwise the Super Commando delivers more than enough stuff for the average commuter."

▲ Road Runner was *Motor Trend*'s 1969 "Car of the Year," and Glenn White (left), Chrysler-Plymouth general manager, accepted the caliper trophy from *MT* publisher Ray Brock. Brock said it was an exciting, influential car that "everybody here liked to drive."

▲ The 'Cuda name marked a new Barracuda enthusiast package and included the 340 or 383 V-8 and dummy hood scoops. Pressure from rival big-block pony cars prompted midyear availability of the 375-bhp 440 Magnum.

▲ 'Cuda was happiest with the 275-bhp 340. Formula S handling was sharp, but most testers reported high-14s. *Hot Rod* got its 340 four-speed with 3.91:1 gears to turn high-13s.

▲ A 'Cuda with the 440 could run the quarter in 14.01 at 103.81 mph. But some testers still called it an underachiever. Its mandatory TorqueFlite didn't shift crisply, and traction off the line was poor.

▲ A 335-bhp 383 'Cuda was more balanced than a 440. It also was cheaper to insure, and still turned ETs in the low 15s at 92 mph

TYPE	CID	BORE × STROKE	BHP @ RPM	TORQUE @ RPM	FUEL SYSTEM	COMP. RATIO	AVAIL.
ohv V-8	340	4.04 × 3.31	275 @ 5000	340 @ 3200	1 × 4bbl.	10.5:1	Barracuda
ohv V-8	383	4.25 × 3.75	330 @ 5200	410 @ 3600	1 × 4bbl.	10.0:1	Barracuda
ohv V-8	383	4.25 × 3.75	330 @ 5000	425 @ 3200	1 × 4bbl.	10.0:1	1
ohv V-8	383	4.25 × 3.75	335 @ 5200	425 @ 3400	1 × 4bbl.	10.0:1	Road Runner
ohv V-8	426*	4.25 × 3.75	425 @ 5000	490 @ 4000	2 × 4bbl.	10.25:1	Road Runner
ohv V-8	440	4.32 × 3.75	350 @ 4400	480 @ 2800	1 × 4bbl.	10.1:1	full size
ohv V-8	440	4.32 × 3.75	375 @ 4600	480 @ 3200	1 × 4bbl.	10.1:1	GTX, Barracuda
ohv V-8	440	4.32 × 3.75	390 @ 4700	490 @ 3200	3 × 2bbl.	10.5:1	Road Runner

1969 PLYMOUTH HIGH-PERFORMANCE ENGINES

* Hemi.

1. Belvedere, Satellite.

▲ Stuffing the 440 into the Barracuda gave Plymouth the largest-displacement pony car of the day. But it left no room in the engine bay for power-assisted steering or the booster needed to operate power front disc brakes. Thus, a 'Cuda with the heavy big-block 440 was a bear to park and required lengthy stopping distances. *Car Life* said a 440 'Cuda was at its best on the highway, where abundant power reserves affording effortless passing, and steering and braking shortcomings were minimized.

▲ Pontiac created The Judge for '69 by stirring GTO's hottest performance extras into a single $332 package, slapping on the decals, and giving it the 366-bhp, 400-cid Ram Air III with open hood scoops.

▶ The new 370-bhp Ram Air IV was a $390 Judge option. A four-speed added $195, hood tach, $63. Rear spoiler, beefed suspension, and Rally II wheels were standard on the $3161 hardtop and $3700 convertible. For '69, 6833 Judges were built.

▲ Except for badges, Judge's interior was regular-GTO. "Air" knob to left of the steering wheel opened and closed the Ram Air hood vents.

▲ Judges were no quicker than similarly equipped GTOs. A Ram Air IV four-speed with 3.55:1 gears turned a 14.4 at 97.8 for *Car Life*.

▲ Trans Am, one of Pontiac's most significant performance cars, bowed in midyear as a $725 option group for the Firebird 400. Just 691 T/A hardtops and eight convertibles were built. All were Polar White with blue stripes. Scoops on hood and vents in front fenders were functional.

▲ A 60-inch spoiler was a T/A trademark. High-effort steering, power front discs, and a beefed up suspension were part of the package.

▲ T/As came with a 335-bhp, 400-cid Ram Air III; optional was a 345-bhp Ram Air IV. A Ram Air IV Trans Am with four-speed and 3.90:1 gears turned a 14.1 at 100.7 mph for *Hot Rod*.

1969 PONTIAC HIGH-PERFORMANCE ENGINES

TYPE	CID	BORE × STROKE	BHP @ RPM	TORQUE @ RPM	FUEL SYSTEM	COMP. RATIO	AVAIL.
ohv V-8	350	3.88×3.75	325 @ 5100	380 @ 3200	1×4bbl.	10.5:1	1
ohv V-8	350	3.88×3.75	330 @ 5100	380 @ 3200	1×4bbl.	10.5:1	2
ohv V-8	400	4.12×3.75	330 @ 4800	430 @ 3300	1×4bbl.	10.75:1	Firebird
ohv V-8	400	4.12×3.75	335 @ 5000	430 @ 3400	1×4bbl.	10.75:1	3
ohv V-8	400	4.12×3.75	345 @ 5400	440 @ 3700	1×4bbl.	10.5:1	3
ohv V-8	400	4.12×3.75	350 @ 5000	445 @ 3000	1×4bbl.	10.5:1	4
ohv V-8	400*	4.12×3.75	366 @ 5100	445 @ 3600	1×4bbl.	10.75:1	GTO
ohv V-8	400*	4.12×3.75	370 @ 5500	445 @ 3900	1×4bbl.	10.75:1	GTO

* Ram Air

1. Tempest, LeMans, Firebird. 2. Tempest, LeMans. 3. Firebird, Trans Am. 4. GTO, Gran Prix

▲ Facelifted Firebird returned with 350- and 400-cid V-8s as popular performance engines. Sales slumped to 75,362 coupes, 11,649 ragtops.

1970

Muscle's pinnacle year, with unmatched power and style. ● AMC issues its strongest engine ever, a 340-bhp 390 for new Rebel Machine ● Mopar's first pony cars—Dodge Challenger and Plymouth Barracuda—storm out of the chute ● Winged Road Runner Superbird follows shelved Charger Daytona...draws Richard Petty away from Ford and wins the NASCAR crown for Plymouth ● FoMoCo unleashes 429-cid Cobra Jet Torinos and Cyclones ● Mustang Boss 302 wins Trans Am title ● Shelby Mustangs die with little fanfare ● GM allows 400-cid-plus engines in intermediates ● Buick responds with its quickest-ever car, the GS 455 Stage 1 ● Chevelle answers with a 454...LS-6 version threatens all comers ● Second-generation Camaro bows with classic Euro styling...Z-28 gets 360-bhp 350 ● 455-cid W-30 is baddest Olds 4-4-2 ● GTO has effortless 455-cid or raucous 400 Ram Air ● Redesigned Trans Am boasts world-class road manners ● NHRA creates Pro Stock class...big names flock ● Top Fuelers run 6.4s...Funny Cars turn 6.8-7.0s

▲ American Motors made good on its "Machine" prototype (page 200) with this production version based on the fastback Rebel SST intermediate. It had a variation of the paint scheme seen on the now-discontinued '69 SC/Rambler compact, but after the first 1000 or so, any colors were available. List price was a reasonable $3475. Only 2326 were built.

▲ AMC used some late-'60s cliché images to promote its Machine. The car came with a 390-cid V-8, hood scoop with vacuum-activated ducts, front discs, E60×15 tires on seven-inch wheels, and a close-ratio Hurst-shifted four-speed; a three-speed automatic was optional. *Road Test*'s 3.91:1-geared Machine turned a 14.57 at 92.77 mph, but wheel hop from the standard raked suspension hampered traction off the line.

▲ The Machine's four-barrel 340-bhp 390 was AMC's most powerful engine ever. It was delivered with a standard Twin Grip axle and 3.54:1 gears, but ratios up to 5.00:1 were available through the dealer.

▲ Machine instrumentation was scanty, though an 8000-rpm tach was built into the rear of the hood scoop. Optional power steering was overassisted, but *Road Test* said the 3800-pound car handled well.

▲ AMX's forte was high-speed road work, but "Ramblin Man" is typical of one set up for the drags. George Warren's '70 390 AMX won the SS/D class at the NHRA Springnationals with an 11.70-second pass at 118.42 mph.

▲ This Machine 390 has custom headers and valve covers, but retains the stock heavy-duty cooling with flexible fan. AMC ads confided that the Machine was slower than a Hemi, but faster than "your old man's Cadillac."

▲ AMX entered its last season as a two-seater with a larger standard V-8 and a front suspension updated to upper/lower ball joints. New hood scoop could host an optional vacuum-activated Ram Air setup.

▲ This 290-bhp, 360-cid V-8 replaced the 225-bhp 290 as AMX's standard engine. A 390-cid V-8 was still optional, and it now had 325 bhp, up by 10. The new Ram Air setup helped the 390 turn out 340 bhp.

225

▼ A mild facelift included front-bumper holes that AMC claimed help cool the brakes. Optional "Go" package for the 390 V-8 added power front discs, E70×14 tires, handling components, stainless steel front spoiler, and a Twin-Grip diff. The standard bucket seats were now high-backs with integral head rests. This AMX is finished in Big Bad Green.

▲ Full-width taillamps marked the last of the two-seat AMXs. AMC would make the car a version of the four-place Javelin after this year.

▲ With a Ram Air 390 like this, an AMX could turn mid-to-low 14-second ETs. *Motor Trend* ran its 325-bhp 390 with 3.54:1 gears to a 14.68 at 92 mph. While it combined good scoot with fine handling, AMX never attracted a wide audience. Production sank to 4116 for 1970.

			1970 AMC HIGH-PERFORMANCE ENGINES				
TYPE	CID	BORE× STROKE	BHP @ RPM	TORQUE @ RPM	FUEL SYSTEM	COMP. RATIO	AVAIL.
ohv V-8	360	4.08×3.44	245 @ 4400	365 @ 2400	1×2bbl.	9.0:1	1
ohv V-8	360	4.08×3.44	290 @ 4800	395 @ 3200	1×4bbl.	10.0:1	2
ohv V-8	390	4.17×3.57	325 @ 5000	420 @ 3200	1×4bbl.	10.0:1	2
ohv V-8	390	4.17×3.57	340 @ 5100	430 @ 3600	1×4bbl.	10.0:1	2

1. Rebel, Javelin, Ambassador. 2. AMX, Javelin, Rebel, Ambassador.

▲ The 1970 GSX was the ultimate expression of Buick's ultimate supercar. With its mighty 455-cid Stage 1 mill and Apollo White or Saturn Yellow paint set off by stripes, spoilers and scoops, it had an extroverted style to match its muscle.

▲ The $1195 GSX package bowed at midyear and included aero cosmetic pieces, a hood tach, stiffer shocks and suspension pieces, and G60×15 tires on mag-style steel wheels. Only 678 were built for 1970; Buick produced 9948 base GS models, 8732 GS 455 hardtops, and 1416 GS 455 convertibles.

▲ Buick's restyled Skylark again hosted the GS models, which started with a 325-bhp, 350-cid V-8. Replacing the 400-cid V-8 was a big-valve, hot-cam 455. Output was 350 bhp. New top dog was the $199 Stage 1 performance package for the 455. It added a higher-lift cam, even larger valves, and tighter compression for 360 bhp with the same earth-moving 510 lbs/ft of torque as the regular 455. A 3.64:1 Posi-Traction axle was included with either the four-speed or automatic. This is the setup that put the GS 455 on the muscle dream team. *Motor Trend*'s Stage 1 turned a 13.38 at 105.5 mph, prompting the editors to crown it "the quickest American production car we had ever tested."

1970 BUICK HIGH-PERFORMANCE ENGINES

TYPE	CID	BORE×STROKE	BHP @ RPM	TORQUE @ RPM	FUEL SYSTEM	COMP. RATIO	AVAIL.
ohv V-8	350	3.80×3.85	315 @ 4800	410 @ 3200	1×4bbl.	10.25:1	1
ohv V-8	455	4.31×3.90	350 @ 4600	510 @ 2800	1×4bbl.	10.0:1	GS 455
ohv V-8	455	4.31×3.90	360 @ 4600	510 @ 2800	1×4bbl.	10.0:1	GS 455
ohv V-8	455	4.31×3.90	370 @ 4600	510 @ 2800	1×4bbl.	10.0:1	2

1. GS, LeSabre, Skylark, Sportwagon. 2. Wildcat, Estate Wagon, Riviera, Electra, LeSabre 455.

▲ Sheetmetal changes freshened Chevelle and the $445 SS package again came with a 396, but it was now the 350-bhp L-34 version. In January, a 350-bhp, 402-cid V-8 replaced it, but the "396" label stuck.

▲ Super Sports got a beefed suspension with a rear stabilizer bar. Seven-inch sport wheels with F70×14 white-letter tires were included, though the tires on this car are not of the period. Body stripes were a common option.

▼ Chevy's response to GM's new displacement rule was to stroke the 427 and create the SS 454 Chevelle. The LS-5 454 had 360 bhp, the LS-6 had 450 bhp and made for one of the quickest supercars ever.

▲ Squarer lines gave SS Chevelles the stance of a street tough. The Super Sport option was available on the coupe, convertible, and El Camino. *Road Test* ran a 350-bhp SS Chevelle with Turbo Hydra-Matic through the quarter in 15.27 seconds at 92.98 mph.

▲ Competition was tough, and Chevelle SS 396 production fell to 53,559. Chevy built 8773 SS 454s, split about evenly between the solid-lifter LS-6, a bargain at $263, and the more manageable LS-5. A limited-slip differential was a $42.15 option.

▲ A popular new option for '70 was the $147 domed hood with a vacuum-operated cowl-induction flap that opened under full throttle. Wide body stripes came with the cowl-induction option.

◄ *Road Test* said the SS package made a Chevelle "worthy of notice by any serious motorist [and] permits the available power to be utilized with safe handling and braking."

▲ With cowl induction, a soft ring sealed the gap between the hood dome and air cleaner. When the flap opened, outside air entered from the low-pressure area at the windshield's base.

▲ *Road Test* doubted cowl induction's utility, branding it a gimmick in normal driving. It said a Chevelle SS 396 without the cowl setup turned "essentially the same speeds" as one with it. Pictured is the base L-34 396. Still available was the 375-bhp L-78 396. It cost $656, or $840 with aluminum heads. Only 18 L-78s were installed.

◄ Super Sport Chevelles shared a revised dash with the new Monte Carlo. A close-ratio four-speed was standard; Turbo Hydra-Matic cost $222, or $290 with the LS-6. Strato-bucket seats added $121, a center console $54, tilt wheel $45, and power steering $105. Special instrumentation, including a tachometer, clock, ammeter, and temperature gauge, totaled $84.30. An AM/FM radio cost $134.

▲ LS-6 ragtop had a beastly beauty. Only the "Rockcrusher" four-speed or heavy-duty M40 Turbo Hydra-Matic could handle its power.

▲ "It has striking performance that you'd never suspect in traffic," said race driver Sam Posey after an LS-6 experience for *Car and Driver*.

▶ "The past is gone, the future may never see a car like this," *Hot Rod* proclaimed after its LS-6 ran a 13.4 at 108.7 mph. *Car Craft* claimed a 13.1 ET. *Car and Driver* said its automatic with 3.70:1 gears turned a 13.8 at 103.8. Compared to the 10.25:1-compression LS-5, which used a Quadrajet four-barrel, the LS-6 (right) had an 11.0:1 squeeze, an 800cfm Holley, forged steel connecting rods, and forged aluminum TRW pistons. Even with a road-ready weight of 4000 pounds, a Chevelle SS 454 LS-6 carried an astonishingly low 8.9 pounds per bhp.

▲ A coupe was now Camaro's only body style. All Camaros handled better this year, but Z-28s benefited further from the stiffer F-41 suspension and F60×15 tires. A Hurst-shifted Muncie four-speed again was standard, but Turbo Hydra-Matic joined as an option. A rear spoiler was included in the $573 Z-28 package price, which made for a $3412 Camaro. Underhood was Corvette's LT-1 350 with solid lifters, hot cam, big valves, extruded aluminum pistons, and a 780cfm Holley four-barrel.

▲ Camaro was redesigned as a 1970½ model. It also was the foundation for what many Chevy fans regard as the finest Z-28 of all. With its new 360-bhp, 350-cid V-8, a Z-28 with the standard four-speed and a 4.10:1 final drive turned a 14.2 ET at 100 mph for *Road & Track*.

◄▲ Camaro's $168 RS package added a unique nose and soft Endura grille surround. The car pictured is a Z-28 Hurst Sunshine Special, a prototype concept car with a sliding fabric sunroof. GM didn't bite, and just three were built.

◄ While the Z-28 had the LT-1 (left), SS Camaros could get a 300-bhp 350, or a 396 with 350 or 375 bhp. Chevy built 137,455 Camaros for the model year, of which 8733 were Z-28s.

▼ Nova's SS package continued with the 300-bhp 350 standard and the 396 (now a 402) a rare option. An automatic Nova SS 350 with stock 3.07:1 gears turned a 16.5 quarter-mile for *Car Life*.

▲ Pennsylvania Chevy dealer and bowtie hyper-power specialist Don Yenko had offered 425-bhp, 427-cid Rat motors in some '69 Novas. But prohibitive insurance rates forced him to dial back to this 360-bhp LT-1 350 for '70.

▲ Yenko named his hot Nova the Deuce LT-1 and offered it for 1970 only. Just 176 were built. All were two-door sport sedans beefed up with the F-41 suspension and Magnum 500 wheels. Interiors were black and had taxi cab-grade rubber floor mats and vinyl bench seats relieved only by silver Yenko stickers on the door panels.

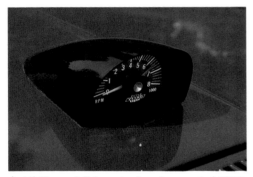

▲ All Deuce LT-1s got a hood-mounted 8000-rpm tach, but an option put water temperature, amp, and oil pressure gauges under the dash. These cars were delivered with a 12-bolt rear end and a 4.10:1 Positraction differential. Buyers chose between a stock four-speed Muncie or a Turbo Hydra-Matic modified with a Hurst floor-shift unit.

▲ Yenko was never shy about dressing up his mounts, and the Deuce's stripes were in keeping with that policy. Yenko called this Nova his "Mini Muscle" car, and compared to the 450-bhp Camaros and Chevelles he was still turning out, it was. But the Deuce certainly was no slouch and could be expected to turn ETs of around 14 seconds flat right out of the box. Interestingly, Yenko didn't do the engine installation himself. Instead, he was able to order LT-1-equipped Novas (with the 4.10:1 Positraction axle) directly from the factory by working them into a fleet order—and by working some valuable Chevy connections.

1970 CHEVROLET HIGH-PERFORMANCE ENGINES

TYPE	CID	BORE× STROKE	BHP @ RPM	TORQUE @ RPM	FUEL SYSTEM	COMP. RATIO	AVAIL.
ohv V-8	350	4.00×3.48	300 @ 4800	380 @ 3200	1×4bbl.	10.25:1	1
ohv V-8	350	4.00×3.48	360 @ 6000	380 @ 4800	1×4bbl.	11.0:1	2
ohv V-8	396	4.09×3.76	350 @ 5200	415 @ 3400	1×4bbl.	10.25:1	4
ohv V-8	400	4.12×3.75	330 @ 4800	415 @ 3200	1×4bbl.	10.25:1	3
ohv V-8	402	4.13×3.76	350 @ 5200	415 @ 3400	1×4bbl.	10.25:1	4
ohv V-8	402	4.13×3.76	375 @ 5600	415 @ 3600	1×4bbl.	11.0:1	4
ohv V-8	427	4.25×3.76	450 @ 6000	460 @ 4000	1×4bbl.	11.0:1	5
ohv V-8	454	4.25×4.00	345 @ 4400	500 @ 3000	1×4bbl.	10.25:1	full size
ohv V-8	454	4.25×4.00	360 @ 4400	500 @ 3200	1×4bbl.	10.25:1	3
ohv V-8	454	4.25×4.00	390 @ 4800	500 @ 3400	1×4bbl.	10.25:1	full size
ohv V-8	454	4.25×4.00	450 @ 6000	500 @ 3600	1×4bbl.	11.25:1	3

1. Camaro, Chevelle, Monte Carlo, Nova, full size.   2. Yenko Nova, Camaro Z-28.   3. Chevelle, Monte Carlo.
4. Camaro, Chevelle, Nova.   5. Yenko Camaro, Chevelle.

Hurst's plushest conversion was the $4200 '70 Chrysler 300-H. All 501 hardtops and two convertibles had a fiberglass hood with air intake.

Rear air foil was fiberglass, too. The 375-bhp 440 hooked to a TorqueFlite and 2.76:1 or 3.23:1 gears, for ETs of 16.8 at 87.3 mph.

Over-the-counter Dodge kits included the "Bee-Liever," (right), with high-rise manifold, carbs, cam, and headers, and the "Top Eliminator," with Six Pack manifold and carbs, hood, transistorized ignition, and electric fuel pump.

This promotional shot combines Dodge and Plymouth models. Clockwise from front is a Dodge Charger R/T; Dodge Challenger; Plymouth Duster 340; Plymouth GTX; and Plymouth Barracuda. Dodge had the "Scat Pack," Plymouth the "Rapid Transit System."

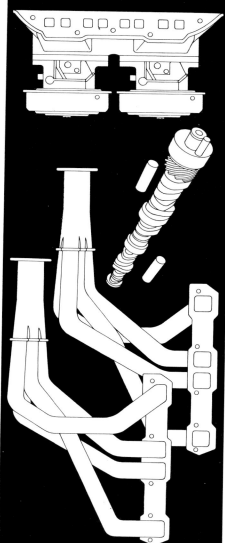

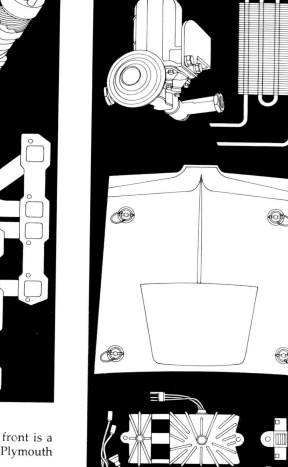

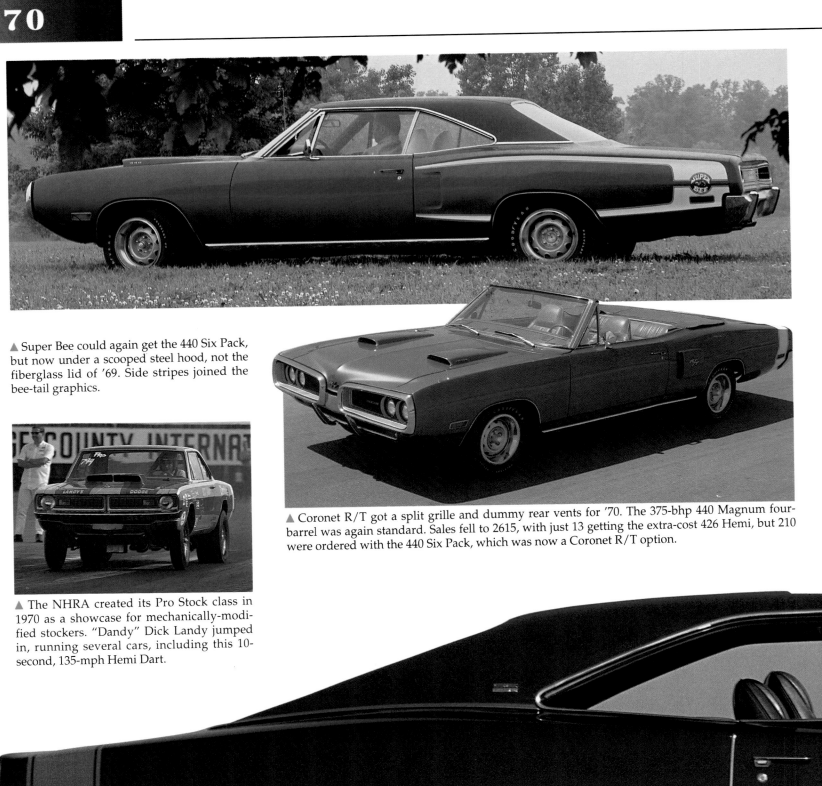

▲ Super Bee could again get the 440 Six Pack, but now under a scooped steel hood, not the fiberglass lid of '69. Side stripes joined the bee-tail graphics.

▲ The NHRA created its Pro Stock class in 1970 as a showcase for mechanically-modified stockers. "Dandy" Dick Landy jumped in, running several cars, including this 10-second, 135-mph Hemi Dart.

▲ Coronet R/T got a split grille and dummy rear vents for '70. The 375-bhp 440 Magnum four-barrel was again standard. Sales fell to 2615, with just 13 getting the extra-cost 426 Hemi, but 210 were ordered with the 440 Six Pack, which was now a Coronet R/T option.

▲ A new chrome loop grille and fake rear-facing door vents marked the '70 Charger R/T. It again got the 375-bhp 440 four-barrel as standard, but added to the optional Hemi an available 390-bhp, 440-cid Six Pack.

▲ This R/T has a Six Pack, but only Hemis got exterior ID. All had special torsion bars and shocks, extra-heavy rear springs, and a front sway bar. TorqueFlite was standard, Hurst-shifted four-speed optional.

▲ The Daytona was gone. Charger 500 returned, though without the aero grille or flush backlight. This black R/T is combined with the optional SE package, which included leather seat facings.

▲ The 426 Hemi added $648 to the Charger R/T's $3711 list price. Again rated at 425 bhp, it now had hydraulic lifters. It went into about 354 Chargers (R/Ts, 500s, and Daytonas) for 1969, but just 112 Charger R/Ts for '70, as some fans defected to the new Hemi pony cars.

▼ Charger R/T production fell by 50 percent for 1970, to 9509. Skyrocketing supercar insurance rates and increased competition were to blame.

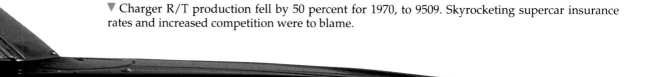

▲ Dodge finally got its pony car: the 1970 Challenger. It used the same unibody platform as Plymouth's new Barracuda, but the Dodge's wheelbase was two inches longer, at 110, to provide slightly more rear-seat room. It was sold in hardtop and convertible form, with the performance model wearing the familiar R/T label. This one's finished in Plum Crazy, one of Dodge's new High Impact hues.

▲ R/Ts came with open hood scoops that didn't feed directly to the engine. Standard was the 335-bhp, 383-cid Magnum. Optional was the 275-bhp 340; the 375-bhp Magnum 440; the 390-bhp 440 Six Pack (shown); and the mighty 425-bhp 426 Hemi. The 440 and Hemi came with a TorqueFlite; ordering the optional four-speed gained them a Hurst shifter and extra-heavy-duty Dana 60 axle with 9¾-inch ring gear. A woodgrain pistol-grip shifter came with the four-speeds. *Motor Trend*'s 383 turned a 15.7 at 90 mph. *Car Craft*'s 440 Six Pack ran a 13.62 at 104. Both were automatics with the standard 3.23:1 axle ratio.

1970 DODGE HIGH-PERFORMANCE ENGINES

TYPE	CID	BORE × STROKE	BHP @ RPM	TORQUE @ RPM	FUEL SYSTEM	COMP. RATIO	AVAIL.
ohv V-8	340	4.04 × 3.31	275 @ 5000	340 @ 3200	1 × 4bbl.	10.5:1	1
ohv V-8	383	4.25 × 3.75	330 @ 5000	425 @ 3200	1 × 4bbl.	9.5:1	2
ohv V-8	383	4.25 × 3.75	335 @ 5200	425 @ 3400	1 × 4bbl.	9.5:1	3
ohv V-8	426*	4.25 × 3.75	425 @ 5000	490 @ 4000	2 × 4bbl.	10.2:1	4
ohv V-8	440	4.32 × 3.75	350 @ 4400	480 @ 2800	1 × 4bbl.	9.7:1	full size
ohv V-8	440	4.32 × 3.75	375 @ 4600	480 @ 3200	1 × 4bbl.	9.7:1	5
ohv V-8	440	4.32 × 3.75	390 @ 4700	490 @ 3200	3 × 2bbl.	10.5:1	4

* Hemi.

1. Dart Swinger 340, Challenger. 2. Coronet, Challenger, full size. 3. Coronet, Coronet Super Bee, Charger, Challenger, Challenger R/T, full size. 4. Charger R/T, Coronet Super Bee and R/T, Challenger R/T. 5. Coronet R/T, Challenger R/T, full size.

▲ Trans Am-series rules required 2500 street versions of a racer. Dodge met that with 2539 Challenger T/As for '70. This one is Panther Pink.

▲ T/As had E60×15 front tires and G60×15 rears. The tail was raised two inches to clear the larger back rubber and standard side-exit exhausts. Front discs, lift-off fiberglass hood with working scoop, and ducktail spoiler were standard. This shade of green was "Sublime."

◄ Real race T/As used a 305-cid four-barrel of 440 bhp, but street T/As had a 340 toughened internally and capped with an Edelbrock aluminum manifold and three Holley two-barrels (shown). It was rated at 290 bhp, but likely made 350. Tranny choices were a four-speed or TorqueFlite. T/As handled well and turned low-14s at 99 mph.

▲ Another of Dick Landy's Pro Stock rides was this outstanding Hemi Challenger. It usually ran high-nines at 140 mph, but its 10.38 at 130.43 was good enough to win the Pro Stock title at the '70 Summernationals. Rules mandated the stock wheelbase and body panels, but allowed some powertrain alterations.

▲ The 426 Hemi and associated hardware added $1227 to the R/T's $3226 base. "In return," said *Road Test*, "you get power that can rattle dishes in the kitchen when you start it up in the driveway." *Car and Driver*'s TorqueFlite with 3.23:1 gears turned a 14.1 at 103.2 and got 7 mpg.

▲ Challenger's ram-air setup cost $97 and mounted to the air cleaner, where it vibrated with the engine—hence the "shaker" name. Hemis went into 287 Challenger R/T hardtops, nine convertibles, and 60 R/T SE hardtops.

▲ With 58.9 percent of its 3890-pound curb weight on the front tires, a Hemi R/T SE didn't corner very well; neither did one with the 440. But road-race types could always order the well-balanced 340. Despite intense competition, a respectable 83,000 Challengers sold for 1970, nearly 20,000 of them in hot R/T guise.

▲ "Special Edition" package added a vinyl roof with smaller formal backlight, plus leather seat facings, an overhead console, and other extras for $232 over a base R/T hardtop.

▲ Boss 302 had new stripes for its second and final year. Its solid-lifter 302 got smaller valves for better driveability, but retained the 290-bhp underrating. Price was $3720. Of 7103 Boss 302s built, 6319 were '70s.

▲ Formerly standard, the "shaker" hood was now a Boss 302 option. Louvers added $65, tail spoiler, $20. *Car and Driver*'s, with a limited slip ($43) and 3.91:1 ($13), ran a 14.9 at 93.4. "Grabber" colors were new.

▲ As did all '70 Mustangs, the Boss 429 got a new twin-lamp face, but it was mechanically unchanged. Its 429-cid engine was a high-rev NASCAR mill, and in stock form, was no quicker than a 428 Cobra Jet on the street.

▲ Rated at 375 bhp, the 429 boasted semi-hemi heads, super-tough internals, and a 735cfm Holly on a high-rise aluminum manifold.

▲ Even with the front suspension altered to fit the big 429, the only room for the battery was in the trunk. It helped weight balance a little.

▲ Ford built just 858 Boss 429s for '69 and 489 for '70, but its legend—and unmet promise— live on. It delivered for $4932 in '70.

▲ The $457 428 CJ returned as Mach 1's big gun. A fake hood scoop was standard, but the $522 Ram-Air version got this shaker.

▲ Among rarest of 1970 Mach 1s are the 100 Twister Specials built for sale by Kansas City dealers.

▲ Mach 1's four-barrel 351 was the new 300-bhp "Cleveland" motor. About half of the Twisters got a fortified 428 called the Super Cobra Jet.

▲ Twisters were Grabber Orange with Traction-Lok and shaker hood. As on all SportsRoofs, spoilers and slats were optional. New rear stabilizer bar aided Mach 1 handling, softer springs improved the ride.

▲ Torino was redesigned on an inch-longer wheelbase (now 117). Its handsome new shape was another venue for the hallowed Cobra name.

▲ New for Ford intermediates was the 429-cid V-8. It replaced the 428 and Boss 429 and came in base, Cobra Jet, and Super Cobra Jet form.

▶ This is the 429 SCJ, which had solid lifters, forged aluminum pistons, and a 780cfm Holley four-barrel. It was variously listed at 370 or 375 bhp, but could be ordered with or without the Ram Air shaker scoop.

▲ The Torino GT came with a 302-cid V-8, fake hood scoop, and steel wheels. Hidden headlamps and Laser side stripe were options. Ford built 56,819 GT SportsRoofs. The GT convertible was Torino's only ragtop, and 3939 were produced. The 390-cid V-8 died, but the better 351-cid Cleveland four-barrel filled its role well.

▲ A 429 CJ Torino Cobra was a comfortable everyday supercar capable of mid-14s at near 100 mph. Black-out hood and grille were standard on Cobra. Shaker scoop was available only with 429 or 351 Cleveland.

▲ Torino Cobra started at $3270 with the 360-bhp 429, competition suspension, ultra-high-rate springs, extra-heavy stabilizer bar, staggered rear shocks, and F70×14 tires. Magnum 500 wheels cost $155.

▼ With an elongated front clip on a Torino SportsRoof body, the King Cobra was to succeed the Talladega as Ford's superspeedway tool. Its aerodynamics were disappointing, however, and a change in Ford policy left little money to develop it. Only a handful were built. Regular '70 SportsRoofs did battle on NASCAR's short tracks, while '69 Talladegas and Spoiler IIs ran the big ovals, but neither was enough to beat the Mopars.

▶ Like the SCJ, the 429 CJ (shown) had 11.3:1 compression, but it used hydraulic lifters, a 700cfm Rochester four-barrel, and made 370 bhp with Ram Air. The base 429 had 360-bhp and a 600cfm Ford quad. The SCJ was combined with a Drag Pack that was otherwise optional. It included a 3.91:1 Traction-Lok or a 4.30:1 Detroit Locker axle.

1970 FORD HIGH-PERFORMANCE ENGINES

TYPE	CID	BORE× STROKE	BHP @ RPM	TORQUE @ RPM	FUEL SYSTEM	COMP. RATIO	AVAIL.
ohv V-8	302	4.00×3.00	290 @ 5800	290 @ 4300	1×4bbl.	10.5:1	Mustang
ohv V-8	351	4.00×3.50	300 @ 5400	380 @ 3400	1×4bbl.	11.0:1	1
ohv V-8	390	4.05×3.78	320 @ 4600	427 @ 3200	1×4bbl.	10.5:1	1
ohv V-8	428	4.13×3.98	335 @ 5200	440 @ 3400	1×4bbl.	10.6:1	Mustang
ohv V-8	429	4.36×3.59	360 @ 4600	480 @ 2800	1×4bbl.	10.5:1	2
ohv V-8	429	4.36×3.59	370 @ 5400	450 @ 3400	1×4bbl.	11.3:1	Fairlane
ohv V-8	429	4.36×3.59	375 @ 5200	450 @ 3400	1×4bbl.	11.3:1	Fairlane
ohv V-8*	429	4.36×3.59	375 @ 5200	450 @ 3800	1×4bbl.	10.5:1	Mustang

* BOSS.
1. Fairlane, Torino, Mustang.   2. Fairlane, Thunderbird, full size.

▲ This Torino Cobra has the standard quick-ratio Hurst-shifted four-speed. Its bucket seats cost $133 extra, and front-disc brakes were $65 options. To the left of the steering column is the unusual, rectangular-shaped 8000 rpm tachometer.

▲ The 1970 Shelby Mustangs were actually leftover '69 models with Boss 302-type chin spoilers, hood stripes, and 1970 serial numbers.

▲ The final year's tally: 286 GT-500s; 350 GT-350s. Ford let the Shelbys wither as it concentrated on its own Boss 302 and big-block Mustangs.

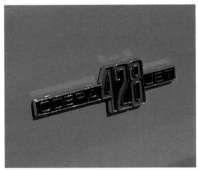

▲ Carroll Shelby had ceased direct involvement in the Cobra ponies.

▲ The '70 GT-500 shared Mustang's 335-bhp 428 CJ-R, but GT-350 stayed with the 351 Windsor, not Mach 1's 351 Cleveland.

▲ Costly, with no big performance edge, the Shelby's focus blurred.

▲ Performance versions of Mercury's redesigned Montego started with the base Cyclone, which had the 360-bhp 429 and cost $3238.

▲ Cyclone options included the 370-bhp 429 CJ or the 375-bhp SCJ. Air cleaner flap and rubber ring show the available Ram Air setup.

▲ Top Cyclone was the Spoiler. It came standard with the 429 CJ Ram Air. *Road Test*'s automatic with 3.50:1 Traction-Lok ran a 14.61 at 99.22.

▲ Positioned between Cyclone and Spoiler was the new Cyclone GT. Hidden headlamps and a 250-bhp, 351 two-barrel were standard.

▲ Spoiler's $3530 price included a four-speed with Hurst T-handle, 3.50:1 Traction-Lok, competition handling package, and G70×14 tires. The SCJ required a Drag Pack with 3.90:1 or 4.30:1 axle.

▲ Spoiler came with a functional hood scoop and front air dam. The optional Select-Shift automatic upshifted at 5600 rpm during full-throttle runs.

▲ All Spoilers got...a spoiler. Inside were high-back buckets, 140-mph speedo, 8000-rpm tach, and gauges for oil pressure, coolant temp, and amps.

▲ Cyclone's 429 had an "exhaust note which is a solid pleasant roar reminiscent of a NASCAR stocker and highly pleasing...." said *Road Test*.

▲ This prototype has a "GT" badge that was never on the Cyclone GT. Similarly, Mercury and Ford said the Boss 429 would be offered in their mid-size '70s. Few, if any, were installed. This is a 429 SCJ.

▲ Tape stripes and one of six "Grabber" colors (blue, orange, yellow, green, coral, and platinum) could dress up a Spoiler or other Cyclone.

▲ Cougar got a new snout. Eliminator (shown) was back as the performance model with the Boss 302 engine, the 351 Cleveland, or the 428 CJ. The 390 and 351 Windsor were gone. Two racing Eliminators got Boss 429s.

243

▲ Eliminator's front air dam may have worked, but its rear spoiler was purely decorative. Hood scoop was functional with the 428 CJ only.

▲ Even with the Super Drag Pack's 4.30:1 Detroit Locker, an Eliminator Boss 302's low ET was 15.0 seconds. The 351 was the best overall choice: lighter than the 428, torquier than the 302.

1970 MERCURY HIGH-PERFORMANCE ENGINES						
TYPE	CID	BORE × STROKE	BHP @ RPM	TORQUE @ RPM	FUEL SYSTEM	COMP. RATIO	AVAIL.
ohv V-8	302	4.00 × 3.00	290 @ 5800	290 @ 4300	1 × 4bbl.	10.5:1	1
ohv V-8	351	4.00 × 3.50	300 @ 5400	380 @ 3400	1 × 4bbl.	11.0:1	2
ohv V-8	428	4.13 × 3.98	335 @ 5200	440 @ 3400	1 × 4bbl.	10.6:1	1
ohv V-8	429	4.36 × 3.59	360 @ 4600	480 @ 2800	1 × 4bbl.	10.5:1	3
ohv V-8	429	4.36 × 3.59	370 @ 5400	450 @ 3400	1 × 4bbl.	11.3:1	Cyclone
ohv V-8*	429	4.36 × 3.59	375 @ 5200	450 @ 3400	1 × 4bbl.	10.3:1	1
ohv V-8	429	4.36 × 3.59	375 @ 5600	450 @ 3400	1 × 4bbl.	10.5:1	Cyclone

* BOSS.
1. Cougar Eliminator. 2. Cougar, Montego, Cyclone. 3. Montego, Cyclone, full size.

▲ W-30s got fiberglass hood with functional scoops; rear deck spoiler could be deleted.

▲ Chrome bars replaced the black-out grille for '70. Hardtop 4-4-2s started at $3376.

▲ Escape machines, indeed. Like this racer, showroom 4-4-2s took their lead from the Hurst/Olds cars and gained a 455-cid V-8 as standard for '70. It was rated at 365 bhp, or 370 with the W-30 option. With the 365-bhp motor, automatic, and 3.08:1 gears, *Motor Trend* turned a 14.8 at 95 mph. *Hot Rod* got serious. Its W-30 had a Hurst Dual-Gate Turbo Hydra-Matic 400 with a high-performance converter, and a 3.91:1 limited slip. Box stock, it ran a 14.10 at 100.5. Removing the air filter element and adding Autolite A42 plugs got it down to 13.98 at 100.7.

▲ Taillamps were fresh, also. All 4-4-2s got stabilizer bars and Polyglas G70 × 14s.

W-30s had air-induction, long-duration cam, aluminum intake manifold, and low-restriction air cleaner. "The 455 W-30 has an almost unholy torque capability," *Hot Rod* said, so launches required "deft throttle work."

▲ Red plastic inner fenders shaved a few pounds from the big-block W-30's nose.

▲ Cutlass Supreme shared 4-4-2's interior, though 4-4-2s got a four-spoke steering wheel. Strato bucket seats, optional on Cutlass, were standard on 4-4-2. Note the tach to the right of the steering column. The factory's was combined with a clock; this is an easier-to-read aftermarket item.

1970 OLDSMOBILE HIGH-PERFORMANCE ENGINES

TYPE	CID	BORE × STROKE	BHP @ RPM	TORQUE @ RPM	FUEL SYSTEM	COMP. RATIO	AVAIL.
ohv V-8	350	4.06 × 3.38	310 @ 4800	390 @ 3200	1×4bbl.	10.3:1	1
ohv V-8	350	4.06 × 3.38	325 @ 5400	360 @ 3600	1×4bbl.	10.5:1	Cutlass
ohv V-8	455	4.13 × 4.25	365 @ 5000	500 @ 3200	1×4bbl.	10.5:1	2
ohv V-8	455	4.13 × 4.25	370 @ 5200	500 @ 3600	1×4bbl.	10.5:1	4-4-2
ohv V-8	455	4.13 × 4.25	375 @ 4600	510 @ 3000	1×4bbl.	10.3:1	Toronado
ohv V-8	455	4.13 × 4.25	390 @ 5000	500 @ 3200	1×4bbl.	10.3:1	full size
ohv V-8	455	4.13 × 4.25	400 @ 5100	500 @ 5100	1×4bbl.	10.3:1	Toronado

1. Cutlass, Vista Cruiser. 2. 4-4-2, Vista Cruiser, full size.

▲ A W-30 4-4-2 convertible paced the Indy 500, and Olds assembled 626 Pace Car Replicas; 358 of them were Cutlass ragtops. This Cutlass replica has the 350-cid V-8 with the 325-bhp W-31 package. The W-31 was also offered in the Rallye 350, a budget-muscle version of the Cutlass pillared coupe. Olds built just 3547 Rallye 350s. All were bright yellow with black and orange stripes and turned ETs in the high-14s. No Hurst/Olds was offered for 1970.

▲ "GTX & Road Runner: No brag. Just fact." That was the tag line for this ad shot of Plymouth's reskinned muscle intermediates. They were part of the division's new "Rapid Transit System" approach to performance.

▲ A new vacuum-operated "Air Grabber" scoop slowly rose at the push of a dash switch to reveal a snarling-shark graphic. It was optional on 440 cars, standard with the Hemi. The 426 went into 152 Road Runners and 72 GTXs for '70. Also, the 440+6 was now offered on GTX, and 678 were ordered.

▲ Road Runner (shown) and its GTX cousin were restyled for '70. With the base 335-bhp 383 V-8, the Road Runner started at just $2896, $49 less than in '69—though a three-speed manual had replaced the four-speed as standard for '70. Also, the optional 426 Hemi got hydraulic lifters for easier maintenance and cleaner emissions.

▲ The biggest "Rapid Transit" member was the $3898 Sport Fury GT. It came with the 440 four-barrel or the 440 tri-carb, the latter good for 16-second quarter-miles.

▼ Echoes of the late Dodge Daytona: Plymouth issued a limited-edition, long-snout Road Runner Superbird to meet NASCAR homologation rules. The 25-inch-tall air foil kept NASCAR racers on track at 190 mph.

◄ Plymouth built 1920 Superbirds for this, their lone model year. All NASCAR racers had Hemis; 135 of the street versions got the 425-bhp 426; 716 the 440+6 (shown); and the rest used the 375-bhp 440 four-barrel. All could have TorqueFlite or a four-speed. *Car and Driver*'s Hemi automatic with 3.23:1 gears turned a 13.5 at 105 mph. *Road Test*'s 375-bhp 440 automatic with a Sure-Grip 3.55:1 ran a 14.26 at 103.7.

► All Superbirds had a black vinyl top that hid scars inflicted during creation of the flush rear window. Fender scoops were decorative on street cars. Dodge Coronet fenders helped mate the aero nose to the body. Curb weight was 3785 pounds, 310 more than a Road Runner hardtop.

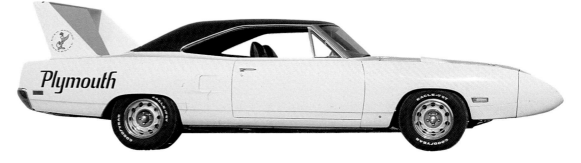

▲ Superbird borrowed Road Runner's "beep-beep" horn, which mimicked the cartoon bird's call. "It's cute," remarked *Road Test*, "but absolutely lacks the authority the car deserves."

▲ Road Runners were transformed into Superbirds by Creative Industries, the aftermarket firm that also built the Dodge Charger 500 and Daytona. These weren't cars for those who shunned attention.

▲ Fiberglass hidden-headlamp pods were set into the Superbird's steel beak. The rear wing was aluminum. Heavy-duty suspension gave the nose-heavy car adequate handling, but the ride was harsh.

▲ Power front discs were included in Superbird's $4298 base price, and extra-cost G60×15 tires could replace the usual F70×14s. Buyers were cool to these cars, and many languished on dealers' lots. Now they're coveted.

▲ In its element: Richard Petty's Superbird on the NASCAR banking. Petty had defected to Ford for '69, but Plymouth's new 'bird won him back to the Mopar flock for '70.

▲ The King himself poses with his restored '70 Superbird at the Petty museum in North Carolina. Petty won 18 NASCAR races in '70, but Bobby Isaac, running a Charger Daytona, took the drivers' championship.

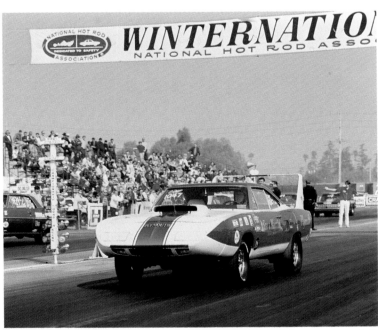

▲ NASCAR would outlaw both the Ford and Chrysler aero specials after the '70 season. But Superbirds still ran at the drags, where their wings were of less value. Here's the Sox & Martin car at the '71 NHRA Winternationals.

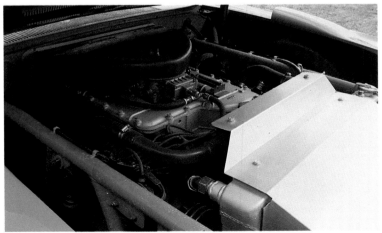

▲ Ducted and tweaked, Petty's NASCAR Hemi pushed his Superbird to almost 200 mph. Pete Hamilton won the '70 Daytona 500 in a Petty-prepped 'bird, and Mopar took 38 NASCAR wins (21 by Superbirds) to FoMoCo's 10 in 1970.

▲ The Barracuda name was on a redesigned line of pony car hardtops and convertibles for '70. The performance versions were tagged 'Cuda.

▲ They shared a platform, but Barracuda's 108-inch wheelbase was two inches shorter than Challenger's, so it had even less rear leg room.

◄ Only 666 'Cudas had Hemis for 1970, and just 14 went into convertibles. *Motor Trend*'s 4.10:1 automatic Hemicuda coupe turned a 13.7 ET at 101.2 mph. The Rapid Transit System approach matched axle ratios, transmissions, and other gear to the likely use of the car. For example, the factory set suspensions on Hemis and 440s to withstand brutal acceleration, while the 340s and 383s got handling-oriented spring rates.

▲ The 440+6 cost $621 less than a Hemi. *Motor Trend*'s 3.54:1 four-speed stayed with a Hemi to 60 mph, but its 14.04 ET at 100 mph was slower.

▲ Just 635 of the 19,515 'Cudas built for '70 were ragtops. A 383 was standard; the optional 340 was as quick, and gave 'Cuda better balance.

1970 PLYMOUTH HIGH-PERFORMANCE ENGINES

TYPE	CID	BORE× STROKE	BHP @ RPM	TORQUE @ RPM	FUEL SYSTEM	COMP. RATIO	AVAIL.
ohv V-8	340	4.04× 3.31	275 @ 5000	340 @ 3200	1×4bbl.	10.5:1	1
ohv V-8	383	4.25× 3.75	330 @ 5000	425 @ 3200	1×4bbl.	9.5:1	2
ohv V-8	383	4.25× 3.75	335 @ 5200	425 @ 3400	1×4bbl.	9.5:1	3
ohv V-8	426*	4.25× 3.75	425 @ 5000	490 @ 4000	2×4bbl.	10.2:1	4
ohv V-8	440	4.32× 3.75	350 @ 4400	480 @ 2800	1×4bbl.	9.7:1	full size
ohv V-8	440	4.32× 3.75	375 @ 4600	480 @ 3200	1×4bbl.	9.7:1	5
ohv V-8	440	4.32× 3.75	390 @ 4700	490 @ 3200	3×2bbl.	10.5:1	4

* Hemi.
1. Duster 340, 'Cuda. 2. Satellite, Barracuda, full size. 3. Satellite, Road Runner, Barracuda, 'Cuda. 4. Road Runner, GTX, 'Cuda. 5. Road Runner, GTX, 'Cuda, full size.

▲ 'Cuda's functional shaker scoop mounted to the air cleaner though a hole in the hood and quivered with the engine. It was standard with the Hemi, but a $97 option for other 'Cuda mills.

▶ Ronnie Sox (left) and Buddy Martin with the Super Stock Hemicuda that took them to their most successful season. The team won 17 major drag events in '70; Sox was wheelman in 13 of them; Herb McCandless handled the rest. Their Hemi had 13.5:1 compression, Holley dual quads, an experimental camshaft, and transistorized ignition. Valves were stock size: 2.25-inch intake, 1.94-inch exhaust. The car weighed 2980 pounds, ready to rock.

▲ Based on Plymouth's new compact fastback, the Duster 340 was a budget-muscle bull's-eye. Its $2547 base price included the tough 275-bhp 340 four-barrel and a three-speed stick. *Car and Driver's* had the $188 four-speed, $42 Sure-Grip with 3.91:1 gears, and weighed 3368 pounds. It ran a very respectable 14.39 at 97.2 mph, despite a balky shifter.

▲ A Pro Stock Barracuda runs the Winternationals. The hood is borrowed from the Challenger T/A.

▲ Elastomeric bumpers and racing mirrors added $94. TorqueFlite was standard with 440 or Hemi; four-speed with Hurst Pistol-Grip was extra.

▲ This illustration shows Plymouth's wild paint palette for '70. Extra-cost High Impact hues were In-Violet, Limelight, Vitamin C Orange, Tor-Red, Lemon Twist, and Moulin Rouge. Far out.

▲ Cousin to Dodge's Challenger T/A was the AAR 'Cuda. Both were built only for 1970 to qualify race versions for the Trans Am series.

▲ Street handling was emphasized, but *Car and Driver's* AAR 'Cuda, with the standard four-speed and 3.55:1, still ran a quick 14.3 at 99.5.

▲ AAR was raked to clear the big G60×15 rear tires and side-exit exhaust. Front tires were E60×15s. Ducktail spoiler and a fiberglass hood with working scoop were standard. TorqueFlite was optional.

▲ Named for Dan Gurney's All-American Racers team, the AAR started at $3966, some $800 above a regular 'Cuda coupe. Just 2724 AAR 'Cudas were built.

◄ Race AARs had a 340-cid V-8 destroked to 305 cid and a single four-barrel. Street AARs used the 340, but with three Holley two-barrels, Hemi-grade valve springs, and 290 bhp. It had heavier main webbing and a stronger head casting than regular 340s.

▼ Pontiac GTO wore a new Endura nose for '70, but the big news was behind it. A 455-cid V-8 was available and had 360 bhp (or 370 when hooked to the standard three-speed manual). It joined the carried-over 400 cid, which made 350 bhp in standard tune, 366 with Ram Air III, and 370 with Ram Air IV.

▲ The Judge gained the Ram Air III 400 as standard, with Ram Air IV optional. It could get the 455 V-8 late in the model year. The Judge's air foil was revised, and the heavy-duty suspension was now a $4.21 option.

1970 PONTIAC HIGH-PERFORMANCE ENGINES

TYPE	CID	BORE× STROKE	BHP @ RPM	TORQUE @ RPM	FUEL SYSTEM	COMP. RATIO	AVAIL.
ohv V-8	400	4.12×3.75	330 @ 4800	445 @ 2900	1×4bbl.	10.0:1	1
ohv V-8	400	4.12×3.75	330 @ 4800	430 @ 3000	1×4bbl.	10.25:1	2
ohv V-8	400	4.12×3.75	345 @ 5000	430 @ 3400	1×4bbl.	10.5:1	3
ohv V-8	400	4.12×3.75	350 @ 5000	445 @ 3000	1×4bbl.	10.3:1	4
ohv V-8	400*	4.12×3.75	366 @ 5100	445 @ 3600	1×4bbl.	10.5:1	GTO
ohv V-8	400**	4.12×3.75	370 @ 5500	445 @ 3900	1×4bbl.	10.5:1	5
ohv V-8	455	4.15×4.21	360 @ 4300	500 @ 2700	1×4bbl.	10.0:1	full size
ohv V-8	455	4.15×4.21	360 @ 4600	500 @ 3100	1×4bbl.	10.25:1	GTO
ohv V-8	455	4.15×4.21	370 @ 4600	500 @ 3100	1×4bbl.	10.25:1	6

* Ram Air. ** Ram Air IV.
1. Tempest, LeMans, Firebird, full size. 2. Firebird Formula 400. 3. Trans Am, Formula 400.
4. GTO, Grand Prix, Firebird, Trans Am. 5. GTO, Trans Am, Formula 400. 6. Grand Prix, Catalina, full size.

◄ Car and Driver called it "a hard muscled... commando of a car." Trans Am was now a full-fledged model and shared the new Firebird's Euro-styling and Endura nose, but added spoilers and air dams. The $4305 base price included a Ram Air 400 rated at 345 bhp; the optional Ram Air IV 400 had 370. The shaker scoop mated to the motor and Pontiac said it drew in cool air from the windshield base. Fender outlets vented the engine bay. Even with its 3782-pound curb weight split 57/43, handling was sharp. With the base engine, standard Hurst-shifted four-speed, and optional 3.90:1 limited slip, Sports Car Graphic turned a 14.6 at 99.5 mph. Turbo Hydra-Matic was optional.

◄ The 455s made their power at lower rpm than the 400s, so they were easier to drive on the street. But an expert driver could wring more from a Ram Air 400. For example, *Car Life*'s base 455 with automatic, 3.55:1 gears, and the $84 Ram Air option turned a 14.76 at 95.9. Its Ram Air III 400 had a four-speed, 3.90:1 axle, and a best ET of 14.6 at 99.5.

▼ The Judge adopted the Goat's fresh metal, plus new multi-hued stripes. The Judge package added $337 to the $3267 price of a base GTO coupe or $3492 GTO convertible. Judge production fell to 3797, of which 168 were ragtops. These cars again were no quicker than similarly equipped GTOs.

▲ Orbit Orange was an exclusive Judge color. "The Judge," observed *Road Test*, "is not for people who are shy about being looked at."

▲ Judge again shared the GTO's interior, except for badging. Buckets were standard; Trans Am steering wheel was a new option. A tach on hood or dash was available. Standard was a three-speed manual, optional was a Hurst-shifted close-ratio four-speed—both with Hurst T-handle shifter. Turbo Hydra-Matic also was an option.

▲ Foam gasket mated Ram Air engines to the hood scoops; underdash knob could cut the air flow. Air conditioning was unavailable with the Ram Air IV engine.

253

1971

The beginning of the end for the age of muscle ... emissions regulations, high insurance costs, changing social climate take their toll ● High-compression engines fade... all GM cars and some Mopars run on regular fuel...Ford not so quick to surrender ● Net horsepower ratings reflect power of engines as installed in cars ● Baby muscle cars, like AMC Hornet SC/360 and Dodge Demon 340 proliferate ● Chevelle's 402-cid V-8 loses "396" designation, drops to 300 bhp; 454 sinks to 365 bhp ● Hemis and 440 Six Packs still available in Dodge and Plymouth pony cars and intermediates, but very rare ● Bloated new Mustang bows...Boss 351 the last of the Boss line... Ford/Mercury 429 still available with Ram Air for 370 bhp ● At NHRA Nationals, Top Fuel ET falls to 6.21; Funny Cars run 6.64; Ronnie Sox captures Pro Stock with a 9.58 in Hemi Cuda ● King Richard Petty takes 21 NASCAR wins for Plymouth, scores his third national championship ● NASCAR nixes Ford Talladega, winged Dodge/ Plymouths, and Mercury Cyclone Spoiler II

▲ Full-bore muscle machines were under attack on many fronts, so Detroit turned to less-obvious performance cars. A 304-cid V-8 had been offered in the 1970 Hornet compact, but it was the underrated '71 Hornet SC/360 that was AMC's real boy racer.

▲ The SC/360's 360-cid V-8 made 245 bhp with a two-barrel. A $199 "Go" package added a Ram-Air four-barrel for 285 bhp. A three-speed or Hurst-shifted four-speed, or an automatic, were offered. SC/360s turned modest 14.9s at 95.3 in the quarter, but handled well.

▲ Starting at just $2663, this was affordable sportiness. Still, of nearly 75,000 Hornets sold for '71, just 667 were SC/360s. Body stripes were standard; dual exhausts, tachometer, handling package, and white-letter tires were optional.

▲ The second-generation AMX was no longer a two-seater or a distinct model. It was now an option package for the Javelin, itself bigger for '71. A new available 401-cid four-barrel had 330 bhp and pulled the heavier AMX to mid-14 quarters at around 93 mph.

▲ The Javelin AMX started at $3432 and weighed 3244 pounds, 100 pounds more than its two-seat predecessor. Front and rear spoilers were standard. Optional were a reverse-flow cowl induction setup and a "Go" pack with power front discs and E60×15 tires.

▲ Production versions of the subcompact Gremlin could have a 150-bhp six-cylinder, at most. With a modified big-block V-8, however, the Gremlin was a decidedly different creature. This full-race variant was AMC's first foray into pro-stock dragging. Painted in the distinctive AMC livery of the day, it was driven by Wally Booth of Amarillo, Texas. He turned consistent 9.40s at 140 mph. Note the narrowed rear axle needed to fit the fat slicks within the stock fender lines, and the castors needed to keep the wheelies in check.

▲ AMC built 2054 AMXs for '71—just seven percent of Javelin production—and only 745 were equipped with the 401 V-8. The nation was rapidly switching over to low-octane, low-lead gas as 1971 unfolded, and the 401's tepid 9.5:1 compression ratio was a sign of the times.

1971 AMC HIGH-PERFORMANCE ENGINES

TYPE	CID	BORE×STROKE	BHP @ RPM	TORQUE @ RPM	FUEL SYSTEM	COMP. RATIO	AVAIL.
ohv V-8	360	4.08×3.44	245 @ 4400	365 @ 2600	1×2bbl.	8.5:1	1
ohv V-8	360	4.08×3.44	285 @ 4800	390 @ 3200	1×4bbl.	8.5:1	1
ohv V-8	401	4.17×3.68	330 @ 5000	430 @ 3400	1×4bbl.	10.2:1*	2

* Early 1971, 9.5:1 late 1971.
1. Hornet, Matador, Ambassador, Javelin. 2. Matador, Ambassador, Javelin, AMX.

▲ As with most muscle cars that survived to see 1971, the Buick GS seemed a little defused. Stricter exhaust-emissions standards and the movement toward low-lead regular-gas were strangling engine outputs. Plus, soaring insurance rates were depressing the demand for performance models.

▼ GS 455 buyers got either the four-speed manual or the THM 400 Turbo Hydra-Matic. The 3.61:1 axle ratio was dropped and the 3.42:1 took over as the top gear. GS models still got functional hood scoops, dual exhaust, heavy-duty suspension, and G60×15 bias-belted tires, though.

▲ GS sales fell more than 50 percent for '71, to 9170. This Bittersweet Mist GS 455 is one of just 902 GS ragtops built that year.

▲ The Stage 1 package was ordered on only 801 GS coupes and 81 convertibles for '71.

▲ Compression, 10.0:1 or more in 1971, was now 8.5:1 for all GS mills. The GS350's 350-cid four-barrel dropped from 315 bhp to 260; the regular 455 (shown) fell from 350 bhp to 315; and the 455 Stage 1 slipped from 360 bhp to 345. *Motor Trend*'s Stage 1 turned a 14.7 ET at 92.5 mph, down 1.3 seconds and 12.5 mph from '70. Still, with more than 450 lbs/ft of torque, the 455s were plenty strong enough to avoid embarrassment.

▲ The Turbo Hydra-Matic's shift points dropped several hundred rpm, to 5000, to keep the retuned V-8 in its best range.

1971 BUICK HIGH-PERFORMANCE ENGINES

TYPE	CID	BORE× STROKE	BHP @ RPM	TORQUE @ RPM	FUEL SYSTEM	COMP. RATIO	AVAIL.
ohv V-8	350	3.80×3.85	260 @ 4600	360 @ 2300	1×4bbl.	8.5:1	Skylark GS, full size
ohv V-8	455	4.31×3.90	315 @ 4400	450 @ 2800	1×4bbl.	8.5:1	1
ohv V-8	455	4.31×3.90	330 @ 4600	455 @ 2800	1×4bbl.	8.5:1	Riviera GS, full size
ohv V-8	455	4.31×3.90	345 @ 5000	460 @ 3000	1×4bbl.	8.5:1	Skylark GS

1. Skylark GS, Riviera, full size.

▲ The Pro-Stock class was NHRA's way of dealing with the trend toward wildly deviant factory race machines by bringing the cars back to recognizable form and still rewarding serious professional effort.

This is Butch Leal's 427-cid Pro-Stock Camaro. It ran in the 9.90s, but was never as competitive as Leal's Plymouths.

▲ Pro Stock allowed engine cross-breeding, so Rich Mirarcki and Bill Blanding put a 327-cid Chevy small-block in a Vega and ran 9.5s at 140.

▲ The 425-bhp 454 LS-6 Chevelle was still available, and *Motor Trend* smoked one to a 14.7 at 89.5. About 19,000 of the estimated 80,000 '71 SS Chevelles built had a 454.

▲ In 1970, Bill "Grumpy" Jenkins was Pro Stock's first top eliminator. He was back for '71 with a 427 Camaro that turned 9.7s at 138 mph.

▲ This is Ray Allen's tough automatic-transmission SS Chevelle ragtop defending its 1970 SS/E world championship. Allen ran in the 12.20s.

▲ Most performance engines were revamped to run on regular fuel for '71. The Camaro Z-28's 350-cid LT-1 got new pistons that dropped compression from 11.0:1 to 9.0:1, and horsepower from 360 to 300.

Power now concentrated between 3000 and 5500 rpm, hampering hole shots. A good one could turn a 14.9 quarter.

▲ The base Chevelle SS dropped its celebrated "SS 396" badge for '71, but the domed hood was again standard and cowl induction returned as a option.

▲ Compression of the optional 454 LS-5 fell from 10.25:1 to 8.5:1, but it gained 5 bhp to 365. SS Chevelles came with larger tires, now F60×15, for '71.

▲ Available on coupe and convertible Chevelles, the basic SS package now cost $357.

◄ A 402-cid V-8 replaced the SS Chevelle's 396-cid mill during '70. It returned for '71 under the Turbo-Jet 400 tag with 8.5:1 compression instead of 10.25:1 and 300 bhp instead of 350. A 350-cid V-8 with 245 or 270 bhp also was offered on SSs.

▲ Monte Carlo, Chevy's "personal-luxury" coupe, bowed for '70. It used the Chevelle platform, but had the 116-inch wheelbase of the sedan and wagon, not the 112-inch span of the coupe and convertible. As in '70, regular Monte Carlos came standard with a 350-cid V-8 and could be ordered with the 400-cid V-8, which had up to 330 bhp. Enthusiasts could opt for the SS 454 iteration, which made it Chevy's "personal luxury/performance" coupe. About 127,000 Monte Carlos were built in each year, but there were only 3823 SS 454 versions for '70; this is one of just 1919 built for '71.

▲ As in the Super Sport Chevelle, the big block in the '71 Monte Carlo SS 454 had 365 bhp. (That was the gross power rating. When Chevy switched to net measurements, the 454's rating dropped to 285 bhp.) A handful of SS 454 Monte Carlos apparently were ordered with the hot LS-6 variant. In either case, Turbo Hydra-Matic was a required option, though some four-speeds may have been fitted. *Motor Trend*'s '71 automatic SS 454 Monte did 0-60 mph in 7.1 seconds and the quarter-mile in 15.0 at 91.5.

1971 CHEVROLET HIGH-PERFORMANCE ENGINES

TYPE	CID	BORE× STROKE	BHP @ RPM	TORQUE @ RPM	FUEL SYSTEM	COMP. RATIO	AVAIL.
ohv V-8	350	4.00×3.48	270 @ 4800	360 @ 3200	1×4bbl.	8.5:1	1
ohv V-8	350	4.00×3.48	330 @ 5600	360 @ 4000	1×4bbl.	9.0:1	Camaro Z-28
ohv V-8	400	4.13×3.75	255 @ 4400	290 @ 2400	1×2bbl.	8.5:1	Monte Carlo, full size
ohv V-8	402	4.13×3.76	300 @ 4800	400 @ 3200	1×4bbl.	8.5:1	2
ohv V-8	454	4.25×4.00	365 @ 4800	465 @ 3200	1×4bbl.	8.5:1	3
ohv V-8	454*	4.25×4.00	425 @ 5600	475 @ 4000	1×4bbl.	9.0:1	4

* LS-6
1. Camaro, Chevelle, Monte Carlo, Nova, full size. 2. Chevelle SS, Monte Carlo. 3. Chevelle SS, Monte Carlo SS, full size. 4. Chevelle SS, Monte Carlo SS

◄ SS 454s got stouter suspension pieces than other Monte Carlos, but exterior ID was confined to discreet rocker-panel lettering. Testers praised the car's ride and quietness, but said the Turbo Hydra-Matic was dangerously slow to kick down for passing. The rare SS 454 Monte Carlo would not return for '72.

▲ A revised grille marked the '71 Dodge Challenger. Base coupes like this one could get the 383-cid four barrel. It now had 300 bhp, down from 335.

▲ Challenger R/T got new stripes. The 383 was again standard, the 275-bhp 340 and 385-bhp 440 Six-Pack optional. Just 71 of the 4630 R/Ts built got Hemis.

▲ The R/T convertible died, so the only '71 ragtops were base models. A 383 Challenger soft top paced the Indy 500; this replica has the 340, however.

▲ In June 1970, LeRoy Goldstein's Ramchargers Challenger became the first sub-7-second Funny Car. By '71, his Dodge was into the 6.70s at 220 mph.

▲ This colorful Pro-Stock Hemi Challenger was owned by Billy Stepp of Dayton, Ohio. Driven by Stu McDade, it was typical of a host of cars that were very competitive in the NHRA's regional action, but never put together the right run at the right time to win a national championship. This car ran in the 9.70s at 140 mph.

▶ Dick Landy continued his hard-charging ways in this '71 Hemi Challenger. This car wears the fiberglass hood first seen on the '70 Challenger T/A. Landy was a key participant in the Dodge Performance Clinics, in which factory-supported racers toured local Dodge dealerships, dispensing go-fast tips to amateur racers and promoting Mopar hop-up parts and accessories.

▲ This Hemi-powered Dart was among the many cars sponsored by Gratiot, a Michigan high-performance parts dealer. With driver Ron Mancini at the wheel, this car ran in the 10.50s at around 131 mph.

▲ Big-time drag racing was a hot sport in Canada, as demonstrated by this Hemi Demon run by popular Canadian Mopar competitor John Petrie.

▲ Dodge followed Plymouth's successful '70 Duster 340 into the junior-muscle market with the '71 Demon 340. Starting at just $2721, it was a devilish value. Optional hood with fake scoops had trendy tie-down pins.

▲ Chrome exhaust tips and optional rally wheels dressed out the Demon 340. Standard Rallye suspension had heavy-duty components; drum brakes were larger than on other Demons, as were the E70×14 Goodyear Polyglas GT tires.

▼ Dodge chose the "Demon" name after rejecting "Beaver." Of 79,757 Demons built in '71, 10,098 were 340s.

▲ As in other Mopars, Demon's 340-cid four-barrel was rated at 275 bhp. It mated with a three- or four-speed manual or TorqueFlite. A range of axle ratios, from 2.94:1 to 4.10:1, was available. Tipping the scales at just 3165 pounds, the scrappy Demon 340 had a pretty decent power-to-weight ratio. A well-driven three-speed with the 3.23:1 gear could do 0-60 mph in 6.5 seconds and the quarter-mile in 14.5.

1971 DODGE HIGH-PERFORMANCE ENGINES

TYPE	CID	BORE×STROKE	BHP @ RPM	TORQUE @ RPM	FUEL SYSTEM	COMP. RATIO	AVAIL.
ohv V-8	340	4.04×3.31	275 @ 5000	340 @ 3200	1×4bbl.	10.2:1	1
ohv V-8	383	4.25×3.75	275 @ 4400	375 @ 2800	1×2bbl.	8.5:1	2
ohv V-8	383	4.25×3.75	300 @ 4800	410 @ 3400	1×4bbl.	8.5:1	2
ohv V-8	426*	4.25×3.75	425 @ 5000	490 @ 4000	2×4bbl.	10.2:1	Challenger, Charger
ohv V-8	440	4.32×3.75	335 @ 4400	460 @ 3200	1×4bbl.	8.8:1	full size
ohv V-8	440	4.32×3.75	370 @ 4600	480 @ 3200	1×4bbl.	9.5:1	Charger, full size
ohv V-8	440	4.32×3.75	385 @ 4700	490 @ 3200	3×2bbl.	10.3:1	Challenger, Charger

* Hemi.
1. Demon 340, Challenger, Charger.   2. Challenger, Charger, full size.

▲ Requiem for a heavyweight: The last home for the Hemi V-8 at Dodge was the redesigned Charger. The 426-cid, 425-bhp legend was offered on the R/T and Charger Super Bee models and added $883.55, not including required extras, such as the Sure-Grip diff. Just 85 were ordered.

▶ Charger wore its new Coke-bottle shape on a 115-inch wheelbase, down two inches from '70. R/Ts got a blackout louvered hood, special door skins with simulated air extractors, and Rallye wheels. Spoilers on rear deck and chin were optional.

▲ The R/T came standard with the 440-cid V-8; the four-barrel had 370 bhp, the Six Pack 385.

▲ Vacuum-operated hood scoop helped feed Hemi's dual quads. It was a stock item, unlike the hood-mounted tach.

◀ For '71, the R/T was still Charger's image leader, but it cost $3777, and was outsold by the $3271 Super Bee model, 5054 units to 3118. The only Charger to retain the car's trademark hidden headlamps was the luxury SE model, which started at $3422.

▲ R/Ts and Super Bees with the 383, 440, or Hemi used the four-speed manual with Hurst pistol-grip shifter or the slap-stick TorqueFlite automatic.

▲ Both the 440 Magnum and 426 Hemi could still turn high 13s at over 100 mph—good numbers for any era.

▲ The mighty Hemi still packed a punch. *Motor Trend*'s turned a 13.7 quarter at 104 mph with a 4.10:1 gear.

▲ Hawaiian Roland Leong's Funny Cars were colorful and quick. Butch Maas drove this blown Hemi in the 6.90s at 220 mph.

▼ Super Bee came standard with the 300-bhp four-barrel 383 detuned to run on regular fuel. It also had a bumble-bee graphic hood bulge.

▲ The last Boss was built from the restyled SportsRoof Mustang. It was kin to the 351-cid four-barrel Mach 1, but the Boss 351 had 330 bhp on 11.7:1 compression and mechanical lifters. The Mach 1 had 285 bhp, 10.7:1, and hydraulic lifters. With its larger tires and a fatter sway bar, the Boss handled better, but it cost $4124, to $3268 for the Mach. Just 1806 Boss 351s were built.

▲ With a four-speed and 3.91:1 gear, the Boss 351 ran 0-60 mph in 5.8 seconds and turned the quarter in 14.1 at 100.6 for *Car and Driver*. Top speed was 117 mph.

▲ The new Mustang's added heft compelled some Pro-Stockers to stick with the svelter '70 models. The Polaris drag team did. Here, its coupe is launched by Jerry Baker at the '71 Winternationals.

▶ Fred Stone, Leonard Woods, and Doug Cooke ran a series of successful A/GS Willys in the '60s, but their Funny Cars never won a national event. Mike Van Sant drove this one.

▼ Boss 351 was quicker and more tractable than the earlier Boss 302, but had less character. Ram Air, F60×15 tires were standard. Magnum 500 wheels, rear spoiler were options.

▲ Mustang's muscle mainstay for '71 was the new Mach 1, offered with six V-8s that required premium fuel. The fun started with the 285-bhp 351 four-barrel and got serious with the 370-bhp 429 Cobra Jet or 375-bhp Super Cobra Jet. "Drag Pack" editions of both 429s had mechanical lifters, a high-lift cam, and 3.91:1 Traction-Loc or 4.11:1 Detroit Locker. The 429 put more than 850 pounds over the Mach's nose, however, and both handling and traction off the line were problems. A Cobra Jet spun 'em badly out of the hole and ran 0-60 in 6.3 seconds with a 14.6 ET at 99.4 for *Sports Car Graphic*. It had the four-speed and 3.50:1 gears.

1971 FORD HIGH-PERFORMANCE ENGINES							
TYPE	CID	BORE×STROKE	BHP @ RPM	TORQUE @ RPM	FUEL SYSTEM	COMP. RATIO	AVAIL.
ohv V-8	351	4.00×3.50	285 @ 5400	370 @ 3400	1×4bbl.	10.7:1	Torino, Mustang
ohv V-8	351	4.00×3.50	330 @ 5400	370 @ 4000	1×4bbl.	11.1:1	Mustang Boss 351
ohv V-8	429	4.36×3.59	370 @ 5400	450 @ 3400	1×4bbl.	11.3:1	Torino, Mustang
ohv V-8	429	4.36×3.59	375 @ 5600	450 @ 3400	1×4bbl.	11.3:1	Torino, Mustang

▲ Wheelbase was up only one inch, but the '71 Mustang was eight inches longer overall, six inches wider, and 600 pounds heavier than the '70 version. Mach 1 came with a "competition suspension" and F70×14 tires. Mag wheels and Ram Air were optional. Note the flexible, body-colored front bumper compared to the Boss 351's chrome piece.

▲ NASCAR banned Mercury's droop-nose Cyclone Spoiler II for '71 (along with the similar Talladega and winged Mopars). But the street Cyclone Spoiler was back with few changes. It was essentially a grand-touring coupe with an attitude. The Spoiler "can best be described as a gentleman's muscle car," concluded *Car and Driver*. Despite its "competition-oriented external appearance [the Spoiler] was carefully developed for minimum intrusion on the occupants' senses," it said.

▲ The senses were in for a rush when the Spoiler had a 429 Cobra Jet (shown). Ford was slower than GM to lower compression ratios, so the CJ still had an 11.3:1 squeeze and 370 bhp. The Super Cobra Jet had an 11.0:1 ratio, mechanical lifters, and 375 bhp. A 370-bhp Cyclone GT did 0-60 mph in 6.4 seconds and the quarter-mile in a respectable 14.5. Standard in the Spoiler was the 285-bhp, 351-cid Cleveland four-barrel. Like the 429s, it required premium gas.

1971 MERCURY HIGH-PERFORMANCE ENGINES							
TYPE	CID	BORE×STROKE	BHP @ RPM	TORQUE @ RPM	FUEL SYSTEM	COMP. RATIO	AVAIL.
ohv V-8	351	4.00×3.50	300 @ 5400	380 @ 3400	1×4bbl.	10.7:1	1
ohv V-8	429	4.36×3.59	370 @ 5400	450 @ 3400	1×4bbl.	11.3:1	Cougar, Cyclone
ohv V-8	429	4.36×3.59	375 @ 5600	450 @ 3400	1×4bbl.	11.0:1	Cougar, Cyclone
1. Cougar, Montego, Cyclone.							

▲ This pre-production Spoiler photographed at Ford's proving grounds borrows hidden headlamps from the Cyclone GT and has a deep, non-production air dam.

▲ Rear spoiler, side stripe, G70×14 tires, a Hurst-shifted four-speed, and 3.25:1 Traction-Lok axle were standard on Cyclone Spoiler.

◄ Olds followed GM's lead and detuned its engines for '71, but the 4-4-2 W-30 package still meant a factory-blueprinted 455-cid with air-induction hood. Note the weight-saving red plastic fender liners on this W-30.

▼ *Motor Trend* ran two '71 W-30s, both with 3.42:1 gears. The automatic did 0-60 in 6.1 seconds and turned a 14.4 ET at 97 mph. The wide-ratio four-speed hit 60 mph in 6.6 seconds and turned a 14.7 at 97.

▲ 4-4-2s now came only as a $3552 coupe weighing 3688 pounds or as a $3743 convertible at 3731 pounds. The W-30 package added $369. The W-32 and the 350-cid W-31 died.

▲ The 455 still was standard on 4-4-2, but under Olds' net horsepower system (measuring output with all accessories in place), the base 455 got a rating of 260 bhp and the W-30 a rating of 300 bhp.

▲ Regular fuel meant a compression drop to 8.5:1. The base 455 four-barrel (shown) had 340 gross bhp, down 25; the W-30 made 350 gross bhp, down 20.

▲ 4-4-2 cabins bespoke upscale sportiness. A Hurst-stirred four-speed was standard. A Turbo Hydra-Matic 400 was optional—and this one has a Hurst dual-gate shifter.

▲ Motor Trend said the 4-4-2 seemed less affected by the switch to regular fuel than many other '71 models, but its acceleration above 60 mph was noticeably weakened.

▲ Motor Trend achieved its best launches with the automatic W-30 by "walking" into the throttle, keeping the tires on the verge of spinning, and manually shifting at 5200 rpm. The performance was still there, but '71 4-4-2 production fell to just over 7500 units, 1304 of them ragtops.

1971 OLDSMOBILE HIGH-PERFORMANCE ENGINES							
TYPE	CID	BORE × STROKE	BHP @ RPM	TORQUE @ RPM	FUEL SYSTEM	COMP. RATIO	AVAIL.
ohv V-8	350	4.06 × 3.39	260 @ 4600	360 @ 3200	1×4bbl.	8.5:1	Cutlass
ohv V-8	455	4.12 × 4.25	320 @ 4400	460 @ 2800	1×4bbl.	8.5:1	Cutlass, full size
ohv V-8	455	4.12 × 4.25	340 @ 4600	460 @ 3200	1×4bbl.	8.5:1	4-4-2
ohv V-8	455	4.12 × 4.25	350 @ 4700	460 @ 3200	1×4bbl.	8.5:1	4-4-2

▶ Plymouth's hot little Duster 340 lost none of its performance, but relinquished a little of its sleeper quality for '71. The grille was flashier, and the side stripe now culminated with "340" numerals on the rear fender. The little hummer's cover could be blown completely by ordering an optional flat-black hood treatment emblazoned with "340" script that had the word "Wedge" stenciled within. Groovy.

▲ Plymouth's popular Duster proved a versatile venue for Mopar power and the NHRA seemed to have a class to accommodate it, regardless of the engine.

▲ Even a near-stock 340-cid Duster could find a home, this one in G/Stock. It was typical of the locally sponsored cars that were the backbone of the sport.

▶ Capitalizing on the popularity of the original Duster 340 was the new Duster Twister. Pictured here with a "Curious Yellow" 340 is a "Sassy Grass Green" example. Twister got the 340's grille, mirrors, and wheels (without trim rings). The blackout, strobe-stripe hood was standard, but the non-functioning scoops were optional. Twisters were offered with a pair of six-cylinder engines or the 230-bhp 318-cid two-barrel V-8, which, Plymouth noted, made it easier to insure and cheaper to fuel than the 340.

▲ Duster sales increased 21 percent in '71, but muscle was waning and sales of the 340 fell by half, to 12,866.

▲ Compression slid fractionally from 10.5:1 to 10.2:1, but Plymouth's 340 four-barrel kept its 275-gross-bhp rating. Its net rating was 235 bhp.

▼ The spare beauty of the 1970 'Cuda gave way to a busy grille and fake fender vents, but V-8s from the taut 340 up to the thundering Hemi could still shake things up.

▲ Road Runner was radically restyled for '71. Wheelbase dropped an inch, to 115, rear track widened by three inches for better handling, and the convertible and pillared coupe were retired. With a base price of just $3147, it was still a good muscle value.

▲ The 383 four-barrel fell 35 bhp, to 300, as compression dipped one point, to 8.50:1. Still, *Motor Trend* said the 383 was an all-round better value than the 440 V-8.

▲ *Motor Trend*'s triple-deuce 440 was not as easy to drive in fluctuating traffic as the 383. The larger engine averaged 10.8 mpg, the 383, 11.1, both with automatic.

▲ A reconfigured interior featured improved ergonomics. This Road Runner has the optional tachometer and 14½-inch diameter Tuff steering wheel.

▲ The burly 440 six-barrel resisted major detuning, dropping only five bhp, to 385 (330 net), and losing just a fraction of compression, now at 10.3:1.

▲ Grabber graphics played to Road Runner's cartoon theme. Performance varied by car and condition. For example, in a heads-up match of '71 automatics, *Motor Trend*'s 383, which cost $4324 with options and had a 3.91:1 gear, turned a 14.84 at 94.5. A 440 six-barrel cost $4638, had a 4.10:1, and managed a 15.02 at 96. In another test, *MT*'s air-conditioned 383 with a 3.23:1 gear and TorqueFlite snoozed to a 15.9 at 84 mph, while a 440 blew its doors with a 14.3 at 100.

▲ The six-barrel 440 added $262, the Air Grabber hood $69, and TorqeFlite $262 to the Road Runner's price. Despite the new skin and the minimally diminished V-8s, Road Runner sales plummeted from 41,484 to 14,218 in '71.

▲ This was the final year for the GTX, but it died with its big-cube boots on. The 440 was again standard, the Hemi was optional, and competitive ETs were guaranteed.

▲ This also was the mighty Hemi's swan-song season. It still ruled with 425 bhp, but times had changed. Only 55 were installed in Road Runners, 30 in GTXs.

1971 PLYMOUTH HIGH-PERFORMANCE ENGINES

TYPE	CID	BORE × STROKE	BHP @ RPM	TORQUE @ RPM	FUEL SYSTEM	COMP. RATIO	AVAIL.
ohv V-8	340	4.04×3.31	275 @ 5000	340 @ 3200	1×4bbl.	10.2:1	1
ohv V-8	383	4.25×3.75	300 @ 4800	410 @ 3400	1×4bbl.	8.5:1	2
ohv V-8	426*	4.25×3.75	425 @ 5000	490 @ 4000	2×4bbl.	10.2:1	3
ohv V-8	440	4.32×3.75	335 @ 4400	460 @ 3200	1×4bbl.	8.8:1	full size
ohv V-8	440	4.32×3.75	370 @ 4600	480 @ 3200	1×4bbl.	9.5:1	GTX, full size
ohv V-8	440	4.32×3.75	385 @ 4700	490 @ 3200	3×2bbl.	10.3:1	4

* Hemi.
1. Duster 340, Barracuda, Road Runner. 2. Barracuda, Satellite, full size. 3. Barracuda, Road Runner, GTX.
4. Barracuda, Road Runner, GTX, Sport Fury GT.

▲ Plymouth advertising was among the most creative of the era and, as this promotional shot shows, whimsy was still afoot in '71.

Plymouth's slice of the full-size muscle-car pie was the Sport Fury GT. It bowed for '70 as a member of the Rapid Transit System and returned virtually unchanged for '71. The 440 four-barrel was standard and the six-barrel optional. All had the high-upshift Torque-Flite, dual exhausts with 2¼-inch-diameter tail pipes, heavy-duty suspension with six-leaf rear springs, and meaty H70×15 fiber-glass-belted tires. The GT went for around $4000 and weighed about 4000 pounds. Few were sold, and the big coupe died after a 1971 production run of just 375.

▲ Firebird changed little after its short '70 model year, though Formula 350 and 455 models joined the Formula 400.

▲ Trans Am's rear spoiler was now an option on all Firebirds. This is a Formula, which started at $3445.

▲ Firebird's 400-cid now made 300 bhp, down 30, after a two-point drop in compression, to 8:2:1. The Ram Air option was back, and the 455 and 455 H.O. were new.

▲ Trans Am's only change was that the 455 H.O. V-8 was now standard. This mill was offered in the cheaper Formula, however, and sales of the $4590 T/A fell to just 2116.

▼ GTOs got a revised fascia for '71, and so did The Judge, though the 455 H.O. was now The Judge's only engine. It had 335 bhp, down from the 360 bhp it made in '70.

TYPE	CID	BORE × STROKE	BHP @ RPM	TORQUE @ RPM	FUEL SYSTEM	COMP. RATIO	AVAIL.
ohv V-8	400	4.12 × 3.75	300 @ 4800	400 @ 2400	1 × 4bbl.	8.2:1	1
ohv V-8	455	4.15 × 4.21	325 @ 4400	455 @ 3200	1 × 4bbl.	8.2:1	1
ohv V-8	455	4.15 × 4.21	335 @ 4800	480 @ 3600	1 × 4bbl.	8.4:1	2

1971 PONTIAC HIGH-PERFORMANCE ENGINES

1. Grand Prix, GTO, LeMans, Firebird, full size. 2. GTO, LeMans, Trans Am.

▲ The Judge ran the quarter in 14.9 at 95 mph for *Motor Trend*, compared to a 15.4 at 92 mph for a 300-bhp 400-cid GTO. Zero-60 times were 7.0 for The Judge, 7.1 for the Goat. Both were '71s with a four-speed and 3.55:1 rear axle.

▼▶ Judges equipped with the new optional Road Package suspension got 1.25-inch-diameter Trans Am-type front and rear stabilizer bars, the Trans Am steering ratio, 60-series tires on 15×7-inch wheels, and front disc brakes. "The result, when coupled with the coarse pitch M-22 close ratio four-speed, is a very well-behaved package that comes within a whisker of the Trans Am's lateral G capability in cornering," said *Motor Trend*. Braking was excellent, the editors said, but the downside was a very harsh ride.

▲ Court adjourned: Insurance rates and changing tastes retired The Judge in midyear after just 357 hardtops and 17 convertibles had been built.

◀ The '71 Ram Air 455 had fewer horses than the previous optional Ram Air 400 IV, but it had much more torque at lower rpm. Not exactly tractable, it was still better behaved on the street than the high-strung 400 IV.

▲ The GTO's standard 400-cid V-8 was rated at 300 bhp. This is one of only 661 GTO convertibles built for '71; 9497 hardtops were produced.

▲ Royal Pontiac had been at it for nearly a decade by '71, and its Ponchos, including this Firebird, were just as formidable in Super Stock as they were on the street.

▲ Nose elevated as the weight transfers; low-pressure slicks wrinkling as they bite; driver hunched forward in concentration—a classic car in a classic pose.

▲ Linda Vaughn, "Miss Hurst Golden Shifter," with the SSJ Hurst. Adding $1150 to a Pontiac Grand Prix J, the conversion included Fire Frost Gold accents, a landau top, a Cadillac Eldorado sunroof, and American Racing wheels. About 450 1970-72 SSJs were built.

1972

Just two years after its peak season, muscle is on the run...All manufacturers now give net horsepower and torque ratings—and even net bhp is down • Nearly all engines now must use low-lead regular gas • Buick GSX is gone...GS 455 Stage 1 continues with 270 bhp • 454-cid V-8 still available in Chevelle and Monte Carlo, but deflated to 270 bhp • Mopar's Hemi and 440 six-barrels are gone • Dodge Charger R/T and Super Bee are gone...meeker Rallye remains • Dodge Challenger R/T is gone...340-cid V-8 is now biggest Challenger/Barracuda mill • Ford's Torino Cobra is gone...GT Sport with 205-bhp 429 is a pale imitation • Mustang big-blocks and Boss 351 are gone...351 H.O. tops out at 275 bhp • Olds demotes 4-4-2 to an option...W-30 package sticks with 455 V-8 • Plymouth GTX is gone...Road Runner continues with 400- and 440-cid V-8s • GTO demoted to Pontiac LeMans option; available with Trans Am's 300-bhp, 455-cid V-8 • Mike Snively turns record 5.97-second ET in rail dragster at Supernationals • Funny Car hits 235 mph for first time at Supernationals

▲ Javelin AMX wasn't as sharp for '72. Base power was downgraded to the 304-cid V-8, and the previous 360 joined the 401 on the options sheet. All '72 Javs got new taillamps, but the basic '71 styling was unaltered.

▲ Post-1970 Javelins had a curved gauge cluster. Pontiac's 1969-72 Grand Prix had something similar—purely coincidence. Unusual concentric clock/tachometer sat to the right of the central speedometer.

1972 AMC HIGH-PERFORMANCE ENGINES							
TYPE	CID	BORE×STROKE	BHP @ RPM	TORQUE @ RPM	FUEL SYSTEM	COMP. RATIO	AVAIL.
ohv V-8	360	4.08×3.44	195 @ 4400	295 @ 2900	1×4bbl.	8.5:1	1
ohv V-8	360	4.08×3.44	220 @ 4400	315 @ 3100	1×4bbl.	8.5:1	1
ohv V-8	401	4.17×3.68	255 @ 4800	345 @ 3300	1×4bbl.	8.5:1	1
1. Matador, Ambassador, Javelin.							

▲ Javelin's 401 V-8 option cost $162 and made 255 *net* bhp for '72, as AMC gave up on gross ratings.

▼ Stage 1 455 was down to 270-net bhp for Buick GS. New fabric sunroof was a rare option.

▲ NHRA founder Wally Parks (right) congratulates David Binisek on winning Stock honors at the '72 Winternationals. A TV was part of his prize.

▲ David Binisek's Buick GS copped Stock Class honors at the 1972 NHRA Winternationals in Pomona with a quarter-mile of 13.39 seconds at 87.97 mph.

1972 BUICK HIGH-PERFORMANCE ENGINES

TYPE	CID	BORE × STROKE	BHP @ RPM	TORQUE @ RPM	FUEL SYSTEM	COMP. RATIO	AVAIL.
ohv V-8	350	3.80×3.85	195 @ 4000	290 @ 2800	1×4bbl.	8.5:1	1
ohv V-8	455	4.31×3.90	225 @ 4000	260 @ 2800	1×4bbl.	8.5:1	2
ohv V-8	455	4.31×3.90	250 @ 4000	375 @ 2800	1×4bbl.	8.5:1	3
ohv V-8	455*	4.31×3.90	360 @ 4000	375 @ 2800	1×4bbl.	8.5:1	4
ohv V-8	455*	4.31×3.90	270 @ 4400	390 @ 3000	1×4bbl.	8.5:1	GS 455

* Stage 1.

1. GS, Skylark, LeSabre. 2. GS 455, Centurion, Electra 225, Riviera, Estate Wagon, LeSabre. 3. Riviera, LeSabre, Centurion, Electra 225. 4. Riviera GS, Centurion.

▲ Optional column-mounted automatic and factory 8-track dressed out the already plush GS cabin.

▲ The GSX died, and Buick built just 8575 GS models for '72. Their hood scoops were functional.

▲ Buick cut prices $60-$70 to spur 1972 GS sales. The hardtop started at $3225. The convertible started at $3406, but just 852 ragtops were built.

▲ Despite lower rated power, the '72 Stage 1 GS was still quick. *Motor Trend* clocked 0-60 in 5.8 seconds and 14.1 at 97 mph for the quarter.

◀▲ This was the last year for true Chevelle Super Sport muscle. The top power option, the 454 LS-5, was down to 270 net bhp; the Turbo-Jet "400" fell to 240. The LS-5 went into just 5333 cars, mostly hardtops. Base SS power was a 130-bhp 307, and docile 165- and 175-bhp 350 small-blocks were optional. Another sign of worsening muscle-car times: The "performance" axle was a 3.31:1. LS-5s again came only with a "Rockcrusher" four-speed. Other V-8s offered three- and four-speed manuals, Hydra-Matic, and even a revived Powerglide option.

1972 CHEVROLET HIGH-PERFORMANCE ENGINES

TYPE	CID	BORE × STROKE	BHP @ RPM	TORQUE @ RPM	FUEL SYSTEM	COMP. RATIO	AVAIL.
ohv V-8	350	4.00×3.48	175 @ 4000	280 @ 2400	1×4bbl.	8.5:1	Monte Carlo, Chevelle
ohv V-8	350	4.00×3.48	200 @ 4400	300 @ 2800	1×4bbl.	8.5:1	Camaro SS, Nova
ohv V-8	350	4.00×3.48	255 @ 5600	280 @ 4000	1×4bbl.	9.0:1	Camaro Z-28
ohv V-8	402	4.13×3.76	210 @ 4400	320 @ 2400	1×4bbl.	8.5:1	full size
ohv V-8	402	4.13×3.76	240 @ 4400	345 @ 3200	1×4bbl.	8.5:1	1
ohv V-8	454	4.25×4.00	270 @ 4000	390 @ 3200	1×4bbl.	8.5:1	2

1. Camaro, Chevelle, Monte Carlo. 2. full size, Chevelle, Monte Carlo.

▶ Chevelle SS lost its prominent central grille bar, but '72 styling was mostly a 1970-71 repeat. The Super Sport package itself was also little changed. Total SS production fell to 24,946, out of 370,000 Chevelles. Overall, though, Chevy built 296,000 SS 396s and 454s for 1968-72. No muscle car enjoyed a better five-year run.

▲ Only 5333 LS-5s went into these last true SS Chevelles; included were a handful of SS 454 convertibles.

◀ Air cleaner decal says "400," but this V-8 was still really the 402-cid extension of Chevy's original mid-'60s 396-cid big-block.

▲ This Cream Yellow SS has the popular optional black vinyl top and stripe group. Mag-type wheels were again part of the SS package. Cowl-induction hood could still be ordered, and some LS-6s were apparently built, as well.

▲ Top mill for Dodge's Charger was a 280-bhp 440 four-barrel. R/T Super Bee, and Hemi died.

▲ *Motor Trend*'s 340 four-barrel/automatic Charger turned an ET of 16.2 seconds at 89 mph.

▼ Dodge built 45,361 of its basic '72 Charger hardtops. Wire wheels and vinyl roof shown here were extras. So was V-8 power in lieu of standard Slant Six.

▼ Rallye option with blackened hood bulge was now the performance Charger. The 340 adjusted to its smog gear and ran better than in '71.

1972 DODGE HIGH-PERFORMANCE ENGINES						
TYPE	CID	BORE × STROKE	BHP @ RPM	TORQUE @ RPM	FUEL SYSTEM	COMP. RATIO	AVAIL.
ohv V-8	340	4.04 × 3.31	240 @ 4800	290 @ 3600	1×4bbl.	8.5:1	1
ohv V-8	400	4.34 × 3.38	225 @ 4800	340 @ 3200	1×4bbl.	8.2:1	Charger SE
ohv V-8	400	4.34 × 3.38	255 @ 4800	340 @ 3200	1×4bbl.	8.2:1	Charger, Coronet
ohv V-8	440	4.32 × 3.75	230 @ 4400	355 @ 2800	1×4bbl.	8.2:1	Monaco
ohv V-8	440	4.32 × 3.75	280 @ 4800	375 @ 3200	1×4bbl.	8.2:1	2

1. Demon 340, Challenger, Charger. 2. Charger, Charger SE.

▲ Rallye's instrument panel had simulated wood and a 150-mph speedometer. An AM/FM stereo radio with 8-track tape player was a $358 option.

◄ Challenger entered its third model year with a more extensive facelift. New Rallye model replaced the hot R/T. Black grille, dummy air vents on hood and front fenders, and bodyside stripes identified it. Only 8123 '72 Rallyes were built, reflecting the fast-falling demand for performance and pony cars. Rallye bowed with a mild 318 V-8 as base power, but some were equipped with the optional four-barrel 340, rated at 240 bhp in that year's newly adopted net measure.

▲ Mustang still offered the Mach 1, but graphics were counted on more and more to signal sportiness. A good example was the new Sprint Decor Option, which had white paint, blue hood and rocker stripes, American flag decals on rear fenders, and color-keyed interior.

► The redesigned Torino put on pounds and inches. The hot model was this GT Sport fastback on a new 114-inch wheelbase. It was offered with the 429, re-rated to 205 net bhp, but the 248-bhp 351 four-barrel was the best choice. A 161-bhp two-barrel 351 turned an ET of 17.9 at 80 mph for *Motor Trend*.

▲ The Boss retired, and Mach 1 lost its big-block options. Base power was now a lowly 302 with 136 net bhp; the top option was a new 275-horse four-barrel 351 High Output with mandatory four-speed. *Car and Driver's* did the quarter in 15.1 seconds at 94 mph.

◄ Mach 1's base price was $3053, and 27,675 were built. Overall Mustang volume was well down even from the depressed '71 total, at a bit over 125,000. Big NACA hood ducts were functional with the $985 351 H.O./four-speed combo.

▲ Mercury's Maverick-clone Comet returned for '72 with new four-door models. The GT option shown here remained exclusive to the two-door and cost $173. Hood scoop was fake, but sporty features mated well with optional 302 V-8.

			1972 FORD HIGH-PERFORMANCE ENGINES				
TYPE	**CID**	**BORE × STROKE**	**BHP @ RPM**	**TORQUE @ RPM**	**FUEL SYSTEM**	**COMP. RATIO**	**AVAIL.**
ohv V-8	351	4.00×3.50	248 @ 5400	299 @ 3600	1×4bbl.	8.6:1	Torino
ohv V-8	351	4.00×3.50	262 @ 5400	299 @ 3600	1×4bbl.	8.6:1	full size
ohv V-8	351	4.00×3.50	266 @ 5400	301 @ 3600	1×4bbl.	8.6:1	Mustang
ohv V-8	351	4.00×3.50	275 @ 6000	286 @ 3800	1×4bbl.	9.2:1	Mustang
ohv V-8	400	4.00×4.00	172 @ 4000	298 @ 2200	1×2bbl.	8.4:1	full size
ohv V-8	429	4.36×3.59	205 @ 4400	322 @ 2600	1×4bbl.	8.5:1	Torino
ohv V-8	429	4.36×3.59	212 @ 4400	327 @ 2600	1×4bbl.	11.3:1	Thunderbird

▶ Mid-size Mercurys were remodeled along Torino lines for '72. Cyclone was gone with the wind, leaving a new Montego GT fastback as the "muscle" model. Base price was $3346 with standard 302 V-8. The hottest power options included the 351 H.O. and big-block 429.

1972 MERCURY HIGH-PERFORMANCE ENGINES

TYPE	CID	BORE × STROKE	BHP @ RPM	TORQUE @ RPM	FUEL SYSTEM	COMP. RATIO	AVAIL.
ohv V-8	351	4.00 × 3.50	262 @ 5400	299 @ 3600	1 × 4bbl.	8.6:1	Cougar
ohv V-8	351	4.00 × 3.50	266 @ 5400	301 @ 3600	1 × 4bbl.	8.6:1	Cougar
ohv V-8	400	4.00 × 4.00	172 @ 4000	298 @ 2200	1 × 2bbl.	8.4:1	full size
ohv V-8	429	4.36 × 3.59	205 @ 4400	322 @ 2600	1 × 4bbl.	8.5:1	Montego
ohv V-8	429	4.36 × 3.59	212 @ 4400	327 @ 2600	1 × 4bbl.	11.3:1	full size
ohv V-8	460	4.32 × 3.85	224 @ 4400	357 @ 2800	1 × 4bbl.	8.5:1	full size

▼ Oldsmobile's 4-4-2 reverted to its original status as an option package and was in fact a Cutlass trim/handling group. Even so, production rose a bit over '71, ending at 9845 units. Among them were the final 4-4-2 convertibles.

▲ A special grille was again part of the 4-4-2 package. This example carries the optional four-barrel 350 V-8, rated now at 180 bhp.

▲ All 4-4-2 engines, this 350 included, had lower compression for '71 to run on low-lead gas. FE2 suspension was part of the 4-4-2 package.

1972 OLDSMOBILE HIGH-PERFORMANCE ENGINES

TYPE	CID	BORE × STROKE	BHP @ RPM	TORQUE @ RPM	FUEL SYSTEM	COMP. RATIO	AVAIL.
ohv V-8	350	4.06 × 3.39	180 @ 4000	275 @ 2900	1 × 4bbl.	8.5:1	1
ohv V-8	455	4.13 × 4.25	225 @ 3600	360 @ 2600	1 × 4bbl.	8.5:1	full size
ohv V-8	455	4.13 × 4.25	250 @ 4000	375 @ 2800	1 × 4bbl.	8.5:1	Toronado, full size
ohv V-8	455	4.13 × 4.25	270 @ 4400	370 @ 3200	1 × 4bbl.	8.5:1	Cutlass, Hurst/Olds
ohv V-8	455	4.13 × 4.25	300 @ 4700	410 @ 3200	1 × 4bbl.	8.5:1	Cutlass, Hurst/Olds

1. Supreme, Cutlass, F-85, full size.

▲ Blueprinted four-barrel 455-cid W-30 with 300 net bhp remained 4-4-2's top power option. Priced at $599, it again included Cold-Air induction hood.

▲ After a two-year absence, the Hurst/Olds returned as a Cutlass Supreme-based hardtop and convertible. Respective production was 499 and 130.

▲ The '72 H/O convertible paced the Indy 500. W-30 engine and special white paint with gold striping were included on all '72 H/Os.

That gleaming 4-4-2 down there may look like a million. But, in reality, it's rock-solid value.

Here's how we pulled it off.

For 1972, we've come up with a special 4-4-2 Sport/Handling Package you can order on four different Olds Cutlass models. You can get it on the lowest priced Cutlass (Hardtop Coupe shown), two different Cutlass S Coupes, or the Cutlass Supreme Convertible.

And here's what that new 4-4-2 package includes: Olds' outstanding heavy-duty FE2 suspension (the imitators are popping up faster than you can say "me, too") with front and rear stabilizer bars.

Heavy-duty 14 x 7" wheels. Hurst Competition Shifter. Louvered hood. Special 4-4-2 grille. Hood and body paint stripes. Plus exterior 4-4-2 identification. And more.

As for engine availability—that's wide open. A spirited 350-cube, 2-barrel V-8 is standard. But you can order a 350-cube, 4-barrel. Or a 455-cubic-incher with 4 barrels, flared dual exhaust outlets, and a specially sculptured rear bumper. Or order our top package, the W-30 with a dual-

intake fiberglass hood and a 455 Cold-Air V-8!

The point is this. Now you can order a low-priced Olds and still wind up with a beautiful performer. 1972 Olds 4-4-2. Go do it.

OLDSMOBILE
ALWAYS A STEP AHEAD

▲ Winged wheel insignia of the Indy 500 graced the Hurst/Olds pace car. All '72 H/Os included firm Rallye suspension, dual exhausts, and power front-disc brakes.

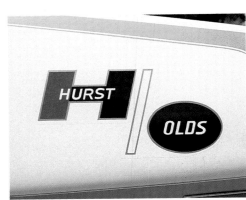

▲ Hurst/Olds badge marked the very rare but still very hot limited-edition 4-4-2 hardtop and convertible. Hurst conversions were carried out at the firm's Southfield, Michigan, Headquarters.

Now there are four ways to get 4·4·2. This is the lowest priced way!

◀ Olds ads stressed the more affordable 4-4-2. It was available on base Cutlass coupe, S coupe and hardtop, and Cutlass Supreme hardtop and convertible. Package price depending on model was $71-$150—not a bad deal.

▲ "Twister" and "340" versions were back for Plymouth's little-changed Duster. This catalog-illustration car has both. The 340 had a 235-bhp two-barrel and 15,681 went out of the factory.

◄▼ Plymouth quarter-mile veteran Butch Leal campaigned this "California Flash" Duster in NHRA's Pro-Stock Class during '72. A Hemi was under the special domed hood. On the street, *Car and Driver*'s 340 with TorqueFlite and 3.23:1 gears did the quarter in 15.6 at 89.5 mph. It cost $4213 with options and averaged 10-12 mpg on 91-octane gas.

▲ Rear-deck stripes and Air Grabber hood were among the options on the '72 Road Runner, but sales declined to just 7628 for the model year.

▲ Road Runner hardtop started at $3095 with a 255-bhp, 400-cid four-barrel. Hemi, 383, and the 440+6 all succumbed to stricter smog laws.

▲ Step-down power for the Road Runner was the 240-bhp (net) 340 small-block, which used a new Carter Thermo-Quad plastic-bodied four-barrel carb.

1972 PLYMOUTH HIGH-PERFORMANCE ENGINES

TYPE	CID	BORE×STROKE	BHP @ RPM	TORQUE @ RPM	FUEL SYSTEM	COMP. RATIO	AVAIL.
ohv V-8	340	4.04×3.31	240 @ 4800	290 @ 3600	1×4bbl.	8.5:1	1
ohv V-8	400	4.34×3.38	255 @ 4800	340 @ 3200	1×4bbl.	8.2:1	2
ohv V-8	440	4.32×3.75	230 @ 4400	355 @ 2800	1×4bbl.	8.2:1	Fury
ohv V-8	440	4.32×3.75	280 @ 4800	375 @ 3200	1×4bbl.	8.2:1	Road Runner

1 Duster 340, Barracuda, 'Cuda, Road Runner. 2 Satellite, Road Runner, Fury.

► Optional "strobe stripes" spilled from side-facing dummy hood scoops. Though Plymouth's plush GTX was gone, the '72 Road Runner offered a "GTX option"—a four-barrel 440 making 280 net bhp. New two-slot grille was unique to the Road Runner.

▲ Barracuda reverted to a 1970-type grille for '72. Twin-scoop black-finish hood was optional.

▲ Don Carlton ran Pro-Stock "Motown Missle" Hemicudas in 1970-71. Here's his '72 at the "tree."

▲ Four-barrel 340 with 240 net bhp was the top power option for Plymouth's 1972 Barracuda. Vinyl top and bodyside tape stripes returned at extra cost. 'Cuda production fell to 7828 for the model year.

▲ As before, the Road Runner's front parking/directional lamps were styled to resemble driving lights. The base 400 was essentially a bored-out 383 and like the 340, it breathed through Carter's novel plastic-bodied Thermo-Quad carb. Road Runners still came with a heavy-duty suspension and brakes, three-speed floor-mounted stick, F70×14 tires, and 150-mph speedometer; a tach was optional. This would be the last year for a Road Runner with anything like the original's sizzle. At least the horn still went "beep-beep."

▼ As with the Olds 4-4-2, Pontiac's GTO was demoted to option status and looked all but identical to the '71 models. No '72 Goat ragtops are known.

▲ GTO production fell to just 5807, but body-color Endura nose remained neat and functional. Wide hood "nostrils" are also functional on this car, which carries the 455 High Output four-barrel with Ram Air, a combo good for 300 net bhp.

▲ *Motor Trend*'s 455 H.O. four-speed with 3.55:1 gears turned a 15.4 at 92 mph. *MT* said the 455's cam shook the whole car at idle. The engine tended to bog so it had to be launched at 3400 rpm, thereby incurring massive wheelspin.

▲ A 300-bhp 455 H.O. topped a limited '72 GTO power slate. That year's base 400 and "regular" 455 option both made 250 net bhp; the latter required automatic. Axle ratios ranged from 3.08 to just 3.55:1.

1972 PONTIAC HIGH-PERFORMANCE ENGINES

TYPE	CID	BORE × STROKE	BHP @ RPM	TORQUE @ RPM	FUEL SYSTEM	COMP. RATIO	AVAIL.
ohv V-8	400	4.12×3.75	200@4000	295@2800	1×4bbl.	8.2:1	LeMans, Catalina
ohv V-8	400	4.12×3.75	250@4400	325@3200	1×4bbl.	8.2:1	1
ohv V-8	455	4.15×4.21	220@3600	350@2400	1×4bbl.	8.2:1	full size
ohv V-8	455	4.15×4.21	230@4400	360@2800	1×4bbl.	8.2:1	LeMans, GTO
ohv V-8	455	4.15×4.21	250@3600	375@2400	1×4bbl.	8.2:1	2
ohv V-8	455	4.15×4.21	300@4000	415@3200	1×4bbl.	8.4:1	3

1. Grand Prix, GTO, Formula 400, LeMans, Catalina. 2. LeMans, GTO, Grand Prix, full size. 3. Trans Am, LeMans, GTO, Firebird Formula 455.

▲ Firebird Trans Am continued as racy as ever, and the price was cut $340 to $4256 list, presumably to spark sales. But the public's continued drift away from performance combined with a factory strike to hold T/A production to just 1286 for the model year.

▶ Trans Am's shaker-hood 455 H.O. returned with 300 net bhp, down from 1971's 335 gross figure. Torque also fell. A four-speed manual replaced a three-speed as standard. *Car and Driver* ran one with 3.42:1 gears to 60 mph in just 5.4 seconds and through the quarter in 13.9 at 104.6 mph.

1973

Horsepower, torque, and compression ratings continue downward spiral ... muscle cars going, going—most are gone ● OPEC oil embargo leads to severe fuel shortage, with long lines, price hikes, and threat of rationing ● Big blocks hold out against the tide ● A 429 is still available in the Ford Torino, but at 201 bhp ● 455s survive in Pontiac Firebird Formula and Trans Am with up to 310 bhp ● Final season for Chevelle's 454, now 245 bhp; 400- and 402-cid engines gone, SS option survives ● Mopar allows 280-bhp 440 four-barrels into Charger and Road Runner ● GM's "Colonnade" styling helps kill off pillarless hardtops and convertibles ●Buick Gran Sport option returns with 270 bhp in Stage 1 ● Big-cube and SS options depart from Camaro; Z-28 drops to 245 bhp from hydraulic-lifter 350 V-8 ● John Wiebe's Top Fuel ET is 6.49 at 227.27 mph...Funny Cars are not far behind: "Soapy Sales" Dodge is quickest at 6.71 (222.77 mph) ● Super Stockers run in the mid-10s; "Grumpy" Jenkins's Pro Stock Camaro turns a 9.02 at 150.25

▲ Javelin AMX was mostly a carryover, but tail/backup lamps were slightly different. Brochures still touted Jav's racing successes, and the 401 V-8 option was back with 255 bhp (net), but comfort, rear-seat room, and even warranty coverage received increasing ad emphasis.

▲ Despite few changes, the Javelin AMX recorded its highest model-year production for 1973, with 4737 units, about 18 percent of the Javelin total. AMC design chief Dick Teague had penned a two-seat AMX with this same basic design, but it was shot down for lack of sufficient anticipated sales.

1973 AMC HIGH-PERFORMANCE ENGINES							
TYPE	CID	BORE × STROKE	BHP @ RPM	TORQUE @ RPM	FUEL SYSTEM	COMP. RATIO	AVAIL.
ohv V-8	360	4.08×3.44	195 @ 4400	295 @ 2900	1×4bbl.	8.5:1	1
ohv V-8	360	4.08×3.44	220 @ 4400	315 @ 3100	1×4bbl.	8.5:1	1
ohv V-8	401	4.17×3.68	255 @ 4800	345 @ 3300	1×4bbl.	8.5:1	1
1. Matador, Ambassador, Javelin.							

▲ Dark blue paint and discreet "PC" front-fender badge identifies this '73 Javelin AMX as having that year's new Pierre Cardin trim package. Mesh over headlamps on car below is not stock.

▲ The 401 four-barrel teamed with a four-speed manual or optional Torque Command automatic. A 195-bhp 360 four-barrel also was a popular AMX choice.

◀▲ Tri-color interior trim dressed out Pierre Cardin-equipped AMX. "Designer editions" were a relatively cheap way to put new sparkle in aging models. Note the matching headliner (left). For more substance, "Go" suspension/axle packages were still available at $428 for the 360 V-8 and $476 for the 401. Power front disc brakes added $79 to Javelin AMX's $3191 base price.

▲ Though not as potent as earlier Stage 1 Gran Sports, Buick's new Century-based 1973 edition was among the rarest: just 728 built. Basic GS package added $173 to Century coupe's $3057 list.

▲ The 455 was available on all Century coupes, but the Stage 1 was a GS exclusive. Priced at $546, it had 270 net bhp via hotter cam and heads, Quadra-Jet carb, twin-snorkel air cleaner, and dual exhausts. Only seven were built with manual transmission; all others had THM 400 automatic.

▲ Black-finish grille and headlamp bezels identified the '73 Gran Sport. Standard 14×7 five-spoke wheels wore low-profile bias-belt tires.

▲ Gran Sport came standard with the same 150-bhp, 350-cid two-barrel as other Centurys, though only GS models could get the 190-bhp four-barrel 350.

▲ All the General Motors intermediates were restyled for '73, but retained the 116-inch wheelbase. Buick resurrected the Century name for its version, and the GS built upon the Colonnade coupe.

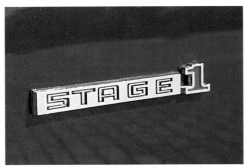

▲ "Stage 1" front-fender badge signaled that 390 pounds-feet of torque awaited in the engine room. A good thing the '73 Stage 1 package included a Positraction rear axle.

1973 BUICK HIGH-PERFORMANCE ENGINES

TYPE	CID	BORE× STROKE	BHP @ RPM	TORQUE @ RPM	FUEL SYSTEM	COMP. RATIO	AVAIL.
ohv V-8	350	3.80× 3.85	190 @ 4000	285 @ 2800	1×4bbl.	8.5:1	1
ohv V-8	455	4.31× 3.90	250 @ 4000	375 @ 2800	1×4bbl.	8.5:1	2
ohv V-8	455*	4.31× 3.90	260 @ 4400	380 @ 2800	1×4bbl.	8.5:1	3
ohv V-8	455*	4.31× 3.90	270 @ 4400	390 @ 3000	1×4bbl.	8.5:1	4

* Stage 1.
1. Gran Sport, Century, LeSabre Centurion. 2. Century, LeSabre, Centurion, Electra 225, Riviera. 3. Riviera, Centurion. 4. Century Gran Sport.

▲ New Chevelle Laguna was Chevy's mid-size. The SS group returned on 28,647 cars at $243; 2500 also had the 454 V-8, another $235.

▲ Chevy's Camaro aimed more toward luxury touring with 1973's new Type LT. RS and Z-28 were still around, but as packages. LT started at $3268.

1973 CHEVROLET HIGH-PERFORMANCE ENGINES

TYPE	CID	BORE × STROKE	BHP @ RPM	TORQUE @ RPM	FUEL SYSTEM	COMP. RATIO	AVAIL.
ohv V-8	350	4.00 × 3.48	175 @ 4000	260 @ 2800	1 × 4bbl.	8.5:1	1
ohv V-8	350	4.00 × 3.48	245 @ 5200	280 @ 4000	1 × 4bbl.	9.0:1	Camaro Z-28
ohv V-8	400	4.13 × 3.75	150 @ 3200	295 @ 2000	1 × 4bbl.	8.5:1	full size
ohv V-8	454	4.25 × 4.00	245 @ 4000	375 @ 2800	1 × 4bbl.	8.5:1	2

1. Camaro, Chevelle, Monte Carlo, Nova, full size. 2. Chevelle, Monte Carlo, full size.

▲ Rallye became a $182 option on Dodge's $3011 Challenger. The 240-bhp 340 four-barrel returned as the top mill and added $181.

▲ Chevelle Laguna shows the new Colonnade look of all '73 GM intermediates. Besides this "hardtop," Laguna also came as a sedan and wagon.

▼ The Dodge Demon was facelifted for '73 to become the Dart Sport. Hot 340 V-8 was standard, again with 240 bhp.

▲ Dodge built only 11,315 Dart Sport 340s for 1973, despite a base price of just $2793. Sunroof and fold-down rear seat were new extras.

► Chrysler's small-block 340 was in its final year for '73, but would return as an upsized 360. Dodge put it in the Dart Sport and in the Rallye versions of the Challenger and Charger. Times had changed since the "Scat Pack" days.

▲ Charger changed little for '73. Luxury SE got hammy triple opera windows, but outsold standard hardtop and coupe. Rallye option ($182), now available with any V-8, again included a beefed chassis and "power bulge" hood.

1973 DODGE HIGH-PERFORMANCE ENGINES

TYPE	CID	BORE × STROKE	BHP @ RPM	TORQUE @ RPM	FUEL SYSTEM	COMP. RATIO	AVAIL.
ohv V-8	340	4.04 × 3.31	240 @ 4800	295 @ 3600	1 × 4bbl.	8.5:1	1
ohv V-8	400	4.34 × 3.38	260 @ 4800	335 @ 3600	1 × 4bbl.	8.2:1	2
ohv V-8	440	4.32 × 3.75	220 @ 3600	350 @ 2400	1 × 4bbl.	8.2:1	full size
ohv V-8	440	4.32 × 3.75	280 @ 4800	380 @ 3200	1 × 4bbl.	8.2:1	2

1. Demon 340 Sport, Challenger, Charger. 2. Charger, Charger SE, Coronet.

1973 FORD HIGH-PERFORMANCE ENGINES

TYPE	CID	BORE × STROKE	BHP @ RPM	TORQUE @ RPM	FUEL SYSTEM	COMP. RATIO	AVAIL.
ohv V-8	351	4.00 × 3.50	246 @ 5400	312 @ 3600	1 × 4bbl.	8.0:1	full size, Torino
ohv V-8	351	4.00 × 3.50	259 @ 5600	292 @ 3400	1 × 4bbl.	7.9:1	Mustang
ohv V-8	429	4.36 × 3.59	201 @ 4400	322 @ 2600	1 × 4bbl.	8.0:1	full size, Torino

▲ Mach 1 was again the hottest Ford Mustang for '73, but that only meant a standard 302 V-8 with 136 net bhp. "Fat" generation was in its final year.

▲ Ford's mid-engine GT40 and Mark IV racers allegedly inspired the sweeping roofline of 1971-73 Mustang fastbacks. Wheels here are not factory-stock.

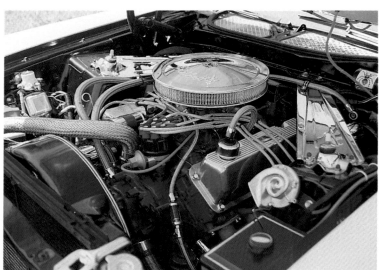

▲ Mustang's top engine for '73 was again the four-barrel 351 Cleveland, shown here, but rated horsepower was down to only about 260 net.

▲ Note tiny "opera" windows on this handsome '73 Hurst/Olds. The H/O was technically an option package W-45 for that year's Cutlass S coupe.

▲ With real muscle nearly extinct, the '73 Hurst/Olds was a standout. A 455 V-8, Hurst Dual-Gate shifter, "wet look" all-vinyl interior, and heavy-duty suspension were included, said Hurst, "for the man in motion."

▲ Hurst built 1097 of the '73 H/Os, all with gold accents. About 40 percent had black paint, the rest were Cameo White. Car shown here also has the rare factory sunroof option. Olds also offered a 4-4-2 for '73, but it was just a $121 cosmetic package with heavy-duty suspension thrown in. Production isn't available, having been lumped in with workaday Cutlass coupe figures.

▲ If real Olds muscle was a thing of the past, at least the Hurst/Olds still looked the part—though the standard half-vinyl top clashed with the image. Still, this was an executive hot rod, not a bad-boy street sweeper. Hurst-brand options included a digital tachometer, air shocks, and anti-theft alarm.

◀ Hurst declined to state horsepower for the '73 H/O, but the figure was likely in the region of 250 net for the "L77" Olds 455. That big-block mated only to a Turbo Hydra-Matic 400 with Hurst dual-gate shifter. Other functional '73 standards were power front-disc brakes, Rallye suspension, Super Stock III wheels, GR60-14 Goodrich Radial T/A tires, and the louvered "Nassau" hood duct. Options included a digital tach, air shocks, alarm system, and "loc lugs," all courtesy of Hurst.

1973 OLDSMOBILE HIGH-PERFORMANCE ENGINES

TYPE	CID	BORE × STROKE	BHP @ RPM	TORQUE @ RPM	FUEL SYSTEM	COMP. RATIO	AVAIL.
ohv V-8	350	4.06 × 3.39	180 @ 3800	275 @ 2800	1×4bbl.	8.5:1	1
ohv V-8	455	4.13 × 4.25	250 @ 4000	370 @ 2100	1×4bbl.	8.5:1	1
ohv V-8	455	4.13 × 4.25	250 @ 4000	375 @ 2800	1×4bbl.	8.5:1	Toronado
ohv V-8	455	4.13 × 4.25	275 @ 3600	360 @ 2600	1×4bbl.	8.5:1	2

1. Supreme, Cutlass, Vista-Cruiser. 2. Delta 88, Delta 88 Royale, Custom Cruiser, 98, 98 Luxury.

▲ Recalling Chrysler circa 1960, Olds offered swivel front bucket seats as a '73 Cutlass option. That year's Hurst/Olds had them standard. H/O dash was pretty much stock Cutlass, so instrumentation wasn't generous.

1973 PLYMOUTH HIGH-PERFORMANCE ENGINES

TYPE	CID	BORE × STROKE	BHP @ RPM	TORQUE @ RPM	FUEL SYSTEM	COMP. RATIO	AVAIL.
ohv V-8	340	4.04 × 3.31	240 @ 4800	295 @ 3600	1×4bbl.	8.5:1	1
ohv V-8	400	4.34 × 3.38	260 @ 4800	335 @ 3600	1×4bbl.	8.2:1	2
ohv V-8	440	4.32 × 3.75	220 @ 3600	350 @ 2400	1×4bbl.	8.2:1	Fury
ohv V-8	440	4.32 × 3.75	280 @ 4800	380 @ 3200	1×4bbl.	8.2:1	Road Runner

1. Duster 340, Barracuda, 'Cuda, Road Runner. 2. Satellite, Road Runner.

▲ Plymouth's Duster 340 lost compression, but survived with 240 bhp. Price was $2822; 15,731 were built.

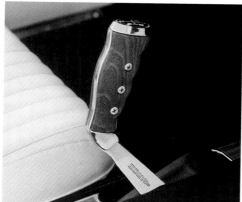

▲ "Pistol grip" four-speed shifter by Hurst was popular on '70s Plymouths.

► A lowly 318 (with dual exhausts) replaced the 400 as standard on the Road Runner. A 440 was still offered. Some 19,000 Road Runners were built for '73. Base price was $3115.

▲ Things were hotter than ever at the drags. Here, Mickey Thompson's '73 Pontiac Grand Am Funny Car smokes away at the Winternationals in Pomona.

▲ Firebird bucked the trend: Sales of the Trans Am (shown) nearly quadrupled, to 4802, while sales of the Formula nearly doubled, to 10,166.

301

The '73 Firebirds were the first to wear the giant "screaming chicken" hood decals, but the real news was underneath. Trans Am retained 455-cid power. The base unit had 250 bhp. Available was the big-port 455 Super Duty, which started the year rated at 310 bhp, but was revised to 290.

▲ Standard on the Formula was a 350-cid two-barrel, but a 400 and both 455s were offered. Both T/A and Formula were among the few really hot cars left.

▲ Formulas with the Ram-Air option got the fiberglass hood with lovely functional scoops. The 455 SD brought the Trans Am hood and rear-facing air inlet, regardless of model.

◄ Both Formula and T/A balanced their big blocks with wide tires and stiff suspensions, so handling was quite competent. Formula came with a three-speed manual, Trans Am a four-speed. Automatic was optional with any mill.

1973 PONTIAC HIGH-PERFORMANCE ENGINES

TYPE	CID	BORE × STROKE	BHP @ RPM	TORQUE @ RPM	FUEL SYSTEM	COMP. RATIO	AVAIL.
ohv V-8	400	4.12 × 3.75	200 @ 4000	310 @ 2400	1 × 4bbl.	8.0:1	full size
ohv V-8	400	4.12 × 3.75	230 @ 4400	325 @ 3200	1 × 4bbl.	8.0:1	1
ohv V-8	455	4.15 × 4.21	215 @ 3600	350 @ 2400	1 × 4bbl.	8.0:1	full size
ohv V-8	455	4.15 × 4.21	250 @ 4000	370 @ 2800	1 × 4bbl.	8.0:1	2
ohv V-8	455	4.15 × 4.21	290 @ 4000	390 @ 3600	1 × 4bbl.	8.4:1	3

1. Grand Prix, GTO, Formula 400, LeMans, Grand Am, Formula 400, Catalina, Bonneville. 2. Trans Am, Grand Prix, full size, GTO, LeMans, Formula 455. 3. Trans Am, Formula 455.

▲ Second-generation Firebird styling, always good, was purest through '73, the last year before safety bumpers.

1974

Fuel crisis eases, but the die is cast for the end of the muscle-car era ● GTO nameplate returns for one final season, but on an embarrassing Nova-like Pontiac Ventura compact ● Pontiac's Super Duty 455-equipped Firebirds carry the torch with 290 bhp...sales soar ● No V-8 is available on the new downsized Mustang II...four-cylinder and V-6 are only engines ● Buick's top Gran Sport 455 enters its final model year, slips to 255 horsepower ● Camaro Z-28 goes into hibernation at the end of the model year ● Laguna Type S-3 replaces the Super Sport Chevelle ● Dodge Challenger enters last season with Mopar's new 360 as top V-8 ● Dodge Charger Rallye can still have 400- or 440-cid V-8 ● Dodge Dart and Plymouth Duster get 360-cid V-8 choice ... Barracuda built for last time ● Road Runner is sole Plymouth with top (275-bhp) 440 option ● Olds 4-4-2 loses solid-lifter V-8 and four-speed; cold air induction remains as an option ● Hurst/Olds paces Indy 500 ● Wayne Gapp's Pro Stock Maverick turns an 8.95 at 153.06 mph ● Top Fuel dragsters hit 5.98 at 247.25

▲ Javelin's swan-song '74s: the base model (background) and sportier AMX. The latter retained its standard 304 V-8, as well as 360- and 401-cid options. AMX production came to only 4980 of nearly 25,000 Javelins built.

▲ AMC never had a well-financed factory drag-racing effort, and its Hornet was an unlikely competitor even in Pro Stock. But the compact did wage war on the strip, including this hatch coupe at the 1974 Gatornationals in Gainesville, Florida.

▲ Another Hornet that aimed its sting at the strip was Maskin and Kanner's 1974 hatch coupe. Here, it approaches the Christmas tree for a qualifying run at that year's NHRA Winternationals in Pomona.

▲ Go-Packages also survived, and included Rally-Pac gauges with a tach and power front disc brakes. A four-speed with Hurst shifter was offered on AMX.

1974 AMC HIGH-PERFORMANCE ENGINES							
TYPE	CID	BORE× STROKE	BHP @ RPM	TORQUE @ RPM	FUEL SYSTEM	COMP. RATIO	AVAIL.
ohv V-8	360	4.08× 3.44	195 @ 4400	295 @ 2900	1×4bbl.	8.25:1	1
ohv V-8	360	4.08× 3.44	220 @ 4400	315 @ 3100	1×4bbl.	8.25:1	2
ohv V-8	401	4.17× 3.68	255 @ 4800	345 @ 3300	1×4bbl.	8.25:1	2
1. Hornet, Matador, Ambassador, Javelin. 2. Matador, Ambassador, Javelin.							

▲ AMX held out to the end with an available big-block in the 255-bhp 401. Starting price was $3299, and improved compatibility with emissions hardware allowed the 3350-pound coupe to turn quarter-miles in the mid-15s.

▲ Starting at $3951, the Type S-3 came with a body-colored rubberized front grille, swivel bucket seats, 15×7 Rallye wheels, and special shocks. Chevy built 15,792 for 1974.

▲ With the proud Super Sport gone for '74, the Laguna Type S-3 carried Chevelle's performance flag with two- or four-barrel 350-cid V-8s, or the available 454 with 235 bhp, the latter capable of high-15-second ETs.

▲ With Mustang gelded, Camaro sales boomed. The $600 Z-28 package returned for its last year with a 245-bhp 350 and ETs in the mid-15s.

▲ Ironically, the only SS Chevy for '74 was a version of the Nova. Trim packages like this "Spirit of America" were more indicative of the times, though.

1974 CHEVROLET HIGH-PERFORMANCE ENGINES

TYPE	CID	BORE × STROKE	BHP @ RPM	TORQUE @ RPM	FUEL SYSTEM	COMP. RATIO	AVAIL.
ohv V-8	350	4.00×3.48	185 @ 4000	270 @ 2600	1×4bbl.	8.5:1	1
ohv V-8	350	4.00×3.48	245 @ 5200	280 @ 4000	1×4bbl.	9.0:1	Camaro Z-28
ohv V-8	400	4.13×3.75	180 @ 3200	290 @ 2000	1×4bbl.	8.5:1	2
ohv V-8	454	4.25×4.00	235 @ 4000	375 @ 2800	1×4bbl.	8.5:1	3

1. Camaro, Chevelle, Monte Carlo, Nova, full size. 2. Chevelle, Monte Carlo, full size. 3. Chevelle, Monte Carlo, full size.

▼ Mopar enlarged its well-regarded 340-cid V-8 to 360 cubes and used the 245-bhp small-block as the Dodge Challenger's top option. The basic Rallye package shown here cost $190 and included fake fender scoops. Challenger wouldn't answer the bell for the '75 round, and hung it up after '74 with a final run of 16,437 units.

▲ A 318-cid V-8 was standard in Challenger, which started at $3143. The 360 V-8 added $259 and was also offered on the base model. A three-speed manual was standard, with a four-speed and TorqueFlite optional. This Rallye package-equipped example wears an optional vinyl roof ($84). Bumper guards were larger this year to comply with the federal 5-mph protection decree.

▲ Rallye trim included side strobe stripes, fake hood scoops, and F70×14 white-letter tires on special cast wheels with trim rings.

▲ Dodge's Dart Sport 340 became a 360 for '74—if you ordered that newly enlarged four-barrel V-8. Few people did: just 3951 for the model year.

1974 DODGE HIGH-PERFORMANCE ENGINES

TYPE	CID	BORE × STROKE	BHP @ RPM	TORQUE @ RPM	FUEL SYSTEM	COMP. RATIO	AVAIL.
ohv V-8	360	4.00×3.58	200 @ 4000	290 @ 3200	1×4bbl.	8.4:1	1
ohv V-8	360	4.00×3.58	245 @ 4800	320 @ 3600	1×4bbl.	8.4:1	2
ohv V-8	400	4.34×3.38	205 @ 4400	310 @ 3400	1×4bbl.	8.2:1	3
ohv V-8	400	4.34×3.38	250 @ 4800	330 @ 3400	1×4bbl.	8.2:1	3
ohv V-8	440	4.32×3.75	230 @ 4000	350 @ 3200	1×4bbl.	8.2:1	full size
ohv V-8	440	4.32×3.75	275 @ 4400	375 @ 3200	1×4bbl.	8.2:1	4

1. Coronet, Charger, full size. 2. Dart 360 Sport, Challenger, Charger. 3. Coronet, Charger, full size. 4. Charger, Coronet.

▲ Charger got a minor facelift, but the 150-bhp 318 V-8 returned as standard. The four-barrel 440 was still around as the top power option, delivering a healthy 275 net bhp, good for ETs in the mid-15-second range. This is the top-line SE model. The Rallye option returned for the base coupe and hard-top; it cost only $100.

◄ Richard Petty won his second straight Daytona 500 in a '74 Charger, and accounted for all 10 of Dodge's NASCAR victories on his way to the driver's title. His mount was a far cry from this SE, which, despite its $3742 base price, was the top-selling model with 36,399 built out of 74,376 Chargers.

▲ Still going strong—or what passed for it in 1974—was the jazzy Hurst/Olds, which was patterned on the '74 Indy 500 pace car. Many of the 380 built were actually used in the Indy fleet, though not necessarily on the track.

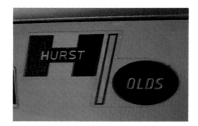

▲ An option package for the '74 Hurst/Olds bore the famous W-30 tag. It included a four-barrel 350 V-8 with about 250 bhp.

▲ The basic Hurst/Olds package was similar to 1973's save the W-30 engine option and modified styling shared with its Cutlass S "parent."

▼ Road Runner was demoted to an option on the base Plymouth Satellite for '74. It still came with a "power bulge" hood—but no more power. New 360 small-block replaced the 340 option, but the 440 four-barrel was back. Base price that year was $3444—again with 318 V-8.

1974 OLDSMOBILE HIGH-PERFORMANCE ENGINES

TYPE	CID	BORE × STROKE	BHP @ RPM	TORQUE @ RPM	FUEL SYSTEM	COMP. RATIO	AVAIL.
ohv V-8	455	4.13×4.25	230 @ 4000	370 @ 2100	1×4bbl.	8.5:1	Toronado
ohv V-8	455	4.13×4.25	250 @ 4000	375 @ 2800	1×4bbl.	8.5:1	1
ohv V-8	455	4.13×4.25	275 @ 3600	360 @ 2600	1×4bbl.	8.5:1	1

1. Cutlass, Vista Cruiser.

▼ Bird decals continued on '74 Road Runners, but former standards like a performance-axle and heavy-duty suspension were now options. Only 11,555 were built for the model year.

▲ Duster remained the most popular Plymouth, but most were the garden variety like this, not the sporty new $3288 Duster 360, which replaced the familiar 340 package and could turn 15.8-second ETs.

▲ Plymouth's Barracuda was beached after a '74 output of just 11,734; only 4989 were 'Cudas (foreground). The 340 was supplanted by the new 245-horse 360 as the "performance" V-8 option.

1974 PLYMOUTH HIGH-PERFORMANCE ENGINES

TYPE	CID	BORE× STROKE	BHP @ RPM	TORQUE @ RPM	FUEL SYSTEM	COMP. RATIO	AVAIL.
ohv V-8	360	4.00× 3.58	200 @ 4000	290 @ 3200	1×4bbl.	8.4:1	1
ohv V-8	360	4.00× 3.58	245 @ 4800	320 @ 3600	1×4bbl.	8.4:1	2
ohv V-8	400	4.34× 3.38	205 @ 4400	310 @ 3400	1×4bbl.	8.2:1	1
ohv V-8	400	4.34× 3.38	250 @ 4800	330 @ 3400	1×4bbl.	8.2:1	3
ohv V-8	440	4.32× 3.75	230 @ 4000	350 @ 3200	1×4bbl.	8.2:1	full size
ohv V-8	440	4.32× 3.75	275 @ 4400	375 @ 3200	1×4bbl.	8.2:1	3

1. Satellite, full size. 2. Duster 360, 'Cuda, Road Runner. 3. Satellite, Road Runner.

1974 PONTIAC HIGH-PERFORMANCE ENGINES

TYPE	CID	BORE× STROKE	BHP @ RPM	TORQUE @ RPM	FUEL SYSTEM	COMP. RATIO	AVAIL.
ohv V-8	350	3.88× 3.75	170 @ 4000	290 @ 2400	1×4bbl.	7.6:1	1
ohv V-8	350	3.88× 3.75	200 @ 4400	295 @ 2800	1×4bbl.	7.6:1	2
ohv V-8	400	4.12× 3.75	200 @ 4000	320 @ 2400	1×4bbl.	8.0:1	full size
ohv V-8	400	4.12× 3.75	225 @ 4000	330 @ 2800	1×4bbl.	8.0:1	3
ohv V-8	455	4.15× 4.21	215 @ 3600	355 @ 2400	1×4bbl.	8.0:1	full size
ohv V-8	455	4.15× 4.21	250 @ 4000	370 @ 2800	1×4bbl.	8.0:1	4
ohv V-8	455	4.15× 4.21	290 @ 4000	390 @ 3600	1×4bbl.	8.4:1	5

1. Ventura, LeMans. 2. GTO, Ventura, LeMans. 3. Grand Prix, Trans Am, Formula 400, LeMans, Grand Am. 4. Grand Am, Grand Prix, full size. 5. Trans Am, Formula 455.

▼ Pontiac's 1974 Firebird was deftly restyled to accommodate new federal "crash bumpers" without ruffling its great-looking feathers. Trans Am remained top of the line with a $4446 base price; 10,255 were built for the model year.

▲ This Buccaneer Red 1974 T/A shows off that year's newly optional "honeycomb" body-color wheels. Just visible is the "screaming chicken" hood decal, which cost $55. Front- and rear-wheel "spats" remained standard for all T/As.

▲ Early second-generation Firebirds had these high-back "Strato" front buckets. Shift console was a separate extra.

▲ T/A's Super-Duty 455 again made 290 net bhp for '74.

1975-93

Performance hibernates... safety, environmental, and fuel issues alter automotive landscape • Big-blocks fade...no V-8 for '74 Mustang...Chevy drops 454 after '76...Firebird loses 455 in '76, 400 in '79...Mopar's 400 dies after '78 • Manufacturers try turbo four- and six-cylinders...best is Buick's Regal Grand National; '87 GNX has true muscle-car performance • Horsepower see-saws: The highest in '75 is 235 in Mopar 440 ... by 1980, only Corvette and Firebird Turbo top 190...several models climb back to 225 bhp in '88... by '92, Dodge Viper is at 400 bhp • Ford leads bang-for-the-buck comeback with 5.0-liter '82 Mustang • Performance takes on a new face with hot front-wheel drive cars using small, multi-valve engines • Sophisticated electronics help late-'80s Camaro, Firebird, and Mustang achieve '60s-like acceleration with best-ever handling, fuel economy, and safety • Top Fuel ET record is 5.97 in '72...4.99 in '88...Kenny Bernstein runs 301.70 mph in '92 • NHRA Pro Stock record falls to 7.86 in '82...7.02 (196.24 mph) in '93

▲ For '75, Road Runner was an option on Plymouth's new mid-size Fury line. Blocky facelift was a snooze, but a hint of performance remained in 180-bhp, 360-cid and 260-bhp, 440-cid four-barrel options.

▲ Pontiac Trans Am's styling changed little for '76, but top 455 V-8 was down to 200 net horsepower.

▲ Sporty Can Am package bowed in mid '77 for Pontiac's LeMans Sport Coupe. It used Trans Am's four-barrel 400 V-8.

▲ Road Runner was a Volaré option after '75. This '77 has "Super Pak" dress-ups, which made it a "Front Runner." Available four-barrel 360 had 175 bhp.

▲ After a two-year absence, Chevy revived the Camaro Z-28 for "1977½." Handling was stressed over pure muscle.

▶ Road Runner ran its last in 1978—again as a collection of trim options for Plymouth's Volaré coupe. This is the $499 "Sport Pack" version; "Super Coupe" ($1417) and "Street Kit Car" groups ($1085) were also offered.

▲ Dodge matched the Road Runner with R/T packages for its '78 Aspen coupe. They cost from $51 to $289. A 175-bhp four-barrel 360-cid V-8 added $439-$463; a four-speed stick added $142.

▲ The mean-looking "Super Coupe" package with a 360 V-8 added $1351-$1420 to a '78 Aspen. As with the Volaré's like-named option, it included firm suspension and lots of body add-ons.

▲ Camaro was restyled for '78, and the '79 Z-28 had front-wheel flares and a 175-bhp 350 four-barrel.

▲ Ford's Mustang II offered a new King Cobra package for 1978. A revived 302 V-8 was included, but this was mostly a "paint-on performance" car.

▲ Tenth Anniversary Pontiac Trans Am of '79 had special trim and a 220-bhp "6.6" (400-cid) V-8. It cost $10,619 and turned 16-second ETs.

▲ Mercury's '79 Capri was a clone of that year's new Mustang. Turbo-four RS was the enthusiast's model.

▲ Camaro Z-28 still looked—and sold—great for 1980. Chevy built 84,877 for '79 and 45,137 for '80.

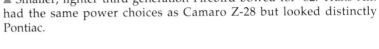
▲ Smaller, lighter third-generation Firebird bowed for '82. Trans Am had the same power choices as Camaro Z-28 but looked distinctly Pontiac.

▲ Z-28 was still the hottest of the redesigned Camaros with its available 165-horsepower 305-cid V-8. New styling would endure more than a decade. A five-speed turned a 17.5 at 81 for *Road & Track*.

▲ Ford rediscovered high performance with a 175-bhp High Output 302 in the '83 Mustang. With its revitalized 5.0-liter V-8, the Boss was back. *Road & Track*'s four-speed ran a 16.3 at 84 mph.

◄ After taking a few years off, the Hurst/Olds returned for 1983 as a limited-edition Cutlass Supreme coupe. Just 3000 were built that model year.

▲ The revived '83 marked 15 years of Hurst/Oldsmobiles. It could do the quarter in 16 seconds at 83 mph.

◄ A four-barrel 307 V-8 packed 170 bhp in the '83 Hurst/Olds. Triple-stick Hurst "Lightning Rod" shifter controlled its three-speed Turbo Hydra-Matic.

▲ Carroll Shelby masterminded the unassuming 1984 Dodge Omni GLH. The letters meant "Goes Like Hell," and the front-drive GLH did. Alloy wheels and tough suspension were included in the bargain $7350 base price.

▲ A tuned 110-bhp Chrysler 2.2-liter four motivated the '84 Omni GLH. It teamed only with five-speed manual. Exact production isn't available for the first-year GLH, but it was certainly limited.

▲ Ford's Special Vehicles Operation brewed up a 2.3-liter intercooled 175-bhp turbo four for the new '84 Mustang SVO. Zero-60 took 7.5 seconds; the quarter-mile, just under 16.

▲ Ford's '84 Mustang SVO aimed for a Euro-style blend of performance and high-speed handling. Unique grille-less nose and working hood scoop helped set it apart from the Mustang herd. Base price was $14,500.

▲ V-6 X-11 was the sportiest early-'80s front-drive Chevy Citation. Here's the final '85 package, which cost $1016.

▲ The reborn Hurst/Olds reversed to silver-over-black for 1984, but was much like the '83 edition otherwise. Production was limited to 3500 units, so it's a possible future collectible. That year's base price was $12,644.

▲ Chevy's '83 Monte Carlo added a reborn SS option. The similar '85 package included a 180-bhp 305 V-8 for $1877.

313

▲ Omni GLH (shown) and GLH Turbo were the basis for Shelby's '86 GLHS, which did 0-60 mph in 6.5 seconds, the quarter-mile in 14.9, and got 20 mpg.

▲ Ford's Mustang SVO never sold as expected. This is one of 1954 built for '85, versus 4508 for '84. SVO vanished after a final 3382 copies for 1986.

▲ Buick fielded one of Detroit's quickest '80s cars in its 1985-87 Regal Grand National. This is the '86, of which 5512 were built. The '85 saw just 2102 copies. Both sold in any color you liked, so long as it was black.

▲ GN's fortified 231-cid Buick turbo V-6 had up to 245 bhp. Zero-60 took 4.9 seconds; the quarter-mile, 13.9.

▲ El Camino pickups like this '86 could get a Monte Carlo SS-type package, but performed better thanks to less-limiting emission controls.

▲ Camaro's use in the International Race of Champions series prompted the IROC-Z for 1987-89. This is an '86. It could do zero-60 in 8.1 seconds and the quarter in 16.5.

► Fastback Monte Carlo SS "Aerocoupe" bowed in early '86 to give Chevy a slicker NASCAR contestant. Street models ran a 180-bhp 305 V-8 with free-flow exhaust and high-lift cam—plus automatic. Aerocoupe lasted only through 1987 and some 6300 copies. It originally sold in the $10,700-$14,300 range.

▲ Dodge's "Shelby" Charger got a 146-bhp turbo 2.2 four in '85-'86. Shelby's "Shelby" Charger had 175 bhp and did 60 in 6.7 seconds, the quarter-mile in 14.9.

▲ Front-wheel drive became prevalent on the street in the mid-'80s, and showed up on the strip, too. Witness this '86 Shelby Charger at Indianapolis.

▲ Pontiac's third-series Trans Am got a smoother nose for '85. The '86 shown here was little different. A 210-bhp 305 V-8 remained the top power option.

▲ Grand Nationals were rare—and rarin' to go. Here's one in NHRA Super-Stock action at Pomona. Showroom models for '87 had 355 pounds/feet of torque at just 2000 rpm and used an overdrive automatic with 3.42:1 gears.

▲ Not all blown Regals were GNs. The same 245-bhp turbo V-6 was optional in lesser models, such as this '87.

▲ Buick proved the renewed mid-'80s demand for Detroit muscle was no fluke by selling 20,193 of its '87 Regal GNs.

▲ An even hotter Grand National called GNX bowed in 1987. Though it started near $30,000, it was quite a buy.

▲ A "smarter" engine-computer chip gave the '87 GNX an estimated 300 bhp. *Car and Driver*'s did 0-60 in 4.7 seconds, the quarter in 13.5 at 102 mph. Those are true muscle numbers.

▲ "Darth Vader, your car is ready," shuddered *Car and Driver*. Among factory '87s, only Porsche's $106,000 911 Turbo Cabriolet could match the GNX's acceleration. Just 547 GNXs were built, all during '87. A few regular '88 Grand Nationals were sold, even though other Regals had gone front-drive.

▲ Chevy's Monte Carlo was in its next-to-last year for 1987. Here's that season's SS Aerocoupe. Like other Montes, it was little changed from '86.

▲ The Hurst/Olds became a reborn 4-4-2 after 1984. The swan-song '87 shown here was a $2577 option on the Cutlass Supreme coupe. About 4210 were sold.

▲ Ford's '87 Mustangs got their first big facelift since the '79 redesign. Zoomy GT again led the herd with a standard 225-horse 302 V-8 for '89. It turned 14.7-second ETs.

▲ Pontiac revived the "2+2" tag for this special "glassback" '86 Grand Prix, a NASCAR-inspired cousin to Chevy's Monte Carlo SS Aerocoupe. The Pontiac saw lower volume of just 200, however. A 180-bhp 305 V-8 was standard.

▲ Dodge's 1989 Daytona Shelby had a 174-bhp turbo 2.2. *Road & Track* took 7.6 seconds 0-60 and 16.0 in the quarter.

▲ A twin-cam, 16-valve "Quad-4" four with 185 bhp was a new mid-1989 option for the front-drive Olds Calais.

▲ A conversion to rear drive made this Calais dragster super sneaky. Here, it is shown at Heartland Park Topeka raceway in 1989.

▲ Camaro IROC-Z rolled into 1990 with newly standard 16-inch wheels and a limited-slip diff. A 230-bhp 350 V-8 repeated as the top power option.

▲ Thunderbird was redesigned for '89 and returned for '90. Supercharged 210-bhp, 232-cid V-6 Super Coupe did 0-60 in 7.4 seconds, the quarter in 15.9 with a five-speed manual.

▲ Camaros had long been hot in quarter-mile action. Here, Joe Scott launches at Heartland Park Topeka.

▲ Z-28 returned as the top '91 Camaro; a 350 V-8 did 0-60 in 6.4 seconds and ran 14.9-second quarter-mile times for *Car and Driver*.

▲ New for 1990, the Dodge Spirit R/T returned for '91 as a real "Q-ship."

▲ A unique 224-horse twincam turbo-four gave Spirit R/T 15-second ET ability.

▲ Chevy served up a Lumina Z-34 coupe for '92 with a 210-bhp twin-cam V-6.

◄ Marking Camaro's 25th birthday in 1992 was the "Heritage Appearance Package" for the convertible and coupe. Unique Heritage features included '60s-style stripes, special emblems, and body-color grille and wheels. Also announced were 602 special Camaros with 270-bhp L98 Corvette 350 V-8s to honor the first 602 Z-28s of 1967, but those were canceled as a wildly shifting market devastated Camaro sales.

▲ Dodge resurrected the Shelby AC Cobra theme in 1992 with the Viper RT/10, a $50,000 "dream car come true." Only 200 were built that year. The plastic-body retro-roadster lacked roll-up windows.

▲ Viper's 400-bhp, 488-cid V-10 hooked to a six-speed manual. The 3400-pound roadster took 4.5-seconds 0-60 and turned the quarter in 13.1 at 108 mph. Lamborghini helped design the engine.

317

▲ Camaro was redesigned for '93 with plastic body panels, standard dual air bags, and available anti-lock brakes. Z-28 got a 275-bhp, 350-cid LT1 V-8.

▲ With tenacious handling and quarter-mile times in the mid-14s at 97 mph, the fourth-generation Z-28 was the best all-around performing Camaro ever.

▲ Chevy invented the muscle truck with its 1990 454 SS. The two-wheel-drive full-size pickup had a fuel-injected 454-cid V-8 with up to 255 bhp.

▲ GMC built 3000 Syclones, all as '91s. With a 280-bhp turbocharged 262-cid inline-six, the compact pickup ran 0-60 mph in 5.3 seconds and turned the quarter in 14.1 for *Car and Driver*.

▲ Trucks were hot in the '90s, and, like Syclone, GMC's $29,000 Typhoon sport-utility had a turbo 4.3 and permanently engaged four-wheel drive. Just 2500 were built for 1991, 2200 for '92.

▲ Ford answered the SS 454 pickup for '93 with this F-150 Lightning and its 250-bhp 351 V-8. It listed for $21,655 and came in two-wheel-drive only.

▲ Mustang GT returned for '93, but was joined by a new V-8 Cobra with 40 extra bhp—245 in all—and chassis mods that made handling even better. It turned 14.5 ETs.

▲ Eras change, but slicks, scoops, and wheelies never die. Jeff Taylor drop-kicks his rear-drive/V-8-conversion Super Stock Olds Achieva.

▲ Olds' front-drive '93 Achieva SCX exemplifies the 1990's budget muscle car with a high-output 185-bhp "Quad-4" engine coded "W-41."

▲ All-new fourth-series Firebirds arrived with the same basic design as Chevy's '93 Camaros, but retained unique Pontiac style. Here's the Trans Am.

INDEX

INDEX